THOSE WHO WORKED

THOSE WHO WORKED

AN ANTHOLOGY OF
MEDIEVAL SOURCES

EDITED BY
PETER SPEED

ITALICA PRESS
NEW YORK
1997

ITALICA PRESS, INC.

595 MAIN STREET

NEW YORK, NEW YORK 10044

LIBRARY OF CONGRESS CATALOGING-IN-PUBLICATION DATA

Those who worked / edited by Peter Speed.
       p.   cm. — (An anthology of Medieval sources)
      Includes bibliographical references and index.
      ISBN 0-934977-40-2
      1. Manners and customs—History—Sources. 2. Civilization, Medieval—Historiography. 3. Social history—Medieval, 500-1500. 4. Manners and customs in literature. 5. Civilization, Medieval in literature. I. Speed, Peter. II. Series: Speed, Peter. Anthology of Medieval sources.
      GT120.T56 1997
      306.3—dc21   97-12493
                                   CIP

Printed in the United States of America

5 4 3 2

Cover Art: Norman servants preparing breads, fowl, and meat for a feast. Detail from the Bayeux Tapestry. Musée de la Tapisserie, Bayeux, France. Giraudon/Art Resource, NY.

Unless otherwise noted, all other artwork used by permission of source cited in List of Illustrations on p. VI.

CONTENTS

ILLUSTRATIONS

ILLUSTRATIONS

THOSE WHO WORKED

ILLUSTRATIONS

PREFACE

My Anthology of Medieval Sources is to consist of three volumes, of which this is the second. Almost everything in the preface of the first volume, *Those Who Fought*, applies here, so there is little point in repeating it. Since this volume treats a subject matter whose vocabulary is no longer current for most readers, I have added one feature not present in the first volume: a glossary of terms. The reader will find this at the end of the volume, just before the bibliography. Along the same lines, I have also "translated" many passages from the Middle English into contemporary English. While specialists may insist upon the purity of this very impure English, I have opted for intelligibility as the surest way to introduce many readers to this material for the first time.

I would like to say once again how pleased I am to write for the people of the United States, since I greatly admire your country. However, I am sure you will agree that one thing missing from it is any considerable feeling of a remote past, which seems strange to us on this side of the Atlantic, because we have reminders of the Middle Ages in nearly all our towns and villages. However, our medieval heritage is also your own, as you recognize by coming to Europe in your tens of thousands every year. Though no substitute for a visit, I hope, none the less, that this anthology will help increase your understanding of our common past.

ACKNOWLEDGMENTS

The author and publishers are grateful to the following for permission to reproduce copyrighted material. Numbers refer to readings: AMS Press, *The Laws of the Salian and Riparian Franks*, translated by Theodore John Rivers, 1986: 141-144; Cambridge University Press, *Social Life in England from the Conquest to the Reformation*, by G.G. Coulton, 1918: 31, 50, 54, 103, 106, 107, 120, 125, 126, 151-154, 156, 158, 160-163, 166, 178-181, 186-188, 191, 193, 196, 207, 220, 221, 224-227; University of Chicago Press, *The Colloquies of Erasmus,* translated and edited by Craig R. Thompson, 1965: 199; Chilton Books, *Great Documents of Western Civilization,* edited by Milton Viorst, 1965: 110; Columbia University Press, *Chaucer's World,* by Edith Rickert, 1948: 57, 72, 76-78, 88, 95, 101, 102, 105, 108, 124, 125, 164, 165, 170, 173-175, 189, 208-209, 211-215, 228, 231, 232; Devin-Adaire, *The Book of Margery Kempe: A Modern Version,* by W. Butler Bowdon, 1944: 96; Garland Publishing, *Catholic Peacemakers: A Documentary History,* VOL. 1: *From the Bible to the Era of the Crusades,* edited by Ronald G. Musto, 1993: 202, 204; Greenwood Press, *Holy Maidenhood,* edited by F.J. Furnival, 1969 (Early English Text Society, 1922): 149, 150; Italica Press, *Norman London,* by William Fitz Stephen, intro. by F. Donald Logan, 1990: 71, 100, 185; W.W. Norton Company, *Medieval Trade in the Mediterranean World,* edited by Robert S. Lopez and Irving W. Raymond, 1967: 137-139; Van Nostrand Company, *The Medieval Town,* edited by John H. Mundy and Peter Riesenberg, 1958: 136; Macmillan Publishing Company (Charles Scribner's Sons), *A Source Book for Medieval History,* by Oliver J. Thatcher and Edgar H. McNeal, 1907: 145; Routledge, Chapman and Hall, *Women's Lives in Medieval Europe: A Sourcebook,* by Emilie Amt, 1993: 89; Methuen, *The Manor and Manorial Records,* by N.J. Hone, 1906: 37-39, 46, 47, 51, 52; *A Source Book of English Social History,* by H.E. Monckton Jones, 1922: 93, 94; *Medieval People,* by Eileen Power, 1963: 155, 157, 159; Ward-Ritchie Press, *The Diseases of Women,* by Trotula of Salerno, translated by Elizabeth Mason-Hohl, 1940: 217, 218, 222, 223; Weidenfeld and Nicolson, *Plantagenet Chronicles,* edited by Elizabeth Hallam, 1986: 84, 203; *Chronicles of the Age of Chivalry,* edited by Elizabeth Hallam, 1987: 197, 230; Yale University Press, *The Poor in the Middle Ages,* by Michael Mollat, translated by Arthur Goldhammer, 1986: 199, 201.

I have tried to locate all holders of copyright, but should I have missed any, I apologize to them. If they will contact me through the publishers, I will do my best to make amends.

Peter Speed
Parkstone, July 1997

CHAPTER 1
AGRICULTURE UNDER THE ROMAN EMPIRE AND DURING THE EARLY MIDDLE AGES

THE ROMANS

In the Roman Empire there were many large estates, known as latifundia, literally "wide farms." The scholar Ausonius (310-c. 395) describes one that he owned, in southern Spain:

1. All hail, little estate, kingdom of my ancestors, which my great-grandfather, my grandfather and my father all cultivated and which this last bequeathed me by his untimely death. Would that I had not had to own it so soon! Certainly it is the law of life that the son should succeed his father, but it is better to enjoy his property with him. Now the work and the care are all mine; formerly I had only the pleasure, and the rest was the concern of my father.

I cultivate 200 yokes of arable, 100 of vineyards and 50 of meadows. My woods occupy twice as much land as the meadows, the vineyards and the fields. I have neither too many nor too few workers. I have a spring, a well, and, moreover, a sparkling river. This last, which is navigable and tidal, brings me home and takes me away. I always keep enough stores to last for two years. He who does not keep a well-stocked larder risks going hungry.

This estate of mine is situated neither too close to the city, nor too far from it, so that I am not bothered by crowds of people; but when boredom makes me change my surroundings, I can leave easily, so that I enjoy the countryside and the city alternately. [*Thanksgiving*]

1

Ausonius's workers were almost certainly slaves. His remark that he owned just the right number was a proud boast, for if there were enough to cope at the peak seasons, then there were too many for much of the year, and he would have had to feed them while they stood idle. This raises the question of how far the villas, or country houses of the wealthy, were associated with villages, which would have provided labor that could be called on when needed. In Britain, it would seem that there were few such links, since villas and villages were, on the whole, in different areas. In Gaul, on the other hand, many villages were close to villas.

Pliny describes methods of storage that Ausonius might well have used:

> 2. The most practical method of storing grain is to keep it in holes which are called silos. These silos must be made in dry soil, and the floor covered with a bed of straw. Moreover, the grain must be kept in the ear. That way, as long as air does not reach it, it is certain that the wheat will suffer no harm. Varro says that wheat kept like this will last for 50 years. He also says that beans and vegetables placed in jars of oil and buried in ashes will last for a long time. [*Natural History*]

The latifundia, like most large estates in all ages, were usually run efficiently, and a symptom of this, perhaps even one of the causes, was that the Romans had books on agriculture. The best known is Virgil's *Georgics*, though the work is remarkable more for its poetry than for its practical value. The following are extracts from a manual of the fourth century AD:

> 3. On buying a field, you must bear in mind whether the previous cultivators have destroyed its fertility by growing

inferior plants; because, although you can rectify this by putting in better, it is more convenient to be without the trouble, than to have the hope of correcting it. With cereals, you can remedy the problem at once. With vineyards, you must pay greater attention, and beware of those who have done a great deal, concerned only to extend their vineyards, and have planted sterile vines, or those which produce grapes which taste unpleasant. It will cost you an enormous amount of work to put matters right, if you buy a field planted with such vines.

4. Trees are like men. You should transplant them from unhealthy places to better ones. After a good wine harvest, prune the vines short, but not so short after a poor harvest. In all the operations of grafting, pruning and cutting, use tools that  are hard and sharp. Do all the work on vines and trees before the flowers and buds appear. In the vineyards, the workman should cultivate with the hoe those places which the plough does not reach. In hot, dry, sunny areas it is not good to strip the vines of young branches, because the plants need to be covered with foliage, and where the Volturno, or some other hostile wind burns the vines, cover them with straw.

The vigorous, but sterile branch which grows in the middle of the olive should be cut out, for it is the enemy of the entire tree. [Paladius, *Treatise on Agriculture*]

THOSE WHO WORKED

THE GERMANS, ACCORDING TO CAESAR AND TACITUS

Outside the Empire, on the other side of the Rhine, farming could hardly have been more different. Caesar wrote:

> 5. The Germans are not great farmers, and live mainly on milk, cheese and meat. No one owns a clearly defined piece of land as his own private property. Instead, the leaders of the tribes allot an area to each clan or kinship group, deciding its size and where it should be, as they think fit. The following year, they make the people move elsewhere. They give numerous reasons for this practice. For example, they do not want their men to become used to living in the same place, lose their warlike spirit and take up farming instead of fighting. They do not want them to covet large estates, so that the strong do not drive out the weak. They do not want them to concentrate on building houses that will protect them from the cold and the heat. They do not want them to become too fond of money, which often causes discord. They also wish to appease the common folk by showing them that even the most powerful are no better off than they are. [*Gallic War*]

A century and a half later, the historian Tacitus wrote of the Germans:

> 6. Their soil will grow good crops of cereals, but not fruit trees. There is plenty of livestock, but most of it is stunted. The Germans take pride in nothing more than the sheer numbers of their animals. They prize them highly, for they are their only wealth.
>
> The bravest and most warlike of the men have no regular work. It is the women, the old men and the weaklings who take care of the homes and the fields.
>
> Land is allotted to groups, in proportion to their numbers. They then divide it among themselves, which causes no problems as there is plenty available. They change their

ploughlands every year, but they still have more than enough. Though land is abundant and fertile, they do not make the best use of it, because they do not cultivate it thoroughly. They do not plant fruit trees, enclose meadows or irrigate their gardens. All they ask of their soil is that it shall give them corn. [*Germania*]

A superabundance of land can often lead to poor farming, as it did on the American prairies, where the first settlers cropped some of the best soils in the world to exhaustion, believing that the supply of virgin land was virtually unlimited. The Germans, too, saw no need to respect the soil, and for the same reason. If Tacitus is right, they, like the Americans, grew only one crop, and it is likely that they solved the problem of soil fertility by the crude technique of "slash and burn." That meant clearing the land, largely with the aid of fire, cropping it until it was no longer worth cultivating, and then repeating the process elsewhere. This might explain the frequent moves mentioned by both Caesar and Tacitus.

THE EARLY MIDDLE AGES

The degree to which the Roman way of life survived the fall of the Empire varied from region to region. In some of the former provinces the conquerors became no more than a new aristocracy, so that the ordinary folk carried on much as before. In Britain, on the other hand, Roman civilization was all but extinguished. Estates may or may not have passed intact to newcomers, but the villas themselves were abandoned. In a rare instance of Roman buildings being occupied, the new owners lived in the barn, once the home of the slaves.

In spite of the regional differences, there was one change that was all but universal. The invaders gave up their nomadic and semi-nomadic habits to lead settled lives. For the most part, and particularly in the great plain of northern Europe, people lived in nucleated villages, that is, villages where the houses were grouped together. Each dwelling had its own toft, or garden, and beyond the tofts there were hundreds of acres of communal fields and meadows. Surrounding the farm land, and separating the villages from each other, there were vast swathes of woodland and waste.

While it is not clear how far Roman villas and villages were associated, almost every medieval village had a manor house, the home of its lord. A nobleman of any consequence owned several manors and lived at each in turn. During his absence, a steward, or some such official, looked after his interests. Each manor house had a demesne, or home farm, which was much the same as the other holdings in the village, save that it was far larger than any of them.

To work his demesne, the lord kept a number of full-time servants, but he also depended on services that the villagers gave him as a form of rent. Some of the people were free, some were slaves and many, usually the majority, were villeins, or serfs, which meant that in status they came somewhere between the other two. But whatever their social position, nearly all the villagers owed the lord services, which could vary from several days work in the week, coupled with deliveries of produce, to carrying the occasional message.

The following is from an inventory compiled at the beginning of the ninth century, during the reign of Charlemagne. It describes a manor house in what is now northern France:

7. At Annapes there is a royal dwelling, well built of stone, with three bedrooms. Running round the house is a landing, leading to eleven small rooms. In the courtyard are seventeen wooden buildings, including a stable, a kitchen, a bake house, two barns and three store rooms. The courtyard has a stout palisade with a stone gateway.

Linen. One set of bedding and a table cloth.

Tools. Two copper basins, two mugs, two copper cauldrons and an iron one, a pan, a pot-hook, a fire-dog, a lamp, two axes, an adze, two augers, a scraper, a plane, a chisel, two scythes, two sickles, two wooden shovels tipped with iron. Many wooden tools.

Farm produce. Spelt from last year, 90 baskets, which will make 450 measures of flour. Barley from last year, 100 muids. Spelt from this year, 100 muids. Spelt from this year, 110 baskets, of which 60 have been sown. Wheat from this year, 100 muids, of which 60 have been sown. Oats, 98 muids. Beans, one muid. Peas, 12 muids.

The five mills yielded 900 small muids, 240 of which have been given to the servants.

The four brew houses yielded 650 small muids.

The two bridges yielded in toll 60 muids of salt and two sous.

The four gardens yielded 11 sous and three muids of honey.

One muid of butter, from dues.

Last year's baconers, 10. This year's baconers, 200, as well as sausages and lard. This year's cheese, 43 loads.

Livestock. Mares; old, 5; three-year-olds, 5; two-year-olds, 7; yearlings, 7. Horses; grown stallions, 3; two-year-olds, 10; yearlings, 8. Oxen, 16. Donkeys, 2. Cows; with calves, 50; heifers, 20; this year's calves, 38; bulls, 3. Pigs; old 250; young, 100; boars, 5. Sheep; ewes with lambs, 150; yearling lambs, 200; rams, 120. Goats; she-goats, with kids, 30; yearlings, 30; billy goats, 3. Geese, 30. Hens, 24. Peacocks, 22. [From A. Boetius, *Capitularia Regum Francorum*]

The following points are of special interest here. Very little money is mentioned. The tolls from the bridges were paid almost entirely in kind, and most of the cash that there was came from the gardens. Was this rent, or were they selling the produce? Most of the metal tools were for cooking and carpentry, and only a few were for agriculture, so it would seem that nearly all the farm work was done with wooden implements. Keeping livestock was an important activity, but no one kind of animal is unduly dominant. Most striking of all, though, are the poor crop yields. That year, 55 percent of the spelt and 60 percent of the wheat had to be kept for seed.

THOSE WHO WORKED

When the Roman Empire was collapsing, people who felt insecure bound themselves to powerful patrons. In the middle of the fifth century, a priest called Salvian of Marseilles wrote:

8. Why do our poor, oppressed people not flee to the barbarians? This is the reason. They have put themselves under the protection of more powerful men. I would not think this was shameful, but would, indeed, praise the rich who undertook the care of the poor, if only they did it from charity and not from greed. But those who are seeking protection must give all they own to their patrons, before they are admitted to their patronage. Thus the sons lose their inheritances, so that the fathers may be protected.

Then there is the dreadful truth that when these wretched people have been deprived of their miserable belongings and driven from their land, they must still pay taxes on what they have lost. They own nothing and taxes destroy them. Therefore many people who have lost their homes and fields, or have fled from the tax gatherers, seek out powerful men and become their serfs. They act like those refugees who, in fear of their enemies, run to fortresses, or any places where they may find refuge. In the same way, those who cannot defend their houses or their children become serfs, depriving themselves not only of their possessions, but also of their position in society. They lose their property and they lose their freedom. [*Governance*]

This trend continued for much of the Middle Ages. On Christmas Day 818, one Perahart gave himself to the monastery of Freising, Bavaria:

9. Perahart made his gift in the following way. In the presence of Bishop Hitton and Count Lippold, as well as many others, he gave himself and all his dependents to the service of the Blessed Virgin Mary and St. Corbinien. This day, he gave all that he owned to the Abbey of the Virgin Mary, that is to say, half a house and half its farm buildings, along with horses, oxen, sheep and pigs, one slave and 30 wagon

CHAPTER 1. EARLY AGRICULTURE

loads of hay. I, Perahart, have done this, so that I may have food and clothing from the Abbey, and if I am given less than I need, I may take what is necessary from my property. [In G. Franz, *Deutsches Bauerntum*]

In many parts of Europe, bondsmen did most of the work on the demesnes. These were some of the services performed for a monastery near Paris in the ninth century:

10. Actard, a villein, and Elgilde his wife, also a villein, have six children called Aget, Teudo, Siméon, Adalside, Dieudonnée and Electard. They hold a free farm, consisting of five bonniers and two ansanges of arable, four arpents of vineyard and four and a half arpents of meadow. In one year they pay four silver sous in lieu of military service, in the second year they pay two sous in lieu of their dues of meat, and in the third year, a ewe and a lamb, in lieu of their dues of fodder. They pay two muids of wine for pannage and four deniers for the right to collect firewood. In lieu of cartage, they give a measure of wood. They plough four perches for the winter grain and two perches for the spring. They must work themselves and with their animals whenever they are needed. They give three chickens and fifteen eggs.

Hadvoud, a slave, and his wife Guingilde, also a slave, have five children, Frothard, Girouard, Airole, Advis and Eligilde. They hold a free farm of one and a half bonniers of arable, three quarters of an arpent of vineyard and a half arpent of meadow. For pannage they pay three muids of wine, a setier of mustard, fifty withies, three chickens and fifteen eggs. They work whenever they are needed. The woman weaves cloth with the master's wool and feeds the poultry whenever she is required to do so.

Ermenolde, a villein and his wife, a slave; Foucard, a slave, and his wife, a slave called Ragentisme. They hold a servile farm of two bonniers and one and a half ansages of arable, an arpent of vineyard and two and a half arpents of meadow. They owe the same services as Havoud and his family. [*Inventory of the Abbey of Saint-Germain-des-Prés*]

9

This document shows there were no neat social divisions, for a
slave was married to a villein, and slaves and villeins shared a holding. Also, there is no link between the status of the people and
that of their holdings. It would not appear, though, that this made
much difference, as they all owed much the same services, save
that the farm first mentioned, being much larger, paid some
money dues.

There was money in circulation here because Paris was close.

The following are the services due from the holdings attached
to the demesne of Friemersheim, a grange of the monastery of
Werden, in the Rhineland. There were 102 holdings, scattered over
five different areas:

11. Rent of each of the farms. One sou on Lady Day, one sou between Martinmas and St. Andrew's Day, one sou at Candlemas,
one sou, three hens and ten eggs in the middle of May.

Services. Two weeks work in autumn, two weeks in late
winter, two weeks in June. Five days work in each week. In
autumn and in late winter a yoke of land must be ploughed
and harrowed. The farm will also have to keep the yokes
free from weeds, and carry out all the work on them, including taking the harvest safely to the barn. Also in the
spring, the farm must plough for a day, for which a setier of
beer and a loaf will be given. During the harvest, the wife
must bind the sheaves and pile them in five stacks. She may
keep four sheaves for herself. Her husband must take two
of the stacks to the barn, the rest being carried by the servants of the grange. During the hay harvest, everyone from
the farm must scythe until noon, when every two men will
receive a loaf and a setier of beer. The hay must be bound
into sheaves and carted to the barn.

Every year, each farm must accept 12 muids of grain, from
which it will brew beer, using its own fuel and cauldron. It
may keep one and a half measures of the beer for itself.
The farm must also accept two muids of rye, which it will
grind and bake. It may keep one loaf out of twenty-four. It
must also grind two muids of barley for dog food.

CHAPTER 1. EARLY AGRICULTURE

Every farm must give five muids of acorns, for pig food. All the farms must take it in turn to help the swineherd look after the pigs. They will be held responsible if a pig is lost between sunrise and sunset, but not between sunset and sunrise.

The farm must accept one sheaf of flax, which it will prepare and from which it will collect the seed. [In G. Franz, *Deutsche Bauerntum*]

This document is part of an inventory of the monastery of San Giulia of Brescia in northern Italy:

12. At Porzano there is a grange with four outbuildings and four kitchens. There is enough arable to sow 300 muids of grain, vines to make fifty jars, meadowland to make twenty-five cartloads of hay, enough woodland to feed twenty pigs. There are thirty-two servants, both male and female. In stock are twenty muids of wheat, fifty-three of rye, seven of peas and beans, 100 of barley and 140 of millet. There are twenty-one jars and one urn of wine. Livestock: six oxen, four cows, two calves, twenty-four pigs, forty sheep, fifteen geese and fifteen hens.

There are three holdings, occupied by three slaves who pay three jars of wine, three pigs and three sheep.

There are thirteen other holdings, occupied by thirteen villeins who, between them pay forty muids of grain, five jars of wine, two pigs, four sheep, twenty-six hens, 130 eggs and twenty-nine deniers. Each of them works for one day a week.

On another holding there are eight villeins who pay one sheep, three hens and fifteen eggs.

There are fifteen free men, who have conveyed their holdings to the grange and each work for one day a week.

There are ten other holdings, whose occupants do no more than carry letters and messages. [In *Codex Diplomaticus Longobardiae*, ed. Porro-Lambertenghi]

Here, the tenants, among them, gave no more that twenty-eight days of work in the week, while the thirty-two servants would have given, presumably, close on two hundred. This is in contrast with the estates in northern Europe, where the servants were few and the bondsmen many. Was this Lombard monastery following the Roman tradition of estate management? There was comparatively little livestock for such a large demesne.

In Spain, sheep rearing was becoming important. Isidore, bishop of Seville in the early seventh century, made these rules for the care of sheep in mountainous regions:

> 13. Those who are charged with the feeding of flocks must take the greatest care with them and be so vigilant and skillful that they are not devoured by wild animals, and are kept from throwing themselves over precipices and cliffs in the mountains. And if, through lack of care, the sheep run into any danger, then the shepherds must cast themselves at the feet of the elders, and, lamenting their fault as if it were the greatest of sins, undergo the appropriate punishment. When that is done, they will supplicate and obtain forgiveness. If the offenders are boys, they will be beaten with canes as their punishment.
>
> There are some who are apt to murmur about those who look after flocks, and say they derive no good from this service, for they are never seen at the gatherings, praying and working. But they must lend an ear to the rules of the Fathers and think in silence, recognizing the examples of their ancestors, that the patriarchs grazed flocks, that Peter followed the calling of fisherman and that St. Joseph, who married the Virgin Mary was a smith [sic]. For this reason, those who look after flocks must take great care of them, since not one benefit, but many, come from them. Through them, the sick are nursed, children are fed, the elderly are sustained, captives are redeemed and travelers and guests are lodged. In these regions, which are much less productive than others, many monasteries would have resources

for hardly three months in the year, if they depended only on their daily bread. For which reason, whoever undertakes the work of shepherd must obey wholeheartedly and be sure that he will receive a great reward, while he who disobeys, puts his soul in danger. [*Regula Communis*]

It will be remembered that the tenants of the grange at Friemersheim had to grind corn for the monastery (page 10). They would have done this slowly and laboriously in hand querns. In fact, Friemersheim was behind the times, for by the ninth century, water mills were proliferating. This was one of the most important advances in agriculture during the early Middle Ages, for the mills saved an enormous amount of work. Most of them were owned by lords, to whom they brought large profits. Here are some regulations that the abbot of Corbie in northern France made for his mills. Clearly, his millers were so important to him that he was willing to cosset them:

14. Every miller shall have a holding of six bonniers of land, to enable him to do what is required of him and pay his proper toll of flour. He must have oxen and all he needs for ploughing, so that he and his family will be able to live, keep pigs, geese and hens, look after the mill, cart the materials for the repair of the mill, cart the millstones, and keep the mill and its leat in repair. We do not want him to perform any other services, neither carting, nor ploughing, nor sowing, nor harvesting, nor haymaking, nor brewing, nor delivering hops or wood, nor doing anything else for the master, so that he can devote himself entirely to his mill. [*Inventory of Abbot Irminon*]

The following document shows that there was progress of another kind, at least on some royal estates. This was the increasing use of marl. Many early settlements were on light soils, because they were easy to cultivate, but they were not the most productive and a way to improve them was to dress them with marl, which is a form of clay.

The document also shows that it might be one thing for a lord to detail the services due from his tenants, and quite another to enforce them:

> 15. Certain tenants on the royal and church estates owe cartage and work services. This they do not deny. But they refuse to cart marl, perhaps because, in former times, marl was not carried. As for works, they are unwilling to thresh in the barn, even though they agree that they owe works. Let them cart all they are ordered to cart, since that is their duty, and let them perform whatever works that may be required of them. [*Edict of Charles the Bald, 864*]

The German estates of Einhard, Charlemagne's biographer, hardly ran like clockwork. In 828 he wrote to one of his agents:

> 16. We are amazed that the things we have told you to do for us should remain undone. We understand that of all the grain you should have sent to Mulinheim to make flour and malt, you have sent nothing; but only 30 pigs and these are not of good quality, nor, indeed, even mediocre, and three muids of beans. Nor is that all. During the whole of this winter we have seen neither you, nor anyone sent by you, who could tell us what was happening over there. If we cannot have any more from Fritzlar than what you have sent us, we cannot see any point in keeping this estate. Therefore, if you value our good will, cease this neglect and tell us at once what we may expect from you. [*Einharti Epistolae*]

CHAPTER 2
AGRICULTURE DURING THE
11TH AND 12TH CENTURIES

POPULATION

It is impossible to find accurate figures for medieval populations. England has more complete records than any other country, but even these are inadequate.

The English historians' chief pride is Domesday Book of 1086, which, being a survey of an entire country, is unique. It was ordered by William the Conqueror, who wished to discover what his new kingdom was worth, and hence what he could hope to levy in taxes. This is a typical entry from Domesday:

> 17. Edward also holds Kinson. Wulfwen held it in the time of King Edward. It paid tax for 13 hides. Land for nine ploughs, of which 5 hides and one virgate of land are in demesne; two ploughs there; 7 slaves.
>
> 18 villeins, 14 cottars and 4 coscets, with 7 ploughs. A mill which pays 5 shillings; woodland, 1 acre; meadow 100 acres less 5; pasture 3 leagues long and 2 leagues wide, less 3 furlongs. Value of these two manors [Canford and Kinson] when he acquired them £50; now £70.

This looks like a splendid source of information, but the difficulties of interpretation are enormous. Here, our main concern is population, and we can see that Domesday lists 43 villagers of various kinds. But, with the possible exception of the slaves, most of them would have been men with wives and children, and estimates of the average size of families vary from 5 to 3.5. If we assume that the higher figure was correct and that slaves were heads of households, then the population of the village was 215.

If, however, we assume that the lower multiplier was correct and that slaves were not heads of households, then the population was 133.

Difficulties increase when we investigate population changes, for there is no equivalent to Domesday in later centuries. There are, indeed, tax lists from the early fourteenth century, known as Subsidy Rolls, but we cannot tell how many people escaped tax and were, in consequence, not listed. Nonetheless, the population trend, at least, is clear enough. For the manor of Up Wimborne, Dorset, Domesday mentions 9 heads of households, while the Subsidy Roll of 1332 lists 17 taxpayers. It is, therefore, reasonable to suppose that there were more people living in Up Wimborne in 1332 than there had been in 1086.

We cannot, of course, generalize about an entire continent from  what happened in one village, but there are scraps of evidence like this from all parts of Europe, so we may safely conclude that there was, overall, an increase in population, though we shall be disappointed if we try to quantify it.

The extra population meant that more food was needed, and this might have been found by improving farming techniques. People in general, though, would rather use their muscles than their brains, so, initially, the Europeans of the Middle Ages increased output simply by bringing more land into cultivation. They did this by extending their frontiers and reclaiming their wastes.

THE EXTENSION OF THE FRONTIERS

After they had long been the victims of raids and invasions, in the eleventh century the people of the heartlands of Europe at last went on the offensive. The Anglo-Normans tried to overrun the

CHAPTER 2. LATER AGRICULTURE

Celtic fringes of the British Isles and, though they conquered Wales, they achieved little in Ireland and nothing at all in Scotland. Other peoples had more success, the Germans, for example, taking a great deal of territory from the Slavs.

When, in the Second World War, the Germans tried to colonize Poland and the Soviet Union, they were following an ancient tradition, for their medieval ancestors had also been tempted by the lands to the east. They were thinly populated and their inhabitants seemed primitive. A German poet-monk gave his view of Poland:

18. The land was uncultivated and covered with woods
And the Poles were poor and lazy,
Using wooden ploughs untipped with iron to stir the sandy soil,
Using only two cows or oxen to pull the plough.
In the entire land there was no town or city,
Only country markets, a neglected field and a chapel beside
   a castle.
Neither salt, nor iron, nor coins, nor metals,
Nor decent clothes, nor even shoes
Did the people have. They simply grazed their flocks.
[*Lubiaz Verses*]

The Germans could not resist the temptation to exploit such people. For example, in the middle of the twelfth century, Albert the Bear carved for himself the Mark of Brandenburg; and his two grandsons, John and Otto, followed in his footsteps:

19. After they had grown to be men, they lived together in harmony, as brothers ought. Their friendship allowed them to destroy their enemies, advance their friends, augment their lands and revenues and gain fame, glory and power. They conquered Barnim, Tetlow and many other lands from the lord of Pomerania, and bought Uckermark. They built Berlin, Frankfurt, New Angermünde, Stolpe, Liebenwalde, Stargard, New Brandenburg and many other towns. They turned the wilderness into fruitful lands and had ample goods of all kinds. [*Cronica Principum Saxoniae*]

The men who conquered new lands had to people them, if they were to draw revenues from them. A chronicler describes the recruiting drive of Count Adolf of Wagria in about 1140:

> 20. His lands were uninhabited, so he sent messengers into many places, Flanders, Holland, Utrecht, Westphalia and Frisia. They said that any who were short of farm land should bring their families into this good, spacious region, which has fertile soil, numerous fish and wild animals and makes excellent pasture. [*Chronicle of the Slavs*]

Settlers were encouraged by excusing them rents or dues, until their farms were productive. Early in the thirteenth century, the bishop of Hildesheim made these terms with some new tenants:

> 21. When someone has felled trees and torn out the undergrowth, he shall owe neither rent nor tithes for as long as he is cultivating the soil with the mattock. As soon as the land is ploughed, and is producing more, he shall pay no rent for seven years. But in the seventh year he must pay two pence, in the eighth four pence, in the ninth eight pence and in the tenth one shilling, which shall be his rent from then onwards. [*Charter of Hermann Balk*]

This gives an insight into the work of reclaiming woodland. Removing the trees and bushes was only the beginning since, before the plough could go to work, the roots had to be hacked out with mattocks.

The Teutonic newcomers were as unwelcome in the Middle Ages as they were in more recent years. A Bohemian chronicler of the fourteenth century looked back to a mythical golden age:

CHAPTER 2. LATER AGRICULTURE

22. It would be better and fairer if the bear remained in the woods, the fox in his lair, the fish in water and the German in Germany. The world was much healthier when the Germans were used as targets for archery practice. In some places their eyes were put out, in others they were hung up by the feet, in others they were driven outside the walls, in others they were compelled to give their noses as toll, in others they were slain to make a spectacle for princes, in others they were made to eat their own ears. [*Dalimil Chronicle*]

RECLAIMING THE WASTES

Broadly speaking, the reclamation of the wastes took two forms. New settlements were founded in virgin territory, and people living in existing settlements extended their fields.

The French king Philip Augustus [r.1180-1223] announces the foundation of a new village, attracting newcomers by promising special privileges:

23. Philip, by the grace of God, king of France. Be it known that we have decreed that the place called Chevrières shall be open to all who wish to dwell there, under these terms. The inhabitants shall be exempt from taille and any other unjust dues. They shall not have to perform any military services which will prevent them returning home on the same day, except in time of war. They shall have the right to gather dead wood in our forest of Cuisse. If they commit offenses, the fines shall be: for an offense of sixty sous, five sous; for an offense of five sous, twelve deniers. Moreover, anyone who wishes to purge himself by taking an oath shall be permitted to do so and will pay nothing. Every year, on St. Rémi's day, every man must give six measures of oats. The rent for a full holding is five sous, and half that for half a holding. [*Acts of Philip Augustus*, 1182]

In 1106, the bishop of Hamburg granted some intractable wastes to people who were likely to make them productive. Again, the settlers were to have special privileges:

> 24. Frederick, by the grace of God, bishop of Hamburg. Be it known to all men that we have made an agreement with men from the other side of the Rhine, known as Hollanders. They have asked for land within our diocese, which is now uncultivated and swampy, and of no use to the people of this country, so that they may bring it into cultivation. Having taken council and believing that this will be of value to us and to our successors, we have agreed.
>
> We have made a contract under which each holding will pay us one denier a year. We think it wise to give the size of the holding, to avoid disputes in the future, and it is 720 rods long and 30 wide, together with the streams that cross the land. They have also agreed to give us a tithe of their produce, that is to say, the eleventh sheaf, the tenth lamb, pig, goat, goose, the tenth measure of honey and the tenth of flax.
>
> So that they will not have to submit to the judgments of prejudiced strangers, they have agreed to pay two marks a year for every hundred holdings, so that they may administer justice themselves. If they cannot agree on a verdict in an important case, they may call on the bishop. They must pay for his subsistence while he is with them. They may then keep two thirds of the profits of justice, and give the third part to the bishop.
>
> We have given them the right to build churches wherever they wish. We will give to each of these churches a tithe of the tithe we receive from them. The congregations, for their part, will endow each church with a holding. [In G. Frantz, *Deutsches Bauerntum*]

Each holding was much longer than it was wide. This was probably to give every farmer a share of every type of land in the area, as well as access to water.

CHAPTER 2. LATER AGRICULTURE

Only men of substance could move to new settlements, because, like the Pilgrim Fathers, they had to equip and stock their holdings and live until they had brought in their first harvest. But all could increase their farm land by encroaching on the woodlands and wastes that surrounded their villages. They might extend their communal fields, or individuals might clear and enclose smaller fields for themselves, which was known as "assarting." Either way, progress was likely to be slow, and it might be centuries before all the available land was occupied. Often, the encroachments were made surreptitiously, for, as a rule, the wastes belonged to the lord and he might well object to losing any of them, especially if his hunting was likely to be affected.

Though this movement was important, it is difficult to assess its progress, because it is not well documented. The landscape itself may well show that reclamation took place, but, as a rule, it is impossible to date it, unless it led to disputes. An English jurist describes a typical case:

> 25. The assize comes to recognize if Elias of Leyburn unjustly disseised Wymar of Leyburn of common of his pasture pertaining to his free tenement in the same town [village] of Leyburn.
>
> The jurors say that the wood was at one time common, in such wise that there were five sharers who had the wood common, and afterwards by their consent partition was made between them that each should have his part in severalty, and it was granted that each might assart his part and grow corn, saving however to each of them common of herbage after the corn was carried, and most of them assarted their part, but the wood whereof complaint was made was not then assarted, and because he to whom the wood pertains has now assarted a part, the said Wymar has brought a writ of novel disseisin.
>
> It is decided that the aforesaid Elias disseised him. And it shall be lawful for each sharer to assart his wood, saving to each of them common of pasture after the corn and hay is carried. [*Bracton's Notebook, 1237*]

Thus we discover, in an oblique way, that much of the woodland at Leyburn was assarted early in the thirteenth century.

As long as villages were surrounded by swathes of woodland, boundaries hardly mattered, but they had to be defined after the woods were cleared. Boundary disputes, then, are another sign of reclamation. This example of 1190 comes from eastern France:

> 26. Matthew, by the grace of God, bishop of Troyes. Be it known to all men that there has been a dispute between the abbot of Montier-en-Der and the abbot of Montier-la-Celle because certain men from Fontenay have built houses at La Brau, a place which the abbot of Montier-en-Der claims is within his parish; the abbot of Montier-la-Celle also claims that it is in the boundaries of his parish. After much debate in my council and with the two abbots, an agreement has been reached, which divides the tithes belonging to the parishes of the abbots, that is to the parish of Chavagne, depending on Montier-la-Celle, and to the parish of Beaufort, depending on Montier-en-Der. This boundary goes in a straight line from Perthe-Aymon, to the apple tree standing by the side of the public road from Beaufort to Margerie, and from that tree it follows the road to the stream of la Brau. It follows the stream to its source, and thence it goes along the valley of Bonon to a tree known to the country folk as Canordel. It then follows the path which runs alongside the house of Robert de Duma, on the outskirts of Chavagnes. [*Charter of the Diocese of Troyes*]

CHAPTER 3
THE MEDIEVAL VILLAGE IN ITS PRIME

FARMING

Since Europe is so varied in its geology, topography and climate, regional differences remained strong and it is not possible to describe them all in a book of this size. What follows is, in the main, a description of farming on the great European Plain, which begins in the heartland of England and extends eastwards, growing ever wider, until it reaches the Urals.

Villages divided their territory into arable, meadow and pasture, and parish boundaries were often drawn to give each settlement a share of land suitable for all these uses. For example, in the chalk downlands of southern England, many of the villages are strung along the spring line towards the foot of the hills. The well-drained hill tops were used as pasture, the damper land, near the river or stream was used as meadow, and the intermediate land was arable.

The crops grown on the arable were mainly cereals, that is, wheat, barley, oats, rye and spelt. Wheat was the most prized, as it made the best bread, but it did not thrive everywhere. In wet climates, like that of Scotland, oats were a safer crop, as was rye on dry sandy soils, like many in northern Germany. Spelt was not much grown in England, but was common in continental Europe, especially northern France. Peas and beans were also grown, to be harvested when dry and used as fodder. Much of the grain was also fed to the animals, though there was no hard and fast line dividing fodder from human food. The gentry might insist on wheaten bread, but the peasant made his bread from what he had, even, if need be, the flour of peas and beans. "Hunger," it was said, "puts his first foot in the horse trough."

The main problem with the arable was to maintain its fertility, since it was no longer possible to abandon it, once it was exhausted.

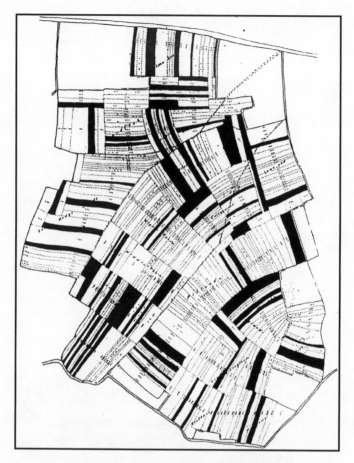

Moreover, there were no artificial fertilizers, and there was but little dung, since most animals had to be slaughtered in the autumn, for lack of fodder. The answer was to allow land to lie fallow, perhaps every other year, perhaps one year in three. Usually, there were three fields, one sown in the autumn, one in the spring, and one resting. The rotation on each field was autumn sowing, spring sowing and fallow. Everyone farmed these fields, taking it in turn to use the communal ploughs, harrows and draught animals. Moreover, though each family had its own plots, there were no enclosures separating them. For that reason, the fields are described as "open." Obviously, there were fences or hedges round the perimeters, to keep straying animals from the crops.

In just a few places, open fields have survived, one of them being at Braunton in Devon. Figure 8 at left shows a map of Braunton Great Field, made in 1841. The field was, and still is, about a mile from north to south. There were 491 strips, or selions, which were shared among 56 families. One holding is shown in black, and all the holdings were scattered in the same way, so that they were completely intermingled. Earlier, the plan of the field was almost certainly even more complicated. At Wigston Magna, Leicestershire, in 1393 there was a holding that consisted of 47 parcels of land, scattered throughout a field, 21 being of one rood, 14 of one and a half roods, and two of two roods. The rood, though far from standard, was about a quarter of an acre. Since the average field covered a square mile, and since the average strip was between a quarter and half an acre, there might well be considerably more than 1,000 strips on a field. The peasants, though, could recognize their own plots as easily as a mother can pick out her own children in a crowd.

As well as the maps drawn in more recent times, there are many references to strip cultivation during the Middle Ages. For example, an inventory of the abbey of Saint-Rémi-de-Reims of 861 records that a certain Giraud "works a plot 40 perches long and three wide," the Law of the Bavarians of 750 states that a "lawful plot" is 40 perches long and 4 wide, and the standard English acre, which is medieval in origin, is a furlong by a chain, or 220 yards by 22. What is not clear is why the fields were divided in this way. There is no shortage of theories, but, as they are not supported by documentary evidence, discussion of them has no place in an anthology of sources. Readers who are interested should consult the work of C.S. and C.S. Orwin, *The Open Fields*.

The meadow gave hay, for winter feed. It was on the lowest and dampest ground, which was difficult to plough, but would give a good crop of grass. Like the arable, the meadow was divided into strips, known as "doles."

The pasture gave summer grazing. Animals grazed in a number of places, the most important of which was the common that lay beyond the open fields. It was land that had not been brought into cultivation, either because it was too poor, or because it was not needed. Secondly, animals could graze the aftermath that grew on the meadow, after the hay had been cropped. Thirdly, there was the fallow field, where the animals roamed at will, feeding on the stubble and any weeds they could find.

As the area under cultivation increased, the common dwindled and there was less and less pasture. The first measure was to "stint" the common, that is to limit the number of animals each villager could graze on it. When, finally, the common vanished, the livestock had to make do with what remained. In fact, it was better off, because an acre of arable would produce more fodder than an acre of unmanaged scrubland on the common.

However great the land hunger, many villages kept a certain amount of woodland. This was pasture of a kind, especially when the acorns fell, a marvelous time for pigs. The following document shows how woods were valuable for this and for other reasons. It is part of a contract made between the monks of a French monastery and their foresters:

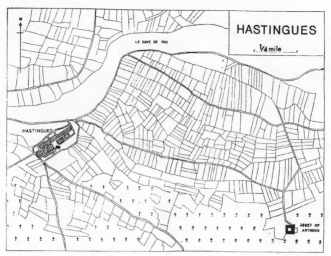

HASTINGUES

LE GAVE DE PAU

¼ mile

HASTINGUES

ABBEY OF ARTHOUS

27. We shall take as much of the living wood as we require for our own use. We may neither sell nor give any growing timber without the leave of the monks. We may collect, sell and give away dead wood.

When there are acorns, we will not run our own pigs in the wood, until the monks have admitted their own. We will never run other men's pigs along with our own. We will not sell acorns or give them away. When the monks admit other men's pigs to fatten them, we shall have the fee. The monks' pigs may graze at any time.

If we trap any game, it shall be ours. If others take it, the monks shall have the shoulder of the boar and the haunch of the deer. If we find bees, we may have them. If anyone else finds them, the monks and the foresters shall have the honey, the wax and half the bees. [*Charters of the Abbey of la Ferté-sur-Grosne*]

As the population grew, and pressure on the land increased, farming had to become more systematic and efficient. There were no startling developments, but methods that had been evolving for centuries became commonplace. This need to farm efficiently produced a number of treatises on agriculture:

28. Sort out your cattle once a year between Easter and Whitsuntide, that is to say, oxen, cows and herds, and let those that are not to be kept be put to fatten. If you spend money to fatten them with grass you will gain. And know for truth that bad beasts cost more than good. If it be a draught beast he must be more thought of than the others and more spared, and because he is spared the others are burdened for his lack. And if you must buy cattle, buy them between Easter and Whitsuntide, for then beasts are spare and cheap. And change your horses before they are too old and worn out or maimed, for with little money you can rear good and young ones. [Walter of Henley, *Husbandry*, 13th century]

29. You must note how much grain has been sown and how much has been reaped. Barley should yield to the eighth grain,

so that from one quarter comes eight quarters; rye to the seventh grain and beans to the sixth grain; and peas to the sixth

grain; and maslin of wheat and rye, if they are equally mixed, must yield to the sixth grain; and if there is more rye than wheat, the yield must be more, and if there is more wheat than rye, less. And wheat should yield to the fifth grain and oats to the fourth.

But the earth does not always yield as much one year as another, so, before every count, you must take note of the soil and what the weather has been. Often, winter sowings take well and spring sowings badly, and another time the spring sowings take well and the winter sowings badly. [*Anonymous Treatise on Rural Economy*, 13th century]

30. Good sons, feed your dung heaps with good earth and mix it with dung. And every fortnight dress the dung from your sheepfold with clay or with good soil from cleansing the ditches. Do not plough your manured land too deep, so that the dung spoils in going down. Now you shall say that you would rather have dung which is mixed with soil, for if the dung is good and pure, it will last two years or three according to whether the soil is cool or warm, but dung mixed with soil will last twice as long.

You should know well that marl lasts longer than manure, for dung spoils in going down and marl in rising.

If you put your dung on the fallow field, it is better for it to be turned under the soil at the second ploughing, so that at sowing time it will be thrown up. If you put it on after the second ploughing, then at sowing time it will be turned into the soil, and will not be worth so much. [Ibid.]

If this excellent advice could have been followed everywhere, medieval farming would have been transformed, but shortage of fodder meant that only a few cattle could be stall fed through the winter, so there was not nearly enough dung for all the arable. But cultivation helps fertility, and, as this document shows, the fallow was ploughed three times, twice during the course of the year, and once before sowing. Yet another treatise describes the work of the ploughman:

31. The plough driver's art consists herein, that he drive the oxen evenly, neither smiting nor pricking nor grieving them. Such should not be melancholy or wrathful, but cheerful, jocund and full of song, that by their melody and song the oxen may in a manner rejoice in their labor. Such a ploughman should bring the fodder with his own hands, and love his oxen and sleep with them by night, tickling and combing and rubbing them with straw; keeping them in all respects, and guarding their forage or provender from theft. If he finds other beasts in their pasture, he must impound them. [*Fleta*]

William Langland took a more realistic view of ploughing:

32. As I went by, weeping with sorrow, I saw a poor man hanging on to the plough. His coat was of coarse stuff which was called cary. His hood was full of holes and his hair stuck out of it. As he trod the soil, his toes stuck out of his worn shoes with their thick soles; his hose hung about his hocks and on all sides he was bedaubed with mud as he followed the plough. He had two mittens made of rough stuff, with worn-out fingers thick with muck. This man bemired himself in mud almost to the ankle, and drove four heifers before him that had become feeble, so that men might count their every rib, so sorry-looking were they.

His wife walked beside him with a long goad, in a shortened cote-hardy looped up full high, and wrapped in a winnowing sheet to protect her from the weather. She went barefoot on the ice so that the blood flowed. And at the end of the row lay a little crumb-bowl, and therein a little child covered with rags, and two two-year-olds were on the other side, and they all sang one song that was pitiful to hear; they all cried the same cry – a miserable note. The poor man sighed sorely and said, "Children be still!" [*Vision of Piers the Ploughman*]

The communal farming gave plenty of chances for cheating. One of Langland's characters says:

33. If I went ploughing, I would skirt my neighbor's strip so closely that I filched a foot or a furrow's breadth of his land; and if I were reaping, I would tell my men to reach over with their sickles, and take in grain that I had never sown. [*Ibid.*]

Village communities tried to ensure good behavior by making rules for the management of their farmland. These two documents are from Tuscany:

34. He who ploughs with oxen or any other animals beside the sown land of another, where wheat or any cereal, or

leguminous crops are to be sown, must leave four furrows beside this sown land, so that, when he turns, he causes no damage. Whoever breaks this rule, shall be fined ten shillings, and will make good the damage he has done. [*Laws of Montepescali*, 1427]

35. The magistrates have ordered that, seeing there is so little pasture in the commune of Bucino, everyone who wishes to keep sheep, goats, pigs or cows, must pay to the treasurer of the commune every year on the calends of November, for every goat, ten shillings, for every pig, five shillings, and for every cow, five shillings. And there shall be a fine of a quarter more for every animal that is not paid.

The magistrates have also ordered that no one shall saddle a donkey, harness oxen, plough, or do any physical work on any of the feasts of Our Lady, the Twelve Apostles, the four Evangelists, Saint Apollinarius, Sundays or Easter Day, without the permission of the mayor, on pain of five shillings per animal.
It shall, though, be allowed for a man to stook the grain in the field, to take a load to the mill and to carry fodder to the animals, save that on Easter
Day, Our Lady's Day and Good Friday, none of these things may be done. [*Laws of Buccine*, 1411]

These rules were made at Wimeswould, in England:

36. If any man tether his horse on any headlands so that it may go into any man's corn, he shall make amends to him that hath harm, and for each foot that is within the corn pay one penny to the church.

If any man shall be taken at night-time destroying other men's corn or grass, he shall be punished as the law decrees and pay fourpence to the church.

If any man be taken at night-time in the field with cart or other carriage, between bell and bell, he shall pay forty pence to the church.

No cattle shall come into the wheat cornfield till the corn be led away; nor into the peas cornfield till the peas be led away, on pain of each beast one penny to the church.

If our hayward pen a herd of stray cattle, he shall take sixpence, for a flock of sheep fourpence, and for each horse, one penny. [*Middleton Manuscripts*, 1425]

Each manor had a court, which enforced the rules:

37. Thomas Brown is presented that he fence the ditch, which is an annoyance to his neighbors, between the Wall Meadow and John Banaster's croft, before the Feast of Pentecost coming, under pain of twelve pence.

And the jurors say that three foul pools are lying at le Holide, not flushed, to the hurt of the neighbors by Butcherfield, by default of Thomas Cotes. He is commanded to amend the same before the Feast of the Ascension of Our Lord, under pain of each not cleansed, fourpence.

Also, it is presented that Robert a London hath five more cows tethered in the common fields than he ought to have; therefore he shall forfeit the penalty thereupon imposed. [*Manor Rolls of Grossall, Staffordshire*, 1502]

38. John atte Cruche in mercy for a trespass made on William Fuller by taking and carrying away a harrow of the said William and detaining it for three days, whereby the land of the said William lies unharrowed to his damage. This trespass he cannot deny.

John Daunsers in mercy for damage done in the lord's wood by breaking and cutting down the lord's thorn bushes. [*Manor Rolls of Brightwaltham, Berkshire*, 1284]

39. John Shad is in mercy for a trespass made at Howelotesfield with his draught cattle, fine threepence.

Rose Newman for a trespass made with her sheep in the meadow, fine threepence.

Sabina Tampan in mercy because she has taken furze in Howelotesfield. Pardoned because she is poor.

The whole village are charged to acknowledge they are wrongdoers, because they have maliciously tied together the feet of the lord's pigs. [*Manor Rolls of Addington, Surrey*, 1433]

THE LORD OF THE MANOR AND HIS VILLEINS

Throughout the Middle Ages, people went on placing themselves in bondage to more powerful men, in order to secure protection. These examples are from fifteenth-century Catalonia:

40. Be it known to all that I, Barchinona, daughter of Maria and Bernat de Nuce, clerk of Villalonga, commend myself completely and entirely, together with my offspring and all my possessions, to you, Lord Galceran de Catllar, to be your woman and that of your successors, and I accept you as my natural lord and subject myself to your rule. [From Miquel Golobardes, *Records of Catalonia*]

41. Be it known to all men, that I, Guillem de les Fonts, son of Maria, who belonged to the parish of St. John of Begur, and my brothers, Pere, Jaume and Berenguer, and our sister Berenguera, together, all of us, who live in the parish of St. Martin of Vilallonga, not having been coerced by force, but of our own free will, recognize, together with all our offspring born and to be born, and all our goods which we have or shall have, that we are the people, complete and entire of you, Lord Galceran de Catllar, and of all your successors for ever; each and everyone of us promises to keep faith with you and yours in all circumstances, and, in recognition of your lordship, we will give you annually, on the feast of St. Andrew, I, the afore-mentioned Guillem, a pound of wax, and each one of us, the

other men, a pair of hens, except for the woman, who does not have to give anything in recognition. [Ibid.]

Both lords and villeins had obligations. William Langland's ploughman says to his lord:

42. I'll sweat and toil for us both as long as I live, and gladly do any job you want. But you must promise, in return, to guard over Holy Church, and protect me from the thieves and wasters who ruin the world. And you'll have to hunt down all the hares and foxes and badgers that break down my hedges, and tame falcons to kill the wild birds that crop my wheat.

Then the knight answered courteously and said, "I give you my word, Piers, as I am a true knight; and I'll keep this promise through thick and thin and protect you to the end of my days."

"Ah, but there's one thing more I must ask you," said Piers. "Never ill-treat your tenants, and see you punish them only when Truth compels you. Even then, let Mercy assess the fine, and be ruled by Meekness. And if poor men offer you gifts, don't ever accept them. It may be that you don't deserve them, and will have to pay them back in a perilous place called Purgatory! Take care that you never ill-use your serfs. It will be better for you in the long run, for although they are your underlings here on earth, they may be above you in Heaven. And it is very hard to tell a knight from a serf when he comes to lie in the church vaults, so take that to heart. [*Vision of Piers the Ploughman*]

A thirteenth-century German friar, Berthold von Regensburg, said,

43. Such as till the earth for wine or corn should live truly towards their lords. You should be true to your lord; yet you do your service so sparingly and slothfully and with such constraint! And, when he scolds you, you leave him and flee to some other master.

Sometimes the lords also are guilty here. You lords, you deal sometimes so ill with your poor folk, and can never tax them too high; you would wish to tax them higher and higher. It is

far better that you should take small taxes every year, and collect these all the more carefully. You cannot till the land yourselves, therefore you should so deal with your folk that they serve you gladly; and it is their duty, too, to serve you truly and live truly with one another. [*Sermons*]

The following extracts from manor rolls and monastery records show some of the restrictions on villeins:

44. It is ordered, as many times before, to take William, son of Richard Gilleson, Alice, daughter of John atte Yate, Alice, daughter of William Childyong and William, son of William Childyong, the lord's bondsmen and bondswomen, who have gone away without license, and to bring them back here until they make fine for their chevage.

45. It is presented that Isabel, daughter of William Childyong, has married one William Cisson, a free man, without license. Therefore let her be distrained to make fine with the lord for her merchet. [*Court Rolls of the Manor of Bradford, Yorkshire, 1354*]

46. Geoffrey the villein who held a tenement of the lord is dead, and the said tenement remains in the hands of Alice his wife for the term of her life. She finds a pledge to do the customs and services due, and for the upkeep of the tenement as is becoming. And the lord hath of heriot, one sheep. [*Court Rolls of the Manor of Brightwaltham, Berkshire, 1307*]

47. I, Guynora de la Mare, give to the monks of Eynsham, the virgate of land in Easton which Roger, my bondsman, held of me. I also give them the same Roger and all his brood. [Will in the *Records of the Abbey of Eynsham*]

Villeins attracted sympathy. Etienne de Fougères, a French cleric
of the twelfth century, wrote:

> 48. The lords receive from the peasants their due rents,
> Which they squander in eating and drinking;
> And they keep their laborers fasting,
> And deceive them and do not preserve the faith they owe them.
>
> When the wretched ones yawn with hunger,
> Their lords rob and tax them;
> They lay burdens upon them, they overwork them;
> The forced labor is never remitted.
>
> For a slight act of disrespect
> The lord strikes the peasant with his fist or with a stake;
> And he thrusts him into prison;
> He takes from him his entire living.
>
> He does not shrink from doing the peasant harm,
> He lays waste and plunders all his property,
> He lets him die without concern;
> He who protects thus knows ill how to protect.
> [*Livre des Manières*]

Eustache Deschamps, a contemporary of Chaucer, wrote:

49. You children, descendants of me, Adam, who, after God,
am the first father, created by Him, are all born from my rib
and that of Eve, your mother. How can it be that one is a villein,
while another assumes the name of gentleman? Whence comes
this title of nobility? I do not know, unless it comes from virtue, and the villeins from all harmful vices. You are all clad in
the same skin.

When God made me from the clay, a mortal man, heavy
and vain, and made Eve from me, he created us naked. But the
spirit inspired us to the full and, for ever, we suffered thirst
and hunger, work, pain, and children born in sorrow. For our
sins, all women give birth in pain. Vilely are you conceived.
You are all clad in the same skin.

CHAPTER 3. MEDIEVAL VILLAGE IN ITS PRIME

> The powerful kings, the counts and the dukes, he who is ruler of the people and sovereign, when they were born, what were they wearing? An unclean skin. Prince, think without disdain of the poor whom death holds in its traces. [*Ballades*]

These are the views of intellectuals, and what the villeins themselves were thinking and feeling is much more difficult to discover, but it would seem that if the average peasant was able to choose between a servile and a free holding, then he took the one with the better land.

THE ADMINISTRATION OF THE MANOR

A great estate was managed by a hierarchy of officials. At its head was the steward, or seneschal, who was responsible for all the manors, as well as the lord's household. Each manor had a bailiff, appointed by the lord or his seneschal. There were also officials elected by the villagers themselves from their own number and who changed every year. Usually, these minor officials included a reeve and a hayward. The reeve supervised the villagers when they were working on the demesne, while the hayward's duty was to safeguard the crops, which he did by making sure the fences were kept in good repair and by impounding stray animals.

A thirteenth-century treatise on estate management describes the qualities these officials should have, though few would have reached such high standards!

> 50. Let the lord then procure a Seneschal; a man circumspect and faithful, provident, discreet and gracious, humble and chaste and peaceful and modest, learned in the laws and customs and in the duties of a Seneschal; one who will devote himself to guard his lord's rights in all matters, and who knows how to teach and instruct his master's bailiffs in their doubts and their errors; merciful to the poor, turning aside from the path of justice neither for prayers nor bribes.
>
> Let the Seneschal see to it that, in every manor, he measure clearly and openly with the common rod how many acres of arable land it may contain, and learn how much seed is needed,

lest cunning reeves should reckon too much. Let him heed that all offices be securely locked, for an easy access often tempts the weaker brethren to sin, and men say, "Fast locks make true hinds."

Let him also inquire concerning the bailiffs of each manor, and of their underlings, how they have borne and demeaned themselves towards their neighbors and the lord's tenants and other folk; and let them be removed from the room during this inquisition, lest the truth be suppressed through fear. Let him inquire whether they have meddled with disseisins, or blows or scuffles or wrestlings; or if they neglect their duties to haunt taverns and wakes by night, whereby the lord may suffer loss.

Moreover, he must forbid the flaying of any sheep or other beast until it has been seen by the bailiff to judge the manner of its death, whether it has been slain of set purpose, or by chance and evil fortune.

The Bailiff of every manor should be truthful in word, diligent and faithful in deed. Let him beware of sloth; therefore let him arise betimes in the morning, lest he seem but lukewarm and remiss. Let him first see to the plough-yoking, and then go round to survey the fields, woods, meadows and pastures, lest damage be done there at dawn. Let him see that the ploughmen do their work diligently and well; and, so soon as the ploughs be unyoked, let him measure forthwith the work that has been done that day. He must watch the ploughmen's labor and shortcomings over and over again, and make sure that such defaults be visited with due correction and punished.

The Reeve, elected by the township to that office as the best manager and tiller, must be presented to the lord or to his Seneschal, who should invest him forthwith with his office. Let him therefore not be slothful or sleepy, but let him effectually and unceasingly strive for his lord's profit.

When the dung is to be carried to the fields, let the Reeve abide all day with the carters, that they may labor and finish their day's work without subterfuge. Let the Reeve cause the beasts and horses to be daily fed by daylight in his own presence; by daylight, I say, lest under cover of night their keepers steal their provender. Let the forage be given in small quantities at a time; if they be too profusely supplied, they will low over it in their fullness, and tread the residue under foot, and blow upon it with their nostrils, whereby they will take it in great disfavor and count it as unclean. Moreover, it is good at times to wash the beasts and comb them when they are dry; it is good also to rub down the oxen twice daily with a wisp of straw, that they may the more lovingly lick themselves.

When, in time of pasture, the milch-cows are parted from the rest, and the good sent to saltmarsh pasture, then the milk of two such heifers should answer for one weight of cheese in four-and-twenty weeks, and half a gallon of butter weekly. But if they be fed in the woods or mown meadows, or in stubble, then three kine shall answer for as much as the two aforesaid. And whatsoever we say of these three kine may also be said of a score of well-kept milch ewes.

Let the threshers and winnowing-women be closely spied upon, lest they steal corn in their shoes, gloves, wallets, bags or satchels hidden near the barn. Let no Reeve remain in office beyond the year, unless he be approved as faithful and excellent; and, so long as he be Reeve, let him look closely to all defaults on the farm, for that which may be amended today for one penny may chance not to be amended in a year's time for twelvepence.

Let the Reeve suffer neither man nor woman to have access to the dairy or carry thence cheese, milk, butter or the like. Nor let him suffer any servant of the manor to hold fairs, markets or disseisins, nor to haunt wakes and taverns, but let him compel all to attend unceasingly to their duties. Let him permit no fire to be brought to the stable or cowshed, nor any lighted candle, except in case of necessity, when it shall be borne by two men at least.

The Hayward should be strong, healthy, stern and faithful. Late and early he must range round and spy upon the woods, the farm, the meadows and fields, and all that belongs to the manor. All cattle found to his lord's damage must be impounded. [*Fleta*]

Much of the administration of the manor was carried out in its court, which all the tenants attended. Usually, the lord's steward presided.

The court had several functions. It was a village council, where tenants could express their views and feelings. It made routine decisions about the farming, deciding, for example, when the reaping should begin, or when the fallow field should be thrown open for grazing. As we have already seen, it made general rules for the conduct of the farming, and enforced them. It also acted as a court of law, trying petty offenses. These are descriptions of typical cases from a thirteenth century treatise on the manor court. The author gives no names, dates or places, but he must have seen cases like the ones he describes, and his accounts are much fuller than the often laconic manor rolls:

51. Of battery and assault
Sir Steward, Henry of Combe complaineth of Stephen Carpenter that, as he was going his way, there came this Stephen and encountered him and assailed him with villain words which were undeserved, in that he called him thief and lawless man, and whatever other names seemed good to him, except his right name, and said he was spying from house to house the secrets of the honest folk of the vill in order that he might come another night with his fellows to break into their houses and carry off their goods. Whereupon Henry answered him civilly and said that he was talking at random, which so enraged the said Stephen that he snatched his staff of holly out of his hand, and gave it him about his head and shoulders and loins and elsewhere all over his body and then made off.

Stephen is awarded to acquit himself at the next court.

52. Of fruit carried off from the garden of the lord

Sir Steward, the bailiff complaineth of William of the Street that, against the peace of the lord, he sent Thomas his son over the walls and commanded him to carry off every manner of fruit at his will; and when the bailiff heard the fruit being knocked down, he marveled who this could be, and at once entered the lord's garden and found the boy right high on a costard tree which he had cultivated for the lord's use, because of its goodness; he made him come down and attached him without doing him any villainy, and debonairly asked him by whose commandment and whose sending he entered the lord's garden over the walls; and the boy answered that William his father bade him enter the garden and urged him on to the trees with the best fruit; so the bailiff suffered the boy to carry off all that he had taken and the lord has damage to the amount of six shillings and shame of half a mark.

And William defends and denies that his son entered the garden and carried off fruit at his bidding. "William," saith the Steward, "at least thou canst not deny that he is thy mainpast nor that he was attached in the lord's garden; how wilt thou acquit thyself that thou didst not make him or bid him to do this?"

"Sir, for the deed of my son and the trespass I am ready to do thy will, and I ask thy favor."

The Court awards that he be at his law six-handed at the next Court.

"That will I, Sir." [*Le Court de Baron*]

Note: to be at his law six-handed – to appear with six others who are ready to swear to his innocence.

CHAPTER 4
AGRICULTURE DURING
THE LATE MIDDLE AGES

DEPOPULATION

In 1348, the bubonic plague, or Black Death, ravaged Europe. This visitation is described in Chapter 17, and all we have to note here is that, in so far as can be judged, between a third and a half of the population died. The loss of so many people had far-reaching results for agriculture.

Farms, and, indeed, entire villages were deserted; over 2,000 abandoned sites have been identified in England alone. Everywhere, it was difficult to find new tenants, and incomes from land fell. The canons of Bordeaux cathedral shed bitter tears:

53. Be it known that the royal steward had received the earnest supplication of the chapter of the Church of St. Andrew of Bordeaux, which reports as follows. There were tenants who were living at St. Julian's, near Bordeaux, who were obliged to pay rents, and also fines on the transfer of properties. These tenants are dead, and none of their heirs has come before the dean and chapter to inform them of their rights, or to pay any rent, and this for the past twenty years. The properties are deserted, to the great loss of the church and its chapter.

The royal steward has made proclamations and public announcements in the cathedral and the fifteen parish churches in Bordeaux, once, twice, three and even four times, saying as follows: "If there are any persons to whom these properties belong, or who believe they have a right to them, through succession, gift, mortgage or any other

43

reason, let them appear before the royal steward to inform him of their rights and to pay the dean and chapter their arrears of rents. If none appears, then the royal steward will allow the dean and chapter to take the properties in hand, and dispose of them as they wish, and impose silence on anyone who may make a claim in the future."

At the days and hours stated in the proclamation, no-one appeared. Accordingly, the royal steward has awarded the properties to the dean and chapter, and given them leave to dispose of them for the benefit of their church.

And be it known that the canons of the chapter of St. Andrew's, the dean being absent, have given by new title, according to the customs of the district of Bordeaux, to Arnold de Longueville, of the parish of St. Eulalie of Bordeaux, that piece of land, where there is a tenement and a half, which is outside St. Julian. [In R. Boutrouche, *La crise d'une société*]

Thus no one who might have had existing rights appeared to claim them, and the canons found only a solitary tenant to occupy a farm and a half. He, it should be remarked, was a townsman.

Following the plague, the surviving laborers soon realized their worth and demanded higher wages. On the manors of Westminster Abbey, for example, the rates for threshing and winnowing increased by nearly 60 percent. Chaucer's friend and fellow poet, John Gower, wrote:

54. The world goeth from bad to worse, when shepherd and cowherd for their part demand more for their labor than the master-bailiff was wont to take in days gone by. Labor is now at so high a price that he who will order his business aright must pay five or six shillings now for what cost two in former times. Laborers of old were not wont to eat wheaten bread; their food was of beans or coarser corn, and their drink of water alone. Cheese and milk were a feast to them, and rarely ate they of other dainties; their dress was of hodden grey; then was the world ordered aright for folk of this sort.

CHAPTER 4. AGRICULTURE: LATE MIDDLE AGES

Three things, all of the same nature, are merciless when they have the upper hand; a water-flood, a wasting fire, and the common multitude of small folk. For these will never be checked by reason or discipline; and therefore, to speak in brief, the present world is so troubled by them that it is well to set a remedy thereunto. Ha! age of ours, whither turnest thou? for the poor and small folk, who should cleave to their labor, demand to be better fed than their masters. Moreover, they bedeck themselves in fine colors and fine attire, whereas, were it not for their pride and their privy conspiracies, they would be clad in sackcloth as of old. [*Mirour de l'Omme*]

Since they could not find servants, the wealthier villagers of Halesowen, Worcestershire, contracted out much of their work, and this had a desirable effect on their behavior. Before the plague, they had been in the habit of assailing all and sundry with fists, feet, teeth and any weapons that came to hand. After the plague, they went on serving their own families in the same way, but assaults on neighbors declined sharply.

THE CONTROL OF WAGES

While the farmers of Halesowen were amending their manners, the reaction of the authorities in many countries was to try to hold down wages by law. The commune of Florence made this decree in the year of the plague:

55. The peasants and tillers of the soil, and all those who work on the land for a wage and by the day, may neither demand nor receive a wage higher than the following: from the calends of November to the calends of February, three sous and six deniers of a small florin per day, or per task, paying their own expenses; from the calends of February to the calends of June, four sous of a small florin per day or per task, paying their own expenses; from the calends of June to the calends of November, they may not demand more than three sous of a small florin per day or per task,

under a penalty of 100 sous for each offense. And if the offender cannot pay the fine, he shall languish for one month in the prison of the commune of Florence. [*Statutum bladi reipublicae fiorentinae*]

The English government was more dilatory than its Florentine counterpart, but Edward III issued this decree in 1349:

56. Because a great part of the people, specially of the workmen and servants, has now died in this plague, some, seeing the shortage of servants, will not serve unless they receive excessive wages. We, weighing the great disadvantages which might arise from a dearth, specially of tillers and workmen, have ordered that every man and woman shall receive only the wages, livery, hire or salaries which he used to be offered in the twentieth year of our reign [1347]. And if such a man or woman so required to serve, refuse to do so, he shall be sent forthwith to the nearest gaol.

And if a reaper, mower or other workman or servant leave his employer without reasonable cause, he shall be imprisoned.

Furthermore no man shall pay to any man, more wages, hire or salaries than is the custom, under penalty of double of that which is so paid.

And because many sturdy beggars, so long as they can live by begging for alms, refuse to labor, living in idleness and sin, and sometimes by thefts and other crimes, no man, under penalty of imprisonment, shall give anything to such as shall be able to labor, or to cherish them in their sloth, so that they may be compelled to labor for the necessaries of life. [*Close Roll,* 23 Edward III]

Cases like these were frequently heard in the courts:

57. Lincolnshire. Item, the jurors present that a certain John Skit was in the service of Sir John Dargentene as plowman last summer, and a certain Roger Swynflete, warden of the manor of the abbot of Seleby, hired the said John Skit out of Sir John's service in this winter for six shillings and for

the sake of unmixed wheat and as much land as he could sow with two bushels, London measure, of wheat for one crop and also one acre of peas sown for one crop, and for the sake of so great a gain he withdrew from the service of the said Sir John until the feast of St. Martin last past. And afterwards the said John Skit suspected that he would be indicted before the justices; so he dared not remain, but withdrew to other parts, and thus the said Sir John lost the service of the said servant by the fault and malice of the said Roger and against the Statute of the lord King.

Item, they present that William de Caburn of Lymburgh, plowman, will not take service except by the day and with board, and will not eat salt meat, but fresh, and for the sake of this he has withdrawn from the town because no one dared hire him after this manner and against the Statute of the lord King. [*Assize Roll,* 26 Edward III]

As usually happens, the laws of economics proved stronger than the laws of kings, so wages remained obstinately at their new levels, or even increased. The earnings of laborers on the manors of the bishop of Winchester were, on average, 2.85 pence a day in the 1350s, and this had risen to 4.03 pence a hundred years later.

THE COMMUTATION OF SERVICES

One way in which lords tried to protect their incomes was by enforcing their dues more severely, but they met opposition. Many holdings were occupied by extended families, and it had been no great hardship to send one of the sons to work for a day or two in the week on the lord's demesne. But if the plague killed several of the sons, the villein found his labor services onerous. He avoided them if he could, and performed them in an off-hand, slipshod way, if compelled.

Eventually, lords recognized that it was better to commute their dues, rather than try to extract them from the unwilling. In 1445, the monks of Cerisy in Normandy wrote to the pope:

58. Whereas from time immemorial, as often as any tenants that were heads of families dwelling on our manors of Cerisy or Littry chanced to die, then, if they had no wives or children, the monastery had the right of taking to itself and applying to its own uses all their moveable goods; if, however, they had wives and children, then such goods were divided into three equal parts between the abbot and convent, the wife, and the children. Moreover, the garments also of the said householders thus deceased were applied to the use and profit of the said monastery, those of Cerisy to the benefit of the sacristy and those of Littry to the granary; and whereas the said parishioners and tenants, having become sorely diminished in their possessions and impoverished by reason of the wars and other miseries which have so long wasted these parts, began to desert the manors aforesaid and betake themselves elsewhere for fear of this burden and servitude; whereas they refused also to marry their daughters on that manor to the great, nay, to the very greatest damage and loss of the aforesaid monastery; and also, by reason of the aforesaid chattels, very many of the inhabitants aforesaid incurred, and long had incurred, the sentence of excommunication by not giving over faithfully the aforesaid moveable goods, but hiding them and thus defrauding the aforesaid monastery, therefore the abbot and monks have agreed with the tenants to commute these dues for a yearly tribute of 20 livres tournois, until such time as the sum of 300 gold pieces might be collected for the final redemption of the burden. [Father Denifle, *Désolation des Églises*]

On the manor of Crawley, Hampshire, in 1449, 3,583 services were due. Of these, 728 were excused, 126 were defaulted, 1,870 were commuted and only 859, or 24 percent, were performed.

The piecemeal commutation of services brought a decline in villeinage, but progress varied from country to country. Bondage was all but dead in England by the sixteenth century, but it survived in France until abolished by the Revolution of 1789, and in parts of Germany until the early years of the nineteenth century.

THE LORDS AND THEIR DEMESNES

Even before the Black Death, lords were tending to give up the direct exploitation of their demesnes. It was easier to let someone else do the work, and simply take a share of the crops, or a money rent. This example is from Northern Germany:

> 59. Otto, by the grace of God, bishop of Hildesheim. Brother Ernst, provost of the monastery of Escher, has, until now, had the manor of Eddinghausen cultivated by his lay brothers. This has not been successful and since, as a faithful steward, he is concerned for the prosperity of his monastery, he has let the aforesaid manor to two farmers, Dietrich Siberingh and Ludolf known as Langheben, for three years. The provost, on behalf of the monastery, shall take a tithe of the manor's produce of crops and animals. Further, the aforesaid farmers shall give to the monastery a third of all their produce. Further, they shall give to the monastery each year at Michaelmas, twelve pigs, a mark of pure silver, 62 chickens, twelve geese, and 1,200 sheep. At the end of the three years, the aforesaid farmers shall return the aforesaid manor to the monastery, in no worse state than it is at present, but just as good and, if possible, somewhat improved. [In G. Franz, *Deutches Bauerntum*]

The Black Death made it even more urgent for lords to dispose of lands that they had in hand:

> 60. Be it known to all men, that the dean and chapter of the church of St. Seurin of Bordeaux hold a parcel of waste vineyard in the Graves of Bordeaux at the place known as à Pradères. They have found that it does not profit them to maintain this vineyard, in view of the great cost of working it.
>
> That is why the canons of the church of St. Seurin (the dean, as everyone knows, being absent and outside the diocese)

meeting in chapter, within sound of the refectory bell, deliver to Arnold Costau, viticulturer of the parish of St. Paul and burgess of Bordeaux, all that waste vineyard in return for two deniers of Bordeaux money as transfer fine, and five sous annual rent to be paid on Christmas Day each year to the rent clerk of the church of St. Seurin.

Arnold Costau has agreed to cultivate this abandoned vineyard, and carry out all the work needed for the care of Graves vines, according to the customs of the district of Bordeaux. [In R. Boutruche, *La crise d'une société*]

Here, again, it is a townsman who takes over the abandoned property. He might well have been engaged in the wine trade with England.

The following table shows changes in the income which the Bishop of Winchester drew from his manor of Crawley:

	1309-10	1408-9	1503-4
Fixed rents	£10 5s 7d	£11 15s 11D	£13 10s 8d
Sale of services	–	2 11 4	2 6 8
Court dues	6 0 10	2 13 1	1 16 10
Animal farming	59 11 7	19 10 0	–
Arable farming	44 12 9	28 18 5	–
Rent of demesne	–	–	21 16 8
TOTAL	£120 10s 9d	£65 8s 9d	£39 10s 10d

It is clear, then, that by the early sixteenth century, the bishop of Winchester was no longer farming actively at Crawley and had become little more than a rent collector.

LEASEHOLDERS AND SHARECROPPERS

With the decline in villeinage, free tenures became more and more common, especially leasehold and share cropping. This is a formula which was drawn up in Brabant, now part of Belgium, in the early 1380s:

61. Be it known to all, that the holy, venerable and prudent man, the lord abbot of the monastery of Villier in Brabant, of the Cistercian order in the diocese of Liège, has given the manor of

Ostin with all its lands, meadows, woods, fishponds, hedges and pastures, to N—, for twelve consecutive years, beginning on St. John the Baptist's Day 1383, according to the following terms.

For rent the aforesaid N— will pay to the monks every year, 100 florins, with two old écus reckoned as four florins of good quality gold and of the proper weight, half to be paid between Christmas and Candlemas, and the other half on St. John the Baptist's Day, though he may deduct ten florins from the first payment, and for these ten florins he must maintain the buildings.

We make it known that the aforesaid N— should prune the woods on the manor once in the twelve years, that is, when each copse reaches the age of twelve years. And he should prune the hedges once in the twelve years, that is, one twelfth part every year. He may not cut trees more than twelve years old, but if one has died, he may fell it and plant two new trees of the  same kind. And the aforesaid N— must at once restore and scour the ditches of the woods and hedges that he has pruned, so that neither his nor anyone else's animals may damage them. And the aforesaid N— must not allow his animals to roam in copses that are less than six years old.

And the aforesaid N— has agreed to maintain the roofs of the buildings with pitch, straw and anything else that might be necessary. And if much timber is needed, the monks will give it to him from their nearest wood and the aforesaid N— will take it and use it at his own expense.

Moreover, the aforesaid N— is subject to the right of lodging and must receive the lord abbot and his company, as a good and honest tenant should, once a year, or twice, if the abbot should choose to visit, and also to receive the monks, lay brothers and people of the household of Villiers whenever they should pass that  way, giving them such food as they may find there.

And during the lease, the aforesaid N— must plough the fields well and faithfully, and fallow with four crop rotations, and the marshland with two rotations, with the fallow properly cut, at the right season.

If [at the end of the lease] he has taken anything from the holding, the monks may pursue him as if he were their villein, at his expense, and pay to any lord whom they may require to hold him, the sum of two pounds in old weight. And if there are any expenses incurred as the result of neglecting any of these agreements, they must be paid by the aforesaid N—, and the monks are to be believed on their word alone. [In L. Genicot and J. Balon, ed., *Formulaire Naumourois du XIV siècle*]

The document also lays down in detail how the tenant should leave the manor on the expiry of the lease, specifying, for example, that the fish ponds should be stocked with 450 year-old fish, 4,000 roach, 600 perch and two female carp. It also states what crops should be sown and how many acres should be devoted to each.

A tenure that suited small men was share cropping, known as *mezzadria* in Italy and *métayage* in France. Instead of paying a money rent, the tenant gave the landlord a fraction of the harvest, usually between a quarter and a half. The following is a *mezzadria* contract:

62. In the name of God, Amen, the 18th of November 1384. Be it known to whoever may read this writ, the I, Recho di Mugnaio, have granted to Andrea de Braccio my property

of Poggio in the parish of Santo Cervagio at Pelagho, with the vineyards and all the parcels of land that belong to that farm. By this agreement: I, Recho, must find half the seed to be sown on the aforesaid farm, and Andrea the other half. And he must give me half of what is harvested on the farm, corn, oats, oil and wine. Andrea must keep two pigs on the aforesaid farm, and he must pay half their pannage, and I, Recho, the other half. And he must give me half the meat. Andrea must also employ two workers every year in my vineyard. And I, Recho di Mugnaio, must lend him fifteen golden florins, for the expense of the oxen, for injuries, from which may God protect him, and for all the work of cultivation. And we wish this agreement to hold for the next four years. And Andrea must give me every year a pair of good capons and ten dozen eggs. And Andrea must make oil from the olives on the farm. [From D. Catellacci, *Archivio Storico Italiano*]

Sometimes only livestock was shared. In 1335 a burgess of Genoa made this agreement with a local farmer:

63. John known as Ravagliano di Bernardini, of Biscia, living at Massa de Luni, has from me, Miliadusso, a sow with black hair, the left shoulder of white hair and the forefeet white, bought by me for ten pounds of money of Lucca.

He must keep her for the next three years. Half the produce of the aforesaid sow shall be the aforesaid John's and the other half mine. Death from natural causes shall be at my risk, death from lack of care at the aforesaid John's. At the end of the three years, half the aforesaid sow shall be the aforesaid John's and half mine. She will be divided at auction. I owe no help when she gives birth to piglets, but I must pay half when she is taken to the boar. [In F. Bobaini, ed., *Archivio Storico Italiano*]

The contracts, with their meticulous detail, described the ideal, but the reality might be different. In 1410 a burgess of Florence listed his receipts from one Chele, the tenant of his farm of Marcia Lunga, and continued:

64. And I have had compensation from him for all the things that he stole from me so often. That is to say, my share of a pig, which he sold without telling me, and the reeds and the wood that he sold for two years, without telling me. Also for the grain: he did not sow his share for two years, and he did not sow what I sent him for my share, or hardly any of it. And there was my share of the pig; my share was not sent. Then for the acorns that were harvested, which he gave to his pig and his sheep and nothing to me. And afterwards for the straw which he took to his house. And for two pieces of plough timber which he stole from me, and the trunk of a walnut tree. Also, for many stakes which he made at home and sold. And then for the beans which he sowed and ate and harvested without giving me any. Then for much of my iron, which he stole from my house. And then for the grain which he stole from me when he had harvested it and hid the sheaves in the wood, here and there, and we found it in different places, as Fruosino di Donato and Monna Nanna his wife, whom I found going by the wood, pasturing his cattle, saw him. There was also the sister of Agnolo di Nanni di Castruccio. It was late one night when we first discovered that Chele and Monna Bella, his wife and all his family came there. Martino and Andrea saw them leaving the place, and

they called me and we caught them. We searched and found grain hidden in various different places. On discovering this evil, I chased him. Wanting to pacify me, he begged Sig. Payolo, our priest, Lolo, Maroccio and other neighbors to be so good as to settle the dispute. In the end, I was satisfied, and, after a lot of argument, Chele confessed that he had stolen all the above mentioned things from me, and he paid me compensation. I have made this memorandum, to remind me what this villain Chele and his family did to me, after I had treated him like a brother or a father. [Ibid.]

THE INFLUENCE OF THE TOWNS

Only a few medieval towns, like Antwerp, Paris and Florence, were commercial centers of European importance. The average town was, by our standards, very small and, moreover, its influence did not extend much further than the distance of a round-trip journey that a horse and cart could make in a day. But, as several documents in this chapter have shown, townsmen of the late Middle Ages were playing a growing part in the countryside. Indeed, they seem to have filled much of the vacuum left by the lords as they withdrew from active farming. There were good reasons for this. An investment in farming could employ surplus capital to produce extra income; a family could make sure of its food supplies; by a share cropping arrangement, a householder could cut out the grain merchant, who was likely to profiteer; a farm could supply goods for manufacture or sale, such as leather, wool and wine.

The countryfolk benefited, too. The towns were useful markets where they could exchange their produce for manufactured goods, such as pottery, clothing, footgear and implements. They were also sources of capital, which might be money, seed corn or livestock. Not the least of their uses was that they were places of refuge in time of war.

CHANGES IN FARMING

In most of Europe, and for most of the Middle Ages, change in farming techniques was painfully slow, but it began to quicken after the middle of the fourteenth century.

The Black Death of 1348 caused such a shortage of workers and tenants that there had to be an immediate response, and the quickest and easiest answer was to abandon fields that were either infertile or difficult to reach. They returned to nature. On land that was still farmed, much of the arable was converted to pasture, since the care of livestock needs far less labor than tillage.

The switch to pasture was to have far-reaching results for the chalk downlands of southern England. They had been important for sheep rearing since Saxon times, but during the years of land hunger, their flanks had been lacerated to make strip lynchets, which gave but indifferent yields of cereals. Now, however, all the downs were allowed to do what they did best, which was to grow grass for sheep. This, in turn, meant that England could play an increasing part in the economy of Europe because, for reasons which are not at all clear, English wool was outstandingly good. The chief woolen manufacturing districts were in the Low Countries, and they looked to Spain for the bulk of their raw wool, but if they wanted quality, they bought from England.

Here again, we see the importance of the towns. If they and their merchants and manufacturers had not been there to cope with the wool, it would have been a waste of time to produce it.

In some places there were changes on the arable. These figures come from the records of the manor of Wistow, part of the estate of Ramsey Abbey, Cambridgeshire:

CHAPTER 4. AGRICULTURE: LATE MIDDLE AGES

Bushels of seed sown at Wistow

	1346	1403
Wheat	37	19
Barley	18	50
Legumes	34	31

The amount of wheat sown was nearly halved, but the legumes, that is, peas and beans, held their own and barley increased considerably. The wheat was for human consumption, while the others were fodder crops.

The farmers of Wistow were responding to the market. The price of wheat was falling, but that of animal products, meat, butter and cheese, remained steady. Yet again we see the influence of the towns, for they took what were, for the Middle Ages, these more luxurious foods.

CONCLUSION

The changes in the medieval countryside well illustrate the principle stated in Sir Henry Maine's *Ancient Law*, 1861, that society proceeds from status to contract.

At one time, most village people were villeins, giving services of various kinds to their lords in return for their farms. The lord, by virtue of being the lord, could require the services; the villein, by virtue of being a villein, was obliged – in theory at least – to provide them.

After the Black Death, lords tended to give up the direct exploitation of their demesnes, and, meanwhile, villeins commuted their services for money payments. When this process had gone far enough, villeins were free to enter into contracts with whom they pleased. Relationships between man and man were no longer determined by their relative status, but by the contracts to which both had freely agreed.

There was more. A peasant might well make a contract with a lord, but lords were becoming little more than rent collectors. The countryman needed an active partner, and he found him in the townsman. There had, of course, always been links between country and town, but the relationship was to strengthen considerably in the late Middle Ages, with fruitful results in the centuries that followed.

CHAPTER 5
THE TOWNS

EARLY GROWTH

During classical times highly developed cities were strung round the Mediterranean like pearls. Moreover, as the Romans expanded their empire, they took their city culture with them, even persuading a minority of the Britons to adopt it. When the Roman Empire collapsed in the west, it survived in the east and its capital Constantinople prospered until the Turks captured it in 1453. Even in the west, many of the Mediterranean cities remained more or less intact, because the barbarians who first invaded were few in number and formed little more than warrior aristocracies in the lands they conquered, leaving the common folk to live much as before. The Arabs, who burst out of the Middle East in the seventh century were, themselves, civilized and more likely to foster cities than destroy them.

It was different in the north. The Romans had never conquered either Germany or Scandinavia, while in Britain their civilization was all but extinguished. A Saxon poet contemplated the ruins of a Roman town, which may well have been Bath:

> 65. Wondrous is this wall-stone; broken by fate, the castles have decayed; the work of giants is crumbling. Roofs are fallen, ruinous are the towers with their gates; frost is on their cement, broken are the roofs, cut away, fallen, undermined by age. The grasp of the earth, stout grip of the ground, holds its mighty builders, who have perished and gone; till now a hundred generations of men have died. Often this wall, grey with lichen and stained with red, unmoved under storms, has survived kingdom after kingdom; its lofty gate has fallen. Bright were the castle-dwellings,

many the bath-houses, lofty the host of pinnacles, great the
tumult of men, many a mead hall full of the joys of men, till
Fate the mighty overturned that. The wide walls fell; days of
pestilence came; death swept away all the bravery of men; their
fortresses became waste places; the city fell to ruin. The mul-
titudes who might have built it anew lay dead on the earth.

Wherefore these courts are in decay and these lofty gates; the
woodwork of the roof is stripped of tiles; the place has sunk
into ruin, leveled to the hills, where in times past many a man
light of heart and bright with gold, adorned with splendors,
proud and flushed with wine, shone in war trappings, gazed
on treasure, on silver, on precious stones, on riches, on possessions, on costly gems, on this bright castle of the broad
kingdom. Stone courts stood here; the stream with its great gush
sprang forth hotly; the wall enclosed its bright bosom; there the
baths were hot in its center. [In R.K. Gordon, *Anglo-Saxon Poetry*]

Eventually, towns of a sort began to appear even in England and
Scandinavia. Alfred the Great founded burghs, or fortified towns, to
combat the Vikings, and the Vikings themselves founded trading
settlements. One of these was Hedeby, in Denmark. In about 950, an
Arab called Ibrahim ibn Ahmed at-Tartushi came here. He was from
Córdoba, then the most advanced city in western Europe, and Hedeby
and its people did not impress him:

CHAPTER 5. THE TOWNS

66. There are fresh-water wells in the town. Its inhabitants are worshippers of Sirius, except for a few who are Christians and have a church there. They hold a feast at which they all gather to honor their god and to eat and drink. Whoever kills a beast as a sacrifice sets up a pole at the door of his house and fastens the animal to it, whether ox, ram, he-goat, or pig; thus people know he has made an offering to his god. The town is poor in goods and treasure. The main food is fish, which is very plentiful there. When a child is born, they often throw it into the sea to save expense. Among them, women have the right to claim divorce, and the woman arranges her own divorce whenever she wishes. Also, there is an artfully made cosmetic for the eyes; when they use it, their beauty does not fade, but, on the contrary, increases. Never have I heard such hideous singing as that of the people of this town; it is a growl that comes from the throat, like the baying of dogs, only even more like a wild beast than that. [*Travels*]

In the eleventh century, as we have seen, the peoples of the heartland of Europe began to expand their frontiers and that, as they did so, they founded agricultural settlements. They also founded new towns, and re-populated old ones. This is an account of the early years of Lübeck:

67. In 1143, Count Adolf came to the place known as Bucu, where he found the walls of an abandoned fortress, and a very large island, enclosed by two rivers. The Trave washes one side, and the Wakenitz the other. On the side followed by the mainland road, though, is a little hill, crowned by the walls of the fort. When, therefore, this wise man saw the advantages of the position and the splendid harbor, he began to build a city there. He called it Lübeck, because it was not far from the old town which Prince Henry had once built.

There was peace in the land, and by God's mercy, the new settlement prospered. Day by day its market increased and its merchants' ships grew in numbers. [*Chronica Slavorum*]

After a few years, Henry the Lion, duke of Saxony, took possession of the town, but it continued to prosper:

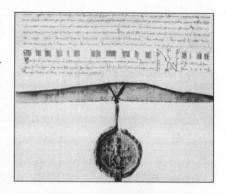

68. At his request, the merchants returned, full of joy, and at once rebuilt the churches and walls of the city. The duke sent his messengers to the cities and kingdoms of the north, Denmark, Sweden, Norway, Russia, promising them peace so that they could come freely to his city of Lübeck. He also established a mint there, and tolls, and granted most worthy civic privileges. From then on, the trade of the city increased and its inhabitants multiplied. [Ibid.]

In Spain, towns that found themselves in disputed territory between Christians and Moslems were usually abandoned by their inhabitants, so that when they were reconquered, they had to be peopled anew. A chronicler describes events at Avila, the like of which have happened in many frontier towns in different countries and in different centuries:

69. When King Alfonso ordered Count Don Remondo to settle people in Avila, there came to the town a great number of good men from the Five Towns and from Lara and some from Covaleda. And those from Covaleda and Lara came first and, on entering the town, they studied the flight of birds. And those who knew how to read the signs saw that it would be good to settle there and they made their homes near the water.

And those of the Five Towns who came after them also studied the birds. And Muño Echaminzuide, who came with them, was a more skillful augur, and he said that those who settled near the water would achieve feats of arms, but they would not be as powerful or as honorable as those who settled up higher, in the middle of the town. And he ordered those who came with him to make their homes there. And the old men told us, and we judged for ourselves when we arrived, that this augur spoke truly. His people did all things well and, serving God and their lord, gained much honor and power.

And because those who came from the Five Towns were the most numerous, they called the other people who came to Avila serranos [mountain dwellers, but used pejoratively]. But God caused the entire population to prosper. And everyone bought, sold and engaged in all kinds of trafficking, so making handsome profits. And those who were called serranos exercised themselves with arms and undertook the defense of the others.

It happened one day, when the serranos were out on patrol, that a powerful force of Moors came to the town. Advancing even to the gates, they took people, cattle, sheep and whatever they wanted. And when the serranos who had been on patrol returned, they told the people that if they would come with them and have faith in God, they would defeat their enemies. And they begged them to accompany them. But when they reached a place called Rostro de la Coliella, the other people turned back, leaving the serranos to press on alone. And they arrived on a hill now called Barva [beard] Azedo, where they saw the Moors resting by a river. They studied the birds and an augur called Azedo learnt from them that the Moors would be defeated and said, "By the beard of Azedo we shall defeat the Moors and put them to flight." That is why the hill is called Barva Azedo.

And they did indeed put the Moors to flight, and killed many of them, and took much booty from them and recovered all they had taken.

And when they came back to the town, the other people who had turned back would not allow them into the town, so they went to a place nearby called Castaño.

Later, those in the town sent to demand their share of the booty, but the serranos would not let them have any, since they had turned back and were not with them when they could have been. They gave them their children, their wives and everything the Moors had taken from them, but they were not satisfied and threatened to fight the serranos.

Meanwhile, this news reached the ears of Don Remondo, who was in Segovia, and he came to Avila and discovered the truth of what had happened. And he ordered that none of the booty should be given to those who had turned back, and expelled them from the town. And he decreed as follows: the mayor, the toll collectors and all other officials should be chosen from among the serranos. And they made so much money as a result, that they gave Count Don Remondo 500 horses. [*Crónica de la población de Avila*]

Eventually, the Spanish towns lost their frontier atmosphere. In the middle of the twelfth century a Moorish geographer gave a glowing account of the cities of Old Castile, and it must be remembered that Christians did not impress Moors easily:

70. Zamora is a famous city and one of the capitals of the Christian territories. It is situated on the north bank of the Duero and is surrounded by strong walls. Its territory is fertile and covered with vineyards. Its inhabitants possess great riches and devote themselves to trade.

León is one of the principal cities of Castile. It is flourishing and its people are very hardy. A most profitable trade is carried on. The inhabitants are fond of saving and are prudent with their money.

Sahagún is well populated and its surroundings are most agreeable.

Burgos is a large city, crossed by a river and divided into districts surrounded by walls. One of these districts is inhabited mainly by Jews. The city is strong, and well adapted for defense. There are bazaars, trade, a large population and many riches. The town is situated on an important route for travelers [the pilgrims' way to Santiago de Compostela]. Its surroundings are covered with vineyards, villages and other dependencies. [El Edrisi, *Geography*]

Even in England there was, by the twelfth century, cause for civic pride:

71. Among the noble cities of the world that are celebrated by Fame, the City of London, seat of the Monarchy of England, is one that spreads its fame wider, sends its wealth and wares further, and lifts its head higher than all others. It is blest in the wholesomeness of its air, in its reverence for the Christian faith, in the strength of its bulwarks, the nature of  its situation, the honor of its citizens, and the chastity of its matrons. It is likewise most merry in its sports and fruitful of noble men. [William Fitz Stephen, *A Description of the Most Noble City of London*]

HOUSES

The following is an inventory of the goods belonging to a London fishmonger who died in 1373. His house was similar to those shown in the illustrations on p. 68:

72. In the chamber

A new bed and tapestry; another bed with a tapestry; 3 quilts and 1 mattress; 3 rugs, 1 framework, 1 tester; 1 blanket, two pillows; four pairs of sheets; 5 feather beds; 5 pillows; panels round the bed; 2 curtains; 2 chests and 2 counters; 1 silver girdle; 2 pairs of amber paternosters.

MEDIEVAL CITIES shared many traits: they formed compact units visibly separated from their surrounding countryside by a ring of walls and gates, the pride of their citizens.

FLORENCE, at right, in a 15th-century view from the north, toward the Arno. Its gates and wall towers date from the mid-14th century and gird a city of monuments: towers of

churches, monasteries, the palazzi of the city's rich commerical oligarchy, the Duomo, Giotto's Campanile, and the Baptistry. The outsider's view is of dense, interlocking and narrow streets: a nexus of power and concentrated energy bubbling upward.

VENICE, below and right, traded stone walls for ones of water: here the sea brings the visitor to a similar nexus, broken by larger piazze and greater monuments: the Doge's Palace and San Marco's (c), the Rialto (r), and the Arsenal (l).

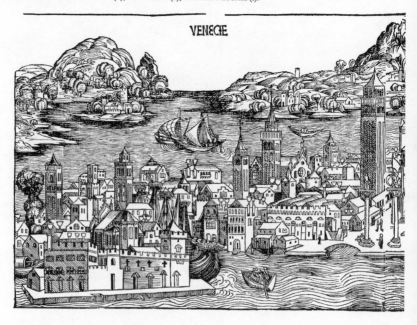

VENECIE

CHAPTER 5. THE TOWNS

COLOGNE, right, was much the same: a commercial center on the Rhine, its cathedral, still unfinished in the 15th century, was a familiar landmark behind its riverfront docks and gates.

CARCASSONNE was a center of Languedoc in the south of France. Though it has been much restored, it typifies the town of the 12th and 13th centuries: its double circuit of walls is rimmed by towers and bastions. Capping a strong defensive position, the town boasts its own castle (at right of photo), thus dominating the countryside both economically and politically.

In the hall

3 dorsers, 3 bankers, 6 cushions; 3 old bankers and 5 old cushions; 1 board, 2 trestles, 5 stools; 3 checker boards; 1 fireplace of iron, 1 pair of tongs; 5 basins, whereof one is round; 7 wash bowls, whereof one is a hanging bowl, 4 candelabras, all weighing ½ cwt 15 lbs.

In the storehouse

7 cloths, 6 hand towels, 4 napkins; 1 cupboard, 4 vats; 5 barrels; 1 gallon jug, 5 pottle jugs, 2 quart jugs, all of pewter, weighing 35 lbs; 2 chargers, 12 small platters, 12 plates, 12 salt cellars, all of pewter, weighing ½ cwt 17lbs; 1 broken silver cup called a biker, 1 silver gilt cup with a silver foot, 4 silver cups without feet, 24 silver spoons, weighing by goldsmith's weight £8 5s; 3 cups with silver feet; 4 broken cups of mazer, 1 broken cup of warre.

In the parlor

1 dorser, 1 banker; 1 board and 1 counter; 1 board for cups called a cupboard.

In the chamber next the parlor

1 aumbry, 3 chairs

In the workmen's room

1 chest, 1 board.

In the solar above the same, called the apprentices' chamber

2 boards, 4 forms.

CHAPTER 5. THE TOWNS

In the kitchen

2 mortars; 2 vats; 1 water tankard; 5 tubs; 1 sieve called a hair sieve; 1 board for a form; 2 large spits, 3 small spits, 2 tripods, 3 gridirons, 1 frying pan, 1 hook, 1 firepan, 4 iron rods for curtains, weighing in all 220 lbs.

5 pitchers, 7 pots, 7 pans, 2 caldrons, all weighing 2 cwt, 3 quarters, 10 lbs. [*Calendar of Plea and Memorandum Rolls,* 1364-1381]

A Spanish woman living at Moguer, in southwest Spain, compiled this inventory in 1414:

73. I, Catalina Fernandéz declare that I have the following possessions: In the first place some houses in the aforesaid town, bounded by the houses and yard of Donna Elvira, and by the houses and yard of the heirs of my brother, Juan Fernandéz, and the streets. And, moreover, a piece of vineyard, which is at the place called Cornejo, on the outskirts of the town, which is bounded by the vineyard of Diego Fernandéz de Betanzos, and by the vineyard of the heirs of the aforesaid Juan Fernandéz, my brother. And, moreover, another piece of vineyard at the place known as de Castillejo, bounded by the vineyard of the heirs of the aforesaid Juan Fernandéz, my brother, and by the vineyard of the heirs of Pero Martinez Amo. And more, three mattresses, three chair backs, and twelve arrobas of wool; and three narrow mattresses; and twelve pillows, seven white and three embroidered; and seven sheets, four of linen and three of hemp; and three pairs of towels, two embroidered and one white; and a linen curtain, bordered with red silk; and a new white quilt; and three pairs of mantillas; and two caldrons, one big and the other small; and a frying pan of iron; and three axes; and one chest; and one chamber pot; and two tin plates; and three jars for wine, clean; and, moreover, two small jars for oil; and two green glazed tubs, one big and the other small; and a sieve; and four boards; and three bedsteads; and wood to make a cupboard; and a

cross bow that Benito Ximénes has; and a tenon saw; and a hand saw, and another small hand saw, which Juan de Garçía de Xeres has at present, and other iron goods, which he has in Lepe; and some jet beads that have a crucifix and a wheel of St. Catherine in silver; and another pair of large jet beads; and some silk sleeves. [*Records of Santa Clara of Moguer*]

People were unlikely to have their houses to themselves:

74. The flea is a little worm and grieveth men most. And escapeth and avoideth peril with leaping and with running, and waxeth slow and faileth in cold time and in summer time it waxeth lively and swift and spareth not kings. [*Trevisa's Bartholomew*]

75. My bed is like the grave, my sheets the winding sheet,
My clothes the mould that I must have to cover me most meet,
The hungry fleas which frisk so fresh, to worms I can compare,
Which greedily shall gnaw my flesh and leave the bones full bare.
[G. Gascoigne, *Good-Night*]

STREETS

There were hazards in the streets:

76. People complained that the alestakes in front of the taverns extended too far over the highway, so as to hinder those riding there and by reason of their weight did tend to the great damage of the houses in which they were placed. All the taverners of the city being summoned, orders were given them that in future no one should have an alestake bearing his sign or leaves, extending over the highway more than seven feet at the utmost. [*London Letter Book H, 1375*]

Folk often advertised that they had drink for sale by putting up a long pole with a bunch of leafy twigs on the end. This led to the expression, "A good wine needs no bush."

77. On Thursday, about the hour of vespers, two carters taking empty carts out of the city were urging their horses apace, when the wheels of one of the carts collapsed, so

that the cart fell on Agnes de Cicestre, who at once died. The carter left his cart and three horses and took flight in fear. The cart was valued by the jury at 6s 8d; the first horse, of a dun color, at 10s 0d, the second, a grey and blind of both eyes, at 4s 0d, and the third, a black, at 6s 0d; also five old sacks and five pounds of candles which were in the cart at 16½d. Total 28s 0½d [*Coroners' Rolls, London,* 1337]

The cart and the horses were valued because of a peculiarity of medieval English law. Anything that was instrumental in causing a death, whether accidental or otherwise, was declared a "deodand," which meant it had to be sold and the money given to the victim's family. There was a jingle which ran, "Whatever's moved to do the deed, is deodand and forfeited." This was a vestige of a primitive belief that inanimate objects could be guilty of offenses and should be punished.

There were attempts to improve the streets:

78. No carter within the City shall drive his cart more quickly when it is unloaded than when it is loaded, for the avoiding of divers perils and grievances, under pain of 40d and of having his body committed to prison at the will of the mayor. [*Liber Albus, London,* 1419]

79. We decree that all public streets outside the city shall be widened and repaired so that all shall be at least two cannae in width. The repair shall be done of the roads leading to the Rhône River from the bishop's tower, from St. Ruffo, from the tannery, from St. Verano and from St. Michael, and from other places situated at a like distance. If, perhaps, beyond these limits, there are found to be roads which are very narrow, then these roads, too, shall be widened if the good and wise men of the city shall see fit. [*Customs of Avignon,* 1243]

80. The year of Christ, 1237, Sig. Rubaconte da Mandella being Podestà of Florence, the new bridge was made in Florence. And during his government, all the roads in Florence

THOSE WHO WORKED

CITY STREETS in medieval towns offer a testament in stone to the perennial urban exchange between public authority and private power, between common aspirations and individual needs.

CANTERBURY, in Kent, was a pilgrimage destination long before Chaucer's *Tales*. Here, the axis of the street called the Mercery brings arriving pilgrims to the end of their quest: Christ Church Gate and Canterbury Cathedral rising beyond it. The view is typical of the medieval town: a narrow street, pressed by the overhanging bays of shops and dwellings, closed off at the end by a public monument. Here the space flows with use and time, perspectives are cut off, and the traveler, or Sunday stroller, is greeted with new views at every turning of a corner. The long perspective views of the modern city are another world away.

SANTIAGO DE COMPOSTELA'S Rua Vilar offers a similar urban sense. Here the view is away from the traveler's goal, the Cathedral of St. James, but the effect is the same.

Early-modern construction takes the place of medieval buildings on the same sites. The street is well paved and lined with arcades to ease the way of travelers. The view again culminates in a large building, here a private palace. At the corner two, even three, new vistas will open up to streets and a plaza, while side streets offer new directions beyond the arcades.

CHAPTER 5. THE TOWNS

Florence may offer the modern visitor the best sense of a medieval city at its prime – provided one can avoid all one's fellow modern travelers. At its medieval core, between the Duomo and the Arno River, the city is a labyrinth of narrow streets and shuttered walls, much like Venice. Twisting streets and overhanging eaves were planned to provide protection from winds in the winter and from harsh summer sun and heat. The effect, once again, is one of continual surprise: ever new vistas around each corner, a piazza opening up, a noble palazzo, or here – as one's eye is drawn up out of the shadows created by centuries of private overbuilding – a sliver view of great public authority and power: the campanile of the Palazzo Vecchio. As in Siena, Bologna, or San Gimignano, the tower was long the symbol of power: at first of feudal families, and then of the public commune. Citizens who lived within range of its bells

were obliged to answer its calls for assembly, for muster to arms, for public emergencies. As medieval communal government gave way to Renaiassnce oligarchy, and then to the principates of families such as the Medici, the campanile became a symbol of princely power and outright tyranny.

Santillana del Mar, in Asturias, on Spain's north coast, mirrors the stone construction and overhanging eaves of Florence. Here the street follows the gentle contours of the hillside. The upper window casements are Renaissance. The

arched doors on the ground floor are medieval. They give access to inner courtyards, shops, stables and storage rooms. As in most medieval towns, ordinances regulated building elevations, plot sizes, street widths, paving, and sanitation.

were paved. Through this work the city of Florence became more clean, and more beautiful and healthy. [Giovanni Villani, *Chroniche Florentine*]

PUBLIC HEALTH AND OTHER PROBLEMS

The following were some of the problems that beset part of London in 1422:

81. These are nuisances and defects found in the ward of Farringdon Without, taken at the wardmoot, before Rankyn Barton, Alderman of the same ward.

First, that the master of Ludgate often puts out dung in the street gutter and stops water from flowing, to the great nuisance of all the folk passing there. Also that a mud wall in the bailey by the High Street falls down piecemeal into the High Street and makes the way foul, to the annoyance of folk passing and dwelling thereabout. Also the pavements before the chamber house in the bailey, and before the door of West, barber, and of Walsh's door, are defective and need to be mended. Also the common privy of Ludgate is very defective and perilous and the filth thereof decays the stone walls, so that it is likely to be very costly and dangerous to those walls in time to come, unless it be put right as soon as possible. Also that the barriers at Shoe Lane End are all broken with water carts, and the pavements defective in divers places in the same parish. Also that John Tavener at Bell is not a freeman of the city. Also that John Whitlock at Bell at Cart Lane and his wife are common bawds, and therefore have been put out of other wards. Also John Swayn and his wife are foregraters, regrators and extortioners often, and especially lately they hired a page of the Queen's household to arrest a boatfull of rushes, and brought it from Queenhithe to Fleet Bridge and there took from it 30 loads of rushes, and then paid the boatman only 26d for 30 loads, whereas he should have been paid for every burden 3d and because of this the boatman made much noise and open slander. Also the taverners of St. Bride's parish set their empty tuns and pipes in the high street to the annoyance of all folk passing there. [*Guildhall MS, Pleas and Memoranda, A 50, m3-7v*]

Towns frequently made regulations for themselves. These measures were taken at Avignon:

82. We declare that Jews or whores shall not dare to touch with their hands either bread or fruit put out for sale, and that if they should do this, that they must buy what they have touched.

Likewise we decree that no one shall have a water pipe emptying into the public street, with the exception of rain water or well water. And if anyone should offend, he shall pay a fine of five sous for every offense.

Likewise we decree that no one shall throw water onto the street, nor any steaming liquid, nor chaff, nor the refuse of grapes, nor human filth, nor bath water, nor indeed any dirt. Nor shall he throw anything into the street under his house nor allow his family to do so. And he who commits this offense shall pay a fine of two sous for every offense; and his accuser shall receive a third of the fine. [*Customs of Avignon*, 1243]

The Emperor Frederick II included the following clause in his *Constitutions of Melfi*, the code of laws that he made for his kingdom of Sicily in 1231:

83. We intend to keep the air healthy, in so far as is possible. Therefore we order that no one may steep flax or hemp in water within a mile of any city or fortress, so that the air may not be contaminated by it. If he does this, the hemp and flax which he has put in the water will be confiscated.

We command that burials of the dead who are not in urns should be half an ell deep. If anyone disobeys this, he will pay us a fine of one augustalis.

We command that anyone who owns a corpse or filth that makes a stench must throw it a quarter of a mile out of the district, or into the sea or a river. If anyone disobeys this, he will pay us a fine of one augustalis for dogs or animals bigger than dogs, and half an augustalis for smaller ones. [*Liber Augustalis*, Title XLVIII]

Since houses were built largely of timber, and were often thatched, there was always a danger of fire. The Venerable Bede describes an incident at Canterbury in 619:

84. It happened that the city of Canterbury, being by carelessness set on fire, was in danger of being consumed by the spreading flames. Water was thrown over the fire in vain. A considerable part of the city was already destroyed, and the fierce flame advancing towards the bishop, when he, confiding in the Divine assistance, where human had failed, ordered himself to be carried towards the raging fire that was spreading on every side. The church of the Four Crowned Martyrs was in the place where the fire raged most. The bishop being carried there by his servants, the sick man averted the danger by prayer, which a number of strong men had not been able to perform by much labor. Immediately, the wind, which blowing from the south had spread the conflagration throughout the city, turning to the north, prevented the destruction of those places that had lain in its way, and then ceasing entirely, the flames were abundantly extinguished. And thus the man of God, whose mind was inflamed with the fire of Divine charity, and who was wont to drive away the powers of the air by his frequent prayers, was deservedly allowed to prevail over the worldly winds and flames, and to ensure that they should not injure him or his. [*Ecclesiastical History*]

Divine help was not always at hand:

85. In the City of London an extraordinary and terrible fire occurred on the southern bank of the River Thames, near

the church of the canons of Our Lady of Southwark. When a large crowd had crossed the river, either to put out the fire or to watch, suddenly the northern part also caught fire as the south wind was blowing, so that those crossing the bridge to go back were prevented by the flames. And so it happened that when the other part of the bridge caught fire, they were trapped. And then, placed as they were between two fires, they were pressed by each in turn, until they expected only death.

Then some ships came to their aid, but so many foolishly rushed into them that the ships were sunk and everyone perished. This was regarded as a great disaster by the people and it was said that three thousand had died either in the fire or in the shipwreck. [*Barnwell Chronicle*, 1212]

CHAPTER 6
SHOPKEEPERS AND CRAFTSPEOPLE

ANY MEDIEVAL TOWN that was at all important contained a great variety of shopkeepers and craftspeople, for example, carpenters, masons, glaziers, wheelwrights, joiners, felt makers, weavers, fullers, tanners, glovers, shoe makers, mercers, brewers, millers, vintners, innkeepers, goldsmiths and, in the more civilized countries like Italy, sculptors, painters, illuminators, book manufacturers and architects.

In about 800 Charlemagne issued an edict to encourage manufactures:

> 86. Let each intendant have good workmen in his district, that is to say, workers in iron, gold and silver; shoemakers, wood turners, carpenters, shield makers, fishermen, soap boilers; men who know how to make beer, cider, perry and all other kinds of drink; bakers to bake bread for our table; workmen who know how to make nets for hunting, as well as for fishing and catching birds, and other types of workmen, that are so numerous that it would be tedious to list them. [*Capitulare de Villis*]

An Anglo-Saxon poet makes a carpenter's tools speak:

> 87. The ship axe said unto the wright;
> Meat and drink I shall thee plight,
> Clean hose and clean shoes,
> Get them wheresoever thou canst.
> Wherefore said the belt,
> With great strokes I shall him pelt;
> My master shall full well then,
> Both to clothe and feed his men.
> Yea, yea, said the twybylle,

Thou speakest ever of thy skill.
Yes, yes, said the wymbylle,
I am as round as a thimble;
My master's work I will remember,
I shall creep fast into the timber,
And help my master within a stounde
To store his coffer with twenty pound.
Then said the whetstone,
Though my master's thrift be gone,
I shall him help within the year,
To get him twenty marks clear;
His axes shall I make full sharp,
That they may lightly do their work;
To make my master a rich man
I shall essay, if that I can.
[*Bodleian Library*]

A fourteenth-century poet gives his opinion of blacksmiths:

88. Swart smutted smiths, smattered with smoke,
Drive me to death with din of their dints;
Such noise on nights ne heard men never.
What with knaven cry and clattering of knocks!
The crooked caitiffs cryen after coal! coal!
And bloweth their bellows that all their brain bursteth.
Huf! puf! saith that one; haf! paf! that other;
They spitten and sprawlen and spellen many spells.
They gnawen and gnashen, they groan all together,
And holden them hot with their hard hammers.
Of a bull-hide be their barm-fells;
Their shanks be shackled for the fiery flinders;
Heavy hammers they have that hard be handled,
Stark strokes they striken on a steely stock,
Lus! bus! las! das! snore they by the row,
Such doleful a dream that the devil it to-drive!
The master loungeth a little and catcheth a less,
Twineth them twain and toucheth a treble,

CHAPTER 6. SHOPKEEPERS & CRAFTSPEOPLE

Tik! tak! hic! hac!, tiket! taket! tyk! tyk!
Lus! bus! las! das!... Christ give them sorrow!
May no man for brenn waters on night have his rest?
[*British Museum, Arundel MS 292*]

The goldsmith's work was more refined:

89. The goldsmith should have a very sharp chisel, so that he can engrave in amber, diamond, marble, jacinth, emerald, sapphire, or pearl, and form many different shapes. He should also have a hard  stone on which he can test metals, and distinguish between iron and steel. He should also have a rabbit's foot for smoothing, polishing and wiping gold and silver. He should collect the fragments of metal in a leather apron. He should also have little boxes and flasks of pottery, and a saw and a file for gold, as well as gold and silver wire, so that he can repair broken objects or make new ones correctly.

The goldsmith must be skilled in feather work as well as in bas-relief, at fusing, as well as hammering.

His apprentice must have a table that is painted or covered with clay, so that he can sketch flowers and make other drawings. He must learn how to tell gold from brass or copper, so that he does not buy them in mistake for gold.
[*Observations of Alexander Neckham in London and Paris*]

The following gives an idea of Arab craftsmanship. It is a description of some gifts that a caliph of Córdoba made to a chieftain whose friendship he was cultivating:

81

90. A large jewel box, ornamented with gilded plates, in relief, its base white and its interior lined with purple.

Nine jars and vessels, full of different perfumes, and, among them, a vessel, round in shape, full of sandalwood mixed with amber; a vessel of white marble, containing incense, adorned with amber; another vessel, also of marble, with silver hinges, which held an Iraqi jar, full of excellent civet; a third marble casket, with silver hinges, containing regal perfumes; a glass casket, with a top and chain of silver, with the powder which kings use against sweating in the summer; a gilded Iraqi bottle with rose water; a silken sheath containing a large sultan's comb, for combing the beard. A container lined with silk and covered with Fez leather, beautifully worked, with four compartments, each containing a silver flask, one with a chequered pattern round its neck, and a top and a chain of silver, the second decorated with floral patterns, with a yellow base and a top and a chain of silver, a third one similar, and a fourth of the same workmanship as the first, with the four excellent caliphal purgatives, broom, yellow grass, white grass and sudorific. And in the compartments of these boxes there was also an Iraqi bottle with califal unguent, and a small silver jewel box with toothpicks and the instruments which kings use after meals. [Ibn Hayyan of Córdoba, *Chronicle of the Caliph 'Abd Arrahman III an Nasir,* early 10th century]

GUILDS

Tradesmen formed guilds. In the largest towns, each trade would have its own guild, but elsewhere numbers would not warrant this. At Dorchester, Dorset, there was only one guild, divided into five sections, clothiers, ironmongers, fishmongers, shoemakers and skinners. Others had to fit in as best they could, for example, carpenters, masons, brewers, butchers and fletchers all joined the fishmongers.

Before becoming a full member of a guild, a young man had to serve an apprenticeship. The following is an indenture made in 1459:

91. This indenture made by John Pentreath of Penzance in the county of Cornwall witnesses that John Goffe has put himself to John Pentreath to learn the craft of fishing, and to stay with him as his apprentice until the end of eight years fully complete. Throughout this time, John Goffe shall well and truly serve John Pentreath and Agnes his wife, shall keep their se-crets, shall willingly do their lawful and honorable commands, shall do his masters no injury, nor see injury done to them by others, but prevent the same as far as he can, shall not waste his master's goods, nor lend them to any man without his special command.

And John Pentreath and Agnes his wife shall teach John Goffe the craft of fishing in the best way they know, chastising him duly, and finding him food, clothing and shoes as befits an apprentice. And at the end of the term aforesaid, John Goffe shall have of John Pentreath twenty shillings. [*Records of the County of Cornwall*]

These are the ordinances of the white tawyers, or leather workers, of London, drafted in 1346:

92. In honor of God, our Lady, and of All Saints, and for the nurture of tranquility and peace among the good folks the Megucers, called "Whittawyers," the folks of the same trade have, by assent of Richard Lacer, Mayor, and of the Aldermen, ordained the points under written.

In the first place they have ordained that they will find a wax candle, to burn before Our Lady in the church of All Hallows near London Wall. Also that each person of the said trade shall put in the box such sum as he shall think fit, in aid of maintaining the said candle.

Also, if by chance any one of the said trade shall fall into poverty, whether through old age or because he cannot labor or work, and have nothing with which to support himself, he shall have every week from the said box sevenpence for his support, if he be a man of good repute. And after his decease, if he have a wife, a woman of good repute, she shall have weekly for her support, sevenpence from the said box, as long as she shall behave herself well, and keep single.

Also that no stranger shall work in the said trade, or keep house in the same city, if he be not an apprentice, or a man admitted to the franchise of the said city.

And that no one shall take the serving man of another to work with him, during his term, unless it be with the permission of his master.

And if any one of the said trade shall have work in his house that he cannot complete, or if for want of assistance such work shall be in danger of being lost, those of the said trade shall aid him, so that the said work be not lost.

And if any one of the said trade shall depart this life, and have not the wherewithal to be buried, he shall be buried at the expense of the common box; and when any of the said trade shall die, all those of the said trade shall go to the Vigil and make offerings on the morrow.

And if any serving man shall conduct himself in any other manner than properly towards his master, and act rebelliously towards him, no one of the said trade shall set him to work, until he shall have made amends before the Mayor and Aldermen.

And that no one of the said trade shall behave himself the more thoughtlessly, in the way of speaking or acting amiss, by reason of the points aforesaid; and if any one shall do to the contrary thereof, he shall not follow the said trade until he shall have reasonably made amends.

CHAPTER 6. SHOPKEEPERS & CRAFTSPEOPLE

And if any one of the said trade shall do to the contrary of any point of the Ordinances aforesaid, and be convicted thereof by good men of the said trade, he shall pay to the Chamber of the guildhall of London, the first time two shillings, the second time forty pence, the third time half a mark, and the fourth time ten shillings and shall forswear the trade.

Also, that the 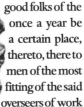 good folks of the said trade shall once a year be assembled in a certain place, convenient thereto, there to choose two men of the most loyal and be- fitting of the said trade, to be overseers of work and all other things touching the said trade for that year, which persons shall be presented to the Mayor and Aldermen and sworn before them diligently to inquire and make search, and loyally to present to the said Mayor and Aldermen such defaults as they shall find touching the said trade, without sparing any one for friendship or for hatred, or in any other manner. And if any one of the said trade shall be found rebellious against the said overseers, so as not to properly make their search and assay, as they ought to do; or if he shall absent himself from the meeting aforesaid, without any reasonable cause, after due warning by the overseers, he shall pay to the Chamber upon the first default, forty pence; and on the second like default, half a mark; and on the third, one mark; and on the fourth, twenty shillings and shall forswear the said trade for ever.

Also that all skins falsely and deceitfully wrought in their trade, which the overseers shall find on sale in the hands of any person citizen or foreigner, shall be forfeited to the said Chamber, and the worker thereof amerced in the manner aforesaid.

Also that no one who has not been an apprentice, and has not finished his term of apprenticeship in the said trade shall be made free of the said trade; unless it be attested by the overseers or by four persons of the said trade, that such person is able, and sufficiently skilled to be made free of the same.

Also that no one of the said trade shall induce the servant of another to work for him in the same trade, until he has made a proper fine with his first master, at the discretion of the said overseers, or of four reputable men of the said trade.

And that no one shall take for working in the said trade more than they were wont heretofore, on the pain aforesaid, that is to say, for the dyker of Scottish stags, half a mark; the dyker of Irish, half a mark; the dyker of Spanish stags, ten shillings; for the hundred of goat fells, twenty shillings; for the hundred of calf skins, eight shillings, and for the hundred of kid fells, eight shillings. [*London Letter Book F,* fol. 126]

The following are from the minute books of the tailors' guild of Exeter:

93. Memorandum that John Rowter received four yards of broadcloth, blue, to make Master Robert Rydon a gown; upon the which the said Master Robert complained of lacking of his cloth; and there was found no cloth wasted, but there was proved three quarters of broadcloth conveyed in pieces, as it appeareth by patterns of black paper in our Common coffer of record, at any time ready to show. For the said defense the said John Rowter submitted himself to the Master and Wardens of the fellowship. [*Records of the City of Exeter,* 15th century]

94. Memorandum that John Sketch, tailor, came before the Master and Wardens and there complained upon William Spicer, tailor, for withholding a pot of pewter weighing four pounds. Item, for sewing of a kirtle without sleeves, and for the stuff of a collar and setting on. For the which offense aforesaid, the Master and Wardens have awarded that the said William shall pay unto the said John Sketch, in full content of all things, from the beginning of the world unto

this day, sixteen pence. And the said John Sketch shall release him of all suits that the said Sketch hath against the said William for all such matter written above. [Ibid.]

One of the main purposes of the guilds was to maintain their monopolies:

95. Henry Wakyngknyght, goldsmith, says that the Mayor of London, at the suggestion of the Wardens of the Craft of Goldsmiths, ordered him to be imprisoned in the Counter in Bread Street. No cause is laid against him, only that he is a stranger occupying his craft in London. They intend to keep him in prison for ever, to his utter destruction and undoing. [*Chancery Proceedings*, 1440]

WOMEN TRADERS

While noblewomen might spend much of their lives in gilded cages, those lower down the social scale had to work. Their freedom to do so, however, varied from country to country.

In England, a wife would help her husband in his trade and, if he died, would manage the business on her own. A single woman might take up a trade, when she was known as a "femme sole" and she might well go on with the same work after she married. If so, she kept her status as femme sole and, if need be, answered for herself in the courts. Her husband was not responsible for her debts. There seems to have been a surplus of women, so that many remained unmarried and had to support themselves all their lives.

An English visionary, Margery Kempe, describes her ventures before she devoted herself to religion. She refers to herself as "this creature":

96. Out of pure greed and the wish to keep up her pride, she began to brew and was one of the greatest brewers in the town for three or four years, till she had lost a good deal of money, for she had never had any experience in brewing. For no matter how good her servants were and clever at brewing, yet things never went well with them. For even when the ale looked so splendid, standing under its head of froth, as anyone might see, suddenly the froth would

sink down so that the ale was ruined, one brewing after another, and her servants were mortified and would not stay with her.

Then this creature thought how God had punished her already, and she refused to be warned, and now again she was punished with the loss of her goods, and then she gave up brewing and did it no more.

Now she thought of a new kind of housewifely venture. She had a horse mill. She got herself two good horses and a man to grind people's corn, and in this way she felt sure she could make her living. This enterprise did not last long, for a short time after the Eve of Corpus Christi, the following marvel occurred. This man was in good health of body, with two horses that were lusty and in good condition, and up till now had drawn well in the mill. Now when the man took one of the horses and put him in the mill as he had done all along, this horse would not drag a load in the mill, no matter what the man did.

When this man saw it was useless, he took the other horse and put him in the mill. And just as his fellow horse had done, so this one did, for he would not pull despite anything the man did. And then this man quit his service and would no longer stay with this creature we have mentioned. As soon as word got around the town that no man or beast would work for that creature, then some people said she was cursed. And some wise men whose mind was more grounded in the love of our Lord said it was the high mercy of our Lord Jesus Christ that commanded and called her from the pride and vanity of the wretched world. [*The Book of Margery Kempe*, 1432]

CHAPTER 6. SHOPKEEPERS & CRAFTSPEOPLE

English women, though, could enter only a few trades in their own right. They were allowed to do almost anything connected with food and drink, both preparing it and selling it. Margery Kempe, as we have seen, tried both brewing and grinding corn. However, she had only a horse mill, since managing a water mill was man's work. Textiles employed large numbers of women, especially spinning, for it took five spinsters to supply one weaver with yarn. But even where women monopolized a trade, as they did spinning, they were not allowed to form a craft guild.

In France, on the other hand, women did form guilds, and made their own regulations along the same lines as the men's. These are the rules of the weavers of silk handkerchiefs of Paris:

> 97. Any woman who wishes to practice the craft of weaving silk handkerchiefs in Paris, will be allowed to do so, provided she is skilled and follows the customary usage.
>
> First, it is ordained that no member of the craft may work on a feast day which is celebrated by the city, and which is ordered by Holy Church.
>
> None may work at night, because it is impossible to do such good work at night as in the day.
>
> No one may have more than one apprentice who is not a relative, and no more than one who is. She may not take an apprentice for less than seven years, with a premium of twenty sous, or for eight years with no fee. If a mistress who is in need should sell her apprentice, she may not take another until her time is finished. If an apprentice should buy her freedom, the mistress may not take another until the time of the one who bought her freedom has expired.
>
> No mistress or journeywoman of the craft may buy silk from Jews, or from spinsters, or anyone else, but only from the appropriate merchants.
>
> If anyone breaks any of these regulations, she must pay a fine of six sous for every fault, four sous to the king, and two sous to the overseers for their trouble.
>
> No member of the craft may put her work, whether finished or unfinished, in pawn to any Jew or Lombard, or to

anyone else. Whoever does so, will pay a fine of ten sous, six sous to the king and four sous to the overseers.

There are three good women and true, sworn and pledged at Châtelet, who oversee the craft for the king, and make public all the infringements of the craft that they find. [Etienne de Boileau, *Le Livre des Métiers*, c. 1270]

The women of Moorish Spain, in contrast, were subjected to all sorts of restrictions:

98. Women are forbidden to do their laundry in the public gardens, for they are dens of fornication.

Women may not sit on the river bank, if men are present.

People may not follow trades in which they are not skilled, especially that of medicine, since that could result in loss of life. A physician buries his mistakes. All must follow their own trades, and not pretend to be skilled in any other, and this is particularly true of women, since they are more prone to ignorance and error.

Only men who are well known as good and trustworthy must buy and sell with women. Tradespeople must be careful about this. The women weavers of brocades must not be allowed in the market, for they are whores.

The manager of the baths must not sit there with women, for this leads to loose behavior and fornication. No woman may be an innkeeper, for this would be veritable fornication.

Prostitutes may not stand outside houses with their heads bare. Respectable women must not dress like them. They may not hold parties for themselves, even when their husbands give permission. Dancing girls may not go bare headed. [Ibn Abdun, *Regulations of Seville*, c. 1150]

As in all ages, some women were driven into prostitution, and towns often tried to regulate them. This edict was issued at Perpignan, then part of the kingdom of Majorca, in about 1440:

99. Always, and especially in holy lent, and most of all in Holy Week, all illegal acts and deviations from the holy life of paradise

should be prohibited. For that reason it has for a long time been ordered every year by the royal officials of the town aforesaid that on Maundy Thursday the public women of the town aforesaid should be placed in the leprosarium situated outside the Canet gate of the town aforesaid, until, and including Good Friday next following, in the charge of certain royal gaolers, to prevent them from carnal sin in the days aforesaid. But experience has shown that, notwithstanding the custody aforesaid, the women aforesaid go on committing illegal acts during the days aforesaid. Moreover, some of them are made to pay heavy fees, both to the gaolers for their custody, and to their hosts. Accordingly we, Johan Borro, Bernat Castello, Mallot Cadany, Guillem Anarell, Johan Viador, consuls of the town aforesaid for the current year, wishing to remedy the ills aforesaid, order Master Guillem Ribba, currently warden of the hospital of the poor, that from now on, every year, during the times aforesaid, the women aforesaid shall be placed by the royal officials aforesaid in the hospital aforesaid. And that during the days aforesaid, they should be given reasonable food and drink, and beds, and that each one should pay the hospital aforesaid, three reales, and that they should not be made to pay more than the three reales aforesaid. [*Records of Perpignan*]

CHAPTER 7
CONDUCTING BUSINESS

BUYING AND SELLING

William Fitz Stephen describes some of the traders of twelfth-century London. His quotations are from Virgil:

100. Those that ply their several trades, the vendors of each several thing, the hirers out of their several sorts of labor are found every morning each in their separate quarters and each engaged upon his own peculiar task. Moreover, there is in London, upon the river's bank, amid the wine that is sold from ships and wine cellars, a public cook-shop. There daily, according to the season, you may find viands, dishes roast, fired and boiled, fish great and small, the coarsest flesh for the poor, the more delicate for the rich, such as venison and birds both big and little. Those who desire to fare delicately, need not search to find sturgeon or "Guinea fowl" or "Ionian francolin," since all the dainties that are found there are set forth before their eyes.

In the suburb immediately outside one of the gates there is a smooth field, both in fact and in name [Smithfield]. On every sixth day of the week there is a much frequented show of fine horses for sale. Thither come all the earls, barons and knights who are in the city, and with them many of the citizens, whether to look on or to buy. It is a joy to see the ambling palfreys, their skins full of juice, their coats a-glisten, as they pace softly, in alternation raising and putting down the feet on one side together; next to see the horses that best befit esquires, moving more roughly, yet nimbly, as they raise and set down the opposite feet, fore and hind, first on one side and then on the other; then the younger colts of high breeding, unbroken and "high stepping with elastic tread," and after them the costly destriers of graceful form and goodly stature, "with quivering ears, high necks and plump buttocks." As these show their paces, the buyers watch first their gentler gait, then that swifter motion, wherein their fore feet are thrown out and back together, and

the hind feet also, as it were, counterwise.

In another place apart stand the wares of the country-folk, instruments of agriculture, long-flanked swine, cows with swollen udders, and "woolly flocks and bodies huge of kine." Mares stand there, meet for the ploughs, sledges and two-horse carts; the bellies of some are big with young; round others move their offspring, new-born, sprightly foals, inseparable followers. [*A Description of the Most Noble City of London*]

A poet calling himself "London Lickpenny" describes a shopping expedition in the early fifteenth century:

101. Then unto London I did me hie;
Of all the land it beareth the prize.
"Hot peascods, " one began to cry;
"Strawberries ripe," others coaxingly advise.
One bade me come near and buy some spice;
Pepper and saffron they gan me bid.
But for lack of money I might not speed.

Then to Cheapside I went on,
Where much people I saw for to stand,

One offered me velvet, silk and lawn;
Another he taketh me by the hand,
"Here is Paris thread, the finest in the land."
I was never used to such things indeed,
And wanting money, I might not speed.

Then went I forth by London Stone,
Throughout all Canwick Street;
Drapers much cloth me offered anon,
Then met I one, cried, "Hot sheep's feet."
One cried, "Mackerel;" "Rushes green," another gan greet.
One bade me buy a hood to cover my head;
But for want of money I might not be sped.

Then to Westminster gate I presently went.
When the sun was high at prime.
Cooks on me they were all intent,
And proffered me bread, with ale and wine,
Ribs of beef, both fat and full fine;
A fair cloth they began for to spread,
But wanting money, I might not be sped.

Then into Cornhill I took my road,
Where was much stolen goods among;
I saw where hung my own hood,

That I had lost among the throng,
To buy my own hood I thought it wrong,
I knew it as well as I did my creed;
But for lack of money I could not speed.
[*British Museum, Harleian MS* 542, fol. 102]

FRAUDS

John Gower describes the wiles of the mercer. The fraud he mentions looks more like high pressure selling to modern eyes, but medieval people had a strong belief in the virtues of the "just price," and a tradesman was condemned, if he used salesmanship to extract more for an article than it was worth:

102. Fraud also of its trickery
Oftentimes in mercery
Cheats people diversely,
Being full of artifice,
Of joking and of nonsense,
To make fools of silly people
So as to get their money.
And smooth and soft he talks to them
And is the best of company
With his mouth, but in his thinking
He is slyly after lucre.
Under pretence of courtesy,

ulum confideration Enutherg / ordon Siber affint fair ro pune quolibet unun poff
'um ad andue u austue .unas rebocus a fair iglhoi eliur nadom uncinom lundif illun

CHAPTER 7. CONDUCTING BUSINESS

He who is born of such a nest
Is never dumb for lack of words,
But cries out like the sparrowhawk,
When he sees people he doesn't know,
Pulls them and drags them with hue and cry,
Saying, "Come on! Come in!
Beds and kerchiefs, ostrich feathers,
Silks and satins and cloths imported,
Come, I will give you a look at them,
For if you are thinking of buying,
You have no need to go farther;
Here is the best in the street!"
But about one thing be careful
In entering his premises;
Have a mind to your buying;
For Fraud does not show his true colours,
But by subtle flattery
Chalk for cheese he can sell you.
You would think by his language
That the wild nettle he offers
Was a precious rose,
So much courtesy he will show you;
But if you wish to go uncheated,
Have no faith in his pretences.
[*Mirour de l'Omme*, c. 1376]

Berthold von Regensburg, a famous German friar of the mid-thirteenth century, addresses cheats, and in the process gives a good idea of the normal run of tradespeople a city dweller could expect to encounter:

103. The first are you that work in clothing, silks or wool or fur, shoes or gloves or girdles. Men cannot dispense with you; men must have clothing, therefore you should do your work honestly; not to steal half the cloth, or to use other guile, mixing hair with your wool or stretching it out longer, whereby a man thinks he has bought good cloth, yet you

have stretched it out longer than it should be, and made good cloth into useless stuff. Nowadays no man can find a good hat because of your cheating; the rain will pour down through the brim into his bosom. There is the same fraud in shoes, in furs, in curriers' work; one man sells an old skin for a new, and how many deceits there are, no man knows as well as you and your master the devil....

The second folk are all such as work with iron tools, gold-smiths, penny-smiths, and other smiths, and carpenters or blacksmiths,... and stonemasons and turners, and all who work with iron.... When they work by the day, they should not stand idle so that they multiply the days at their work. If you labor by the piece, then you should not hurry so that you may be rid of the work as quickly as possible.... You should work it truly, as if it were your own. You, smith, you will shoe a steed with a shoe that is worthless; and the beast may perhaps go scarce a mile before it is broken, and the horse may go lame, or the rider may be taken prisoner or lose his life. You are a devil and an apostate....

The third are those who are busied with trade. We cannot do without them. They bring from one kingdom to another what is good cheap there, and whatever is good cheap beyond the sea they bring to this town, and whatever is good cheap here, they carry over the sea. Thus some bring to us from Hungary, others from France; some on ships, some on wagons; driving beasts or bearing packs. However that may be, they should all follow the same code. You, trader, should trust God that He will find you a livelihood with honest gains,...yet you swear so loudly how good your wares are, and what profit you give the buyer; more than ten or thirty times you take the names of all the saints in vain...for wares worth scarcely five shillings. That which is worth five shillings you sell, perhaps, sixpence higher than if you had not been a blasphemer of our Lord, for you swear loud and boldly, "I have already been offered far more for these wares;" and that is a lie....

CHAPTER 7. CONDUCTING BUSINESS

The fourth are such as sell meat and drink, which no man can disregard. Therefore it is all the more needful that you should be true and honest.... If you offer measly or rotten flesh that you have kept so long until it is bad, then you are perhaps guilty of one man's life, perhaps of ten.... The same I say to him that sells fish. You keep the fish in water until Friday comes, they are then rotten, and a man eats his death by them, or some great sickness. So are certain innkeepers and cooks in the town, who keep their cooked flesh too long, whereof a guest eats and falls sick for his life long. So do certain others betray folk with corrupt wine or moldy beer, or give false measure, or mix water with wine. Certain others, again, make rotted corn into bread, whereby a man eats his own death; and they salt their bread, which is most unwholesome.

Some men are deceivers and liars, like the craftsmen. The shoemaker says, "See, these are two most excellent soles;" and he has  burned them before the fire, and lies and cheats you of your money. And the baker floods his dough with yeast, so that you, who thought you had bought bread, have bought mere air for bread. And the huxter pours beer sometimes, or water, into his oil; and the butcher will sell calves' flesh saying, "It is three weeks old;" and it is scarcely a week old.... [*Sermons*]

CONTROL OF TRADERS

The emperor Frederick II made these rules for the tradesmen and
craftsmen in his kingdom of Sicily:

104. We order that master craftsmen should work legally
and honestly. Gold and silversmiths, workers in bronze and
iron, those who make catapults and bows, should all work
to the best of their skills and abilities. Above all, we instruct
makers of shields and saddles to ensure the safety of their
customers by strengthening their wares with strong orna-
ments. We order that butchers and fishmongers, who can in-
jure not only
property but
people, should be
honest in their
dealings. They
must not dare to
sell breeding sows
for pork, or dis-
eased meat, or
what has been
kept for several
days, or anything corrupt, unless they warn the purchasers.
We also decree that fishmongers must keep faith by not selling rotten fish, and by not keeping it for several days, without
due warning to the customer. None should sell food that was
prepared the day before, and reheated the following day, without telling the customers. Candle makers should work carefully, and not include anything [other than beeswax] in their
candles, and if they do, they must inform their customers.

We forbid innkeepers and vintners to sell watered wine
as pure.

No one may do work in gold with an alloy that contains
less than eight ounces of pure gold to the pound. Similarly,
no one may work with an alloy of silver that contains less
than eleven ounces of pure silver to the pound. This rule

must be obeyed, whether the craftsmen are using their own materials, or materials supplied by others, in which they sometimes mix other metals.

We order that in every region, the bailiffs should appoint two trustworthy men, who will report the frauds of craftsmen to our court. Anyone taken in fraud for the first time, if he makes false goods, or sells rotten food, or watered wine, will pay one pound of pure gold to our treasury. If he cannot pay, he must be beaten. For a second offense, he must lose a hand, and for a third he must suffer death on the forks.

We order that all traders must use the lawful weights and measures. If anyone has used a false weight or measure, or has cut a length from a piece of cloth, he must pay one pound of pure gold to our treasury. If he cannot pay, he should be flogged in public throughout the place where he  committed the fraud, with the weight or measure hung round his neck, as a warning to others. For a second offense, he must lose a hand, and for a third, he must be hanged. [*Constitutions of Melfi*, 1231]

The following extracts come from the London records:

105. For of old it has been the custom to hold in the City of London on every feast day, two markets called eve-cheapings, one in Westcheap and the other in Cornhill, and that, too, by daylight only, between the first bell rung and the second for the said markets ordained.

And now William Standon, the mayor, and the aldermen of the said city have been given to understand that divers persons at night and by candle-light do sell in the common hostels there and in other places, in secret, divers wares that have been larcenously pilfered and some falsely wrought and some that are old as being new, and that other persons do there practice the sin of harlotry under color of the sale of their said wares, to the very great damage and scandal of good and honest folks of the said city. Therefore the said Mayor and aldermen, in order to put the said markets under good control and governance, have ordained that from henceforth on every such market night each of the two bells shall be rung by the beadle of the ward where it is hung, one hour before sunset, and then half an hour after sunset. At which second ringing, all the people shall depart from the market with their wares, on pain of forfeiture of all such wares. [*London Letter Book H, 1393*]

106. Robert Porter, servant of John Gibbe, baker, was brought into the Guildhall, before Nicholas Extone, Mayor, John Hadle and other aldermen, and questioned for that, when the same Mayor on that day went into Chepe, to make assay there of bread, according to the custom of the City, he, the said Robert, knowing that the bread of his master, in a certain cart there, was not of full weight, took a penny loaf, and in it falsely and fraudulently inserted a piece of iron, with intent to make the said loaf weigh more, in deceit of the people.

Wherefore, inquiry was made of the same Robert, how he would acquit himself thereof; upon which he acknowledged that he had done in manner aforesaid. And for his falsity and deceit, it was adjudged that he should be taken from thence to Cornhill, and be put upon the pillory there, to remain upon the same for one hour of the day, the said loaf and piece of iron being hung about his neck. And precept was given to the sheriffs to have the reason for such punishment publicly proclaimed. [*London Letter Book H, 1387*]

107. John de Brykelesworthe, who prosecuted for the King and Commonalty of the City of London, said that John Ryghtways

and John Penrose sold red wine to all who came there, unsound and unwholesome for man, in deceit of the common people, and in contempt of our Lord the King, and to the shameful disgrace of the officers of the city; and to the grievous damage of the Commonalty. The judgment was that the said John Penrose shall drink a draught of the same wine which he sold to the common people, and the remainder of such wine shall then be poured on the head of the same John; and that he shall forswear the calling of vintner in the City of London for ever, unless he can obtain the favor of our Lord the King as to the same. [*London Letter Book G, 1364*]

108. On the eighth day of May, five men of the county of Somerset came before the Mayor, sheriffs and certain aldermen, and showed to them two pieces of cooked fish, rotten and stinking and unwholesome for man, which they had bought of John Welburgham, a cook in Bread Street at noon of the same day, and which the said cook had warranted to them to be good and wholesome for man and not putrid.

And hereupon the said John Welburgham was immediately sent for, and, being questioned, he said he did sell to the complainants the said fish so cooked and that he warranted it to them as being good and wholesome, and still did warrant it. Whereupon the Mayor caused to be summoned twelve good men, neighbors of the cook, who said upon oath that the said pieces of fish were rotten, stinking and unwholesome for man. Whereupon it was ordered that the said John Welburgham should repay the sixpence he had received for the fish, that he should have the punishment of the pillory for one hour, and that the said fish should then be burned beneath him. [*London Letter Book H, 1382*]

CHAPTER 8
TOWN GOVERNMENT

TOWNS AND THEIR LORDS

Originally all towns had feudal lords, who, in the early years, at least, exercised considerable powers. An anonymous chronicler describes the refoundation of the town of Sahagún by Alfonso VI of Castile late in the eleventh century:

109. When the aforesaid king ordered that the town should be founded, there came from all parts of the universe citizens of many different trades, that is to say, blacksmiths, carpenters, tailors, skinners, shoemakers, sculptors and men skilled in many arts and trades, and, moreover, people from many different foreign lands, that is to say, Gascons, Bretons, English, Burgundians, Normans, Toulousains, Provençals, Lombards and many from divers nations, speaking foreign languages, and thus the town was well-populated.

And then the king decreed and ordered that none who dwelt in the town, within the estate of the monastery, should hold by right of inheritance a field, a vineyard, an orchard or a mill, unless the abbot granted any of these things to anyone. But they could have a house in the town, and, on account of that, should pay, each one, one sueldo a year for rental, and in recognition of the abbot's lordship. And if any one of them cut in the forest which belongs to the monastery as much as a single branch, he should be thrown into prison and held at the will and mercy of the abbot. Moreover, he ordered that all should go to bake their bread in the monastery oven, which was a serious inconvenience for the burgesses and inhabitants, who begged the abbot to allow them to bake wherever it suited them, and offered, in return, that every one of them would pay him a sueldo every year, which was granted and set out in writing, that is to say, every year each of the burgesses and inhabitants should pay the monastery two sueldos, one at Easter on account of the oven, and one on All Saints' Day on account of the rent and the lordship.

Moreover, the king ordered that no count or noble should have a house or dwelling in Sahagún, save only French and Castilians, and if, peradventure, by the agreement and authorization of the abbot, any noble did obtain a house or dwelling, he should obey the abbot, just like any other citizen, and pay the same rent. [*Crónicas Anónimas de Sahagún*]

Towns and their lords were frequently at odds and sometimes this led to serious trouble as, for example, at Cologne in 1074 when the people rebelled against the archbishop. They had long been discontented and a riot flared when some of the archbishop's men commandeered a barge:

110. The owner of the barge had a son, notable both for audacity and strength, and popular among the leading citizens. He took his servants, and all the young men of the city he could enlist in the heat of the moment, and, hastening to the barge, he drove off the archbishop's men.

News of the riot was brought to the archbishop. He sent in haste to stop the disturbance, and threatened in his anger, that he would punish the riotous young men as they deserved to be punished. He was a man of many virtues, and had often proved his worth in affairs of both Church and State, but he had one vice which displayed itself among his virtues like a small mole on a beautiful body. When he exploded in anger, he was unable to control his tongue, and would hurl bitter taunts and insults all round, without respect for persons. But afterwards, when his anger had abated a little, he would blame himself for his fault.

Meanwhile, the young man, wild and elated by his first triumph, continued to fan the disturbance. He went up and

down the city, spreading stories among the people about
the insolence and severity of the archbishop – his unjust
decrees, his robbing the innocent of their property, his
dreadful insults to the best citizens of Cologne. He found
his task easy. It is no difficult matter to turn a crowd wherever you wish, like leaves driven before the wind. The mob
was wild with passion. Carried away with the spirit of the
devil, men cried, "To arms!" all over the city. No longer
content with expelling the archbishop, they determined to
put him to death in torment.

Later that evening, drink was added to the people's anger, like oil to a fire. The mob rushed to the archbishop's
palace and began a savage attack. Many men saw the de-
mon who had begun all this tumult, running ahead of the
furious crowd, in helmet and breastplate, flashing like lightning with his fiery dagger, and standing out among the
throng. Then, in the act of sounding a trumpet to summon
the laggards, and the very heat of battle, just as he was rushing to break down the gates, he suddenly disappeared.

The archbishop's men rescued their master with difficulty
from the ranks of the enemy and the clouds of missiles, and
hurried him from the palace to the church of St. Peter. Here,
they tried to secure the gates, piling blocks behind them. Meanwhile, in the palace, the mob roared and raged, pillaging all
the rooms. They poured out the wines, which were there in
abundance, and suddenly found the cellar filled, so that they
were almost in danger of drowning.

Finding the archbishop had fled to St. Peter's church, the
mob besieged it. They did their best to break down the walls,
and threatened to set it on fire if the archbishop was not at
once surrendered. But there was a narrow way from the
church to the dormitory, and from the dormitory into the
house of one of the canons, which abutted on to the city
wall. A few days before the riot, the canon had asked the archbishop for license to make a breach in the wall and erect a
small postern gate; and this, in God's mercy on the archbishop,

now offered him an escape. The archbishop rode unrecognized in the darkness and reached the town of Neuss, twenty miles down the Rhine.

The archbishop now summoned his knights and returned to besiege Cologne. The citizens begged for mercy. But many of the merchants failed to present themselves to offer any satisfaction. The archbishop's knights could not stomach this affront; and without the knowledge of the archbishop, they took arms. They broke into houses, pillaged goods, killed some of those they found, and threw others into prison. The son of the merchant who had first incited the people to rebellion, and a few others, were blinded. Some were beaten and tortured.

Thus was a city, which a little time before had been crowded with citizens and counted as being, next after Mainz, the chief of cities of the Rhineland, suddenly reduced almost to a wilderness. Where once the streets could scarcely hold the thronging crowds of wayfarers, there was now seldom a man to be seen, and silence and horror possessed all the places which had once belonged to pleasure and delight. [Lampert of Hersfeld, *Annales*]

CHARTERS

Rebellion and reprisal were not the usual ways of resolving differences between a town and its lord. The normal method was for the lord to trade privileges for money, as we have seen at Sahagún, where the bishop allowed the townsfolk to bake bread where they wished, in return for an annual payment. Kings, too, could grant exemptions from royal dues, on similar terms. Nearly all such agreements were set out in charters.

CHAPTER 8. TOWN GOVERNMENT

As a town accumulated privileges over the years, it gradually gained its independence. Poole, on the south coast of England, is an interesting case study. The origins of the place are obscure, for it is not mentioned in Domesday Book, 1086, but its name appears in a list of 1224, giving the principal ports of the south of England. Poole was part of the manor of Canford, whose lord in 1284 was William Longespée. He wanted to go on a crusade, for which he needed funds, so he granted Poole a charter:

III. Know those present and those to come that I, William Longespée, have given and granted, and by this my present charter have confirmed for me and my heirs, to my burgesses of Poole and their heirs, all manner of liberties and free customs and acquittances as well of their bodies as of their goods from toll and all other customs and suits to be done without my borough of Poole to me or my heirs, belonging as free citizens or burgesses of the cities or boroughs of the lord the king have throughout all England as fully as to me or my predecessors or heirs in any manner was known through all my land upon the land, sea ports and passages, saving to me and my heirs for every ship going to foreign parts beyond the seas two shillings.

I have also granted to the same burgesses for me and my heirs that out of themselves as often as need shall require they may choose for the government of my said borough of Poole six burgesses from whom I and my heirs will appoint our portreeve who shall faithfully upon his oath preserve the rights of us and our burgesses, who truly if he be found less diligent in our business we will remove and require another according to the form aforesaid to be chosen in his place.

Moreover, the bailiffs of me and my heirs six times in a year shall hold in the said borough our pleas for the breach of measures and assize and all other things which to us of right appertain, that is to say on the morrow of the Circumcision [five other dates follow] so that if during any of the said term or terms or whilst the public pleas are holden within the said borough according to the custom of the borough and cities of the lord the king the said pleas shall be heard and brought to judgment by our said bailiffs the amerciaments therefrom arising according to the offense shall be taken by our bailiffs for our use.

Moreover, if it should happen that any of our said burgesses in the fixed terms of our court should be disabled from attendance through the hindrance of the sea, our bailiffs shall in no wise account their absence by default, but when they return and any pleas opened against them meanwhile shall be holden according to the aforesaid custom they shall be compelled by right to appear before our bailiffs.

Moreover when the king whomsoever he shall be shall take tallage of his cities or boroughs according to the custom of his cities and boroughs it shall be lawful for me and my heirs to take tallage of my said burgesses.

I will also for me and my heirs that the said burgesses shall have well and peaceably their cattle quit of herbage in my heaths as always they have been accustomed, and necessaries for their firing in the heaths and turbaries by the view of my bailiffs.

And for this grant and concession and the confirmation of this present charter the aforesaid burgesses have given to me by their hands seventy marks whereof I and my heirs are held to warrant for ever the said liberties of the said burgesses and their heirs and in order that all the aforesaid may obtain strength in perpetual validity I have given corroboration to this charter by the putting of my seal. [*Records of the Borough of Poole*]

It is clear from the opening paragraph that this charter was not the first grant of privileges, for it mentions "free burgesses." A free burgess, unlike a villein, did not owe his lord work or produce, but was the master of his own time and possessions. The charter confirms these freedoms, claiming in their place a levy of two shillings on every ship leaving the port. "Foreign parts" would have included other places in England.

Allowing six elected burgesses to manage the town was an important step towards self government, though the lord had the right to name one of them as portreeve. Here, "port" signifies "town," and a portreeve was like a mayor, though with less dignity and power. Other clauses show that the lord still had considerable control over the town and still regarded it as his milch cow, from which he extracted fines and taxes.

The mark, worth two thirds of a pound, was not a coin, but a unit of account. If, as was likely, the seventy marks were paid in silver pennies, they would have weighed over 46 pounds.

In 1249, the year after granting the charter and collecting his money, William Longespée duly went on a crusade. In 1250, he was killed leading the English contingent at the Battle of Mansoura, in Egypt.

Step by step, over the centuries, the burgesses of Poole increased their powers. In 1312, the lord of the manor commuted his dues for a fixed annual payment of 13 marks. In 1364, the Winchelsea Certificate, granted by the crown, gave Poole an admiralty court, over which the mayor presided as admiral of the port. Sixteenth-century records state that the court exercised jurisdiction over the northern part of the harbor and the open sea "from the North Haven Pynte as farre seaward as an humber barrell maie be seen and descried in the sea." The court dealt with pirates, or, at least, those who were not in league with the burgesses. It also prosecuted fishermen who dredged for oysters out of season or used small mesh nets "to the distruction of the small ffrye of fyshe." The mayor of Poole was allowed a share of the profits from wrecks and anything found floating in the sea, including "any dead bodye havinge or about hyme any gold, silver, jewell, or other ritches."

This Winchelsea Certificate is the first surviving document to mention the office of mayor of Poole. If a town had a mayor, this usually indicated that it had won a good measure of independence.

A royal charter of 1433 made Poole a Port of the Staple, which meant its merchants could engage in the wool trade, England's most important commerce. The same year, the town was given a license to fortify itself. Twenty years later, another royal charter granted a Thursday market and two fairs a year. To regulate the markets and fairs there was a Court of Pie Powder. This expression was the best that Englishmen of the day could make of the French "pieds poudrés," or "dusty feet," which referred to the state of the shoes of the tradesmen who brought their goods along medieval roads.

Poole's so-called Great Charter, granted by Elizabeth I in 1568, marked the end of this step-by-step progress towards self-government. The town gained almost complete freedom from its lord of the manor and it became a county in its own right, with its own sheriff, so that the only outside authority to which it had to answer was the crown. The next logical step would have been to secure independence of the crown itself, becoming a separate city state. Many European towns took this step, especially in Germany and Italy, but none did in England. Not even London would have aimed so high.

The progress towards greater privileges and increased self-government could sometimes go into reverse. When Thomas, earl of Leicester, succeeded his father, Edmund, he extended the practice of farming his dues from the town. That meant he sold the right to collect the dues to men known as "farmers" in return for fixed, annual sums. That suited the earl who knew just what his income would be, and was saved the trouble of collecting it. But the farmers squeezed the townsfolk, in order to make maximum profits, and in 1322 the burgesses complained to the crown:

112. In the time of Edmund, late earl of Leicester, the men of the town who were in the guild gave nothing for the sale of cloth and other goods, but in the time of Thomas, earl of Leicester, by distraint of farmers, they were compelled to make heavy fines yearly.

Further, in the time of Edmund, the fullers gave nothing for exercising their craft, but in the time of Thomas they were made to pay 40 shillings a year, so that none remain in the town save one, and he is poor.

Further, in the time of Edmund, the farmers used to have the dung found in the high road, but not in the lanes; in the time of Thomas they collected and took the dung in all the lanes.

In the time of Edmund, the burgesses used to have their court at the Portmanmoot; in the time of Thomas the farmers refused to grant their court.

Further, in the time of Edmund, buyers of wool used to hire carts to carry wool at their will; in the time of Thomas they were made to give the farmers 1d on each sack and could hire only at the will of the said farmers.

Further, in the time of Edmund, the foresters of le Frith used not to interfere with the collection of dry wood; in the time of Thomas they taxed those who bought at doors from poor women carrying dry sticks on their heads.

Further, in the time of Edmund, the brewers used to be fined once a year, according to their guilt, at the rate of 6d or 12d at the most; in the time of Thomas, the farmers fined them at their will, from one, half a mark, and from another, 10 shillings.

Further, in the time of Edmund, the weavers used to give nothing for exercising their trade; in the time of Thomas, the farmers took from every weaver 40d for permission to work in broad cloth.

Further, in the time of Edmund, the vendors of salt herrings and fish could sell their goods by themselves, giving nothing except toll; in the time of Thomas, they were not allowed to sell their goods, but the servants of the farmers sold the same and took great sums of money. [*Miscellaneous Inquisitions, 1322*]

A city-state might succumb to a tyrant:

113. Our valiant but unlucky army, which had fought against Lucca, returned. Lucca surrendered to the Pisans. The Florentines considered their situation and recognized that Micer [Giovanni] Malatesta, our captain, had not acted well during the war. In order to be safer, they chose as captain and

protector of the people, Micer Gualterio, duke of Athens and count of Brienne, in France. This was at the beginning of June 1342. He was granted, for the term of one year, the same salary and the same mounted and foot soldiers as Micer Malatesta. The duke, whether for convenience or guile, or for what will shortly be revealed, wished to return to Santa Croce, the residence of the Friars Minor [in Florence]. His people camped around him. Later, on the calends of August, the duke added to his offices that of commander-in-chief in time of war, and the power to administer justice both within and without the city. He realized that the city was divided. This nobleman, being greedy for money, of which he stood in need, since he was a wanderer, and of which he was very fond, in spite of his title of Duke of Athens, accepted advances from some of the great men of Florence. These, along with certain plebeians of importance, tried to continue undermining the rule of the people, wishing to lord it over them and not give rewards where they were due. Accordingly, they went to Santa Croce to advise the duke. The duke, for the reasons given, and being greedy for power, began to follow this bad advice and turned himself into a cruel tyrant. He used the pretext of administering justice, but, in truth, he wanted to be feared, so that, in the end, he could make himself master of Florence. [Giovanni Villani, *Chronicles*]

OLIGARCHIES

Most towns were governed by narrow oligarchies, a practice that was defended by a prominent Italian humanist, Gasparo Contarini, in his account of the constitution of Venice:

114. The whole authority of the city from whose decrees and laws the senate and all other magistrates derive their power and authority, is in that council, into which all gentlemen of the City, over the age of 25, are admitted.

First of all, I will tell you how and with what wisdom our ancestors decreed that the common people should be excluded from this assembly, which has authority over the entire common-wealth. It was because many troubles and popular tumults arise in those cities whose government is influenced by the common people, as we have read, and as we have seen for ourselves. Yet many were of a different opinion, thinking it would be fitting that the commonwealth should be governed by those of ability and wealth. But here they met absurdities and problems, for it often happens that those of the basest sort, yea, the very scum of the people, scrape together great wealth, as do those who practice filthy trades, never sparing themselves arduous toil and wearing themselves out, but making unbearable economies and denying themselves any of the pleasures of life in order to increase their wealth. On the other hand, honest citizens, who have had an enlightened upbring-ing, often fall into poverty. Therefore our ancestors, in their wisdom, decreed that power should be given according to

nobility of descent, rather than wealth. [*The Commonwealth and Government of Venice, 1534*]

Sometimes the ruling clique had to resort to force, in order to keep its authority. The following describes a mayoral election in London in 1384:

115. The 12th day of October was the date on which the Aldermen and leading citizens of London were accustomed to choose their new Mayor, and Sir Nicholas Brembre, mayor for the previous year, did not want the election disturbed by any disturbances or riots. Accordingly, he concealed some armed men in rooms adjoining the Guildhall, instructing them that if any dissension or discord should break out during the election, they were to emerge at once and put down those who were being quarrelsome and disorderly. He hoped that fear of imprisonment would restrain those guilty of riot and verbosity, and bring them back to concord and unity. What else shall I say?

The leading burgesses met together in the Guildhall for the election of the new Mayor. One group shouted, "Twyford! Twyford!" hoping to have him as Mayor. But another group shouted even louder, "Brembre! Brembre!" When this discord erupted, Sir Nicholas Brembre signaled to his armed men to come out of hiding and put down the troublemakers, whereupon those who had been shouting for Twyford fled. After peace had been restored, those who remained, re-elected Sir Nicholas Brembre as Mayor.

When that was done, Nicholas Brembre went through Cheapside with his armed men, to see if any had congregated there to disturb the peace. They then patrolled other streets, so that they might arrest seditious persons, and put them in chains in Newgate prison, as an example to others.

This, then, is how the election was conducted. Even though there were people who impugned it, Brembre remained as Mayor during the following year, with the support of the king. [*Westminster Chronicle*]

CHAPTER 8. TOWN GOVERNMENT

The king at the time was Richard II, and Sir Nicholas Brembre was one of his most loyal supporters. This was to cost him dear. In 1388 the Lords Appellant convicted him, wrongly, for high treason, and he was hanged, drawn and quartered.

CHAPTER 9
TWO SPANISH CHARTERS

THOUGH IN MANY WAYS similar to the other regions of Western Europe, the Iberian Peninsula had its own special problems. The most important of these derived from having been almost entirely overrun by the Moors in the eighth century. A string of independent Christian states appeared in the north, and, gradually, they won back the entire peninsula. This "reconquista" was slow, mainly because the Christians fought among themselves, even forming alliances with Moorish kingdoms from time to time. But once an area had been reconquered, it had to be made attractive to settlers, which was best done by granting privileges. A further problem was what to do with the Moors who remained under Christian rule, for many of them were valuable citizens and it would have been unwise to persecute them. A third problem was agricultural. Herds of cattle and, more important, flocks of sheep, moved up and down the peninsula with the changing seasons; they had to be controlled or they would have caused havoc in the settlements through which they passed.

The charters are as much codes of laws as grants of privileges, and some of the laws are fairly crude. The charters, too, are crude in their way. There is little attempt at a proper division into paragraphs, while the order in which the various clauses appear is sometimes untidy.

Both of the following charters were granted to the town of Jaca, the first in 1077. This town had never fallen to the Moors, and, in the eighth century, had played a leading part in resisting them. It survived a bitter siege and the inhabitants still hold a festival in May each year to celebrate the heroism of the women and girls in defense of their town. After the victory, the local people formed the County of Aragon, even though they held no more

119

than a few Pyrenean valleys. Then, in 1035, Aragon became a kingdom with Jaca as its capital. The place was also an episcopal seat and an important route center:

116. In the name of Our Lord Jesus Christ and of the indivisible Trinity, Father, Son and Holy Ghost, Amen. This is the charter granted by me, Sancho, by the grace of God, King of Aragon and Pamplona. Be it known to all men from east to west and from north to south that it is my wish that my town of Jaca shall become a city. To this end I revoke all the unsatisfactory charters which you have held until today. And as I wish that the city should be well populated, I ratify and grant to you and to all who come to dwell in my city of Jaca all those good laws which you have sought from me and which are as follows: That everyone should build his dwelling as well as he can. That if any one of you should wound another in my presence, or in my palace while I am there, he shall pay a thousand sueldos, or lose a hand. But if anyone, be he gentleman, burgess or countryman wounds another, but neither in my presence nor in my palace, even though I am in Jaca, he shall not pay this penalty, but the one prescribed by the law which applies when I am not in Jaca. That if anyone in Jaca is killed while committing theft, then the killing shall not be deemed homicide. I grant and concede with good will to you and your successors, that when you go with the army you shall not be obliged to take with you provisions for more than three days, and that only when there is full-scale war, or when I or my successors are besieged by the enemy; and if the head of the family does not want to go to war, he can send an armed laborer in his place. That if any of you should acquire property, in Jaca or outside it, you shall hold it freely without let or hindrance; and if, after you have held it for a year and a day, anyone should begin a lawsuit for its recovery, or evict you from it, he shall pay me 60 sueldos and confirm your right to the farm. That you shall have the right to pasture your animals and collect firewood for as far as you can go and

return in a day, in all directions and within all boundaries, as the people of the neighboring villages may do within your boundaries. That you shall not be obliged to accept challenges to judicial duels, unless both parties are willing, and you may not accept them from outsiders without the consent of the people of Jaca. That none of you shall be imprisoned, provided he gives the proper sureties. That if any of you should sin with an unmarried woman, with her agreement, you shall pay no penalty. But if you use violence, you must provide her with a husband, or marry her yourself. If the woman who has been outraged asks for justice on the first or second day, let her prove her case with trustworthy witnesses of Jaca; but if she allows three days to pass without bringing her case, she shall have no rights. That if any of you, angry with his neighbor, takes up arms, a lance, a sword, a mace, or a knife, let him pay 1000 sueldos, or lose a hand. If anyone should kill another, let him pay 500 sueldos. If he only hurts him with his fist, or seizes him by the hair, let him pay 25 sueldos, and if he hurls him to the ground, 250 sueldos. That my steward shall not collect any dues or fines from anyone of Jaca without the consent of six of the best men of Jaca. That none of the men of Jaca shall be obliged to appear before a judge in any place other than Jaca. That anyone who has false weights or measures shall pay 60 sueldos. That all may take their grain to be ground in whatever mill they like, save Jews and those who make bread for sale. That none of you shall give or sell your farms to the church or to minors. That if any man is to be imprisoned for debt, he who wants him confined must arrange it with my steward, who will have him imprisoned in my palace, in the care of my jailer. After three days, he who had him imprisoned must take the prisoner a daily ration of bread, and if he fails to do so, my jailer shall set the prisoner free. That if any man should seize a Moor, let him be kept in my palace, and the owner of the Moor must give him a proper ration of bread and water, for he is a human being, and must not be left without food as if he were an animal.

And if anyone should have the temerity to amend this charter which I grant to the people of Jaca, be he of my line or of any other, let him be excommunicated, anathematized and excluded from all association with God.

Amen, amen, amen.

I, Sancho, by the grace of God, king of Aragon and Pamplona, order the above and herewith affix my seal.

[Damaso Sangorrín, *El Libro de la Cadena del Consejo de Jaca*]

The following charter was granted to Jaca just over a hundred years later, in 1187. The need now is more to regulate trade and protect property than to establish order:

117. In the name of God and with His divine mercy, I Alfonso [II], by the grace of God, king of Aragon, count of Barcelona and marquis of Provenza, approve, concede and confirm, with the counsel of Ricardo, venerable bishop of Huesca, of Sancho de Orta, of Fortún de Bergua, of Marco Ferriz and of many other good men, the ancient customs and rights of Jaca and of all the land that there is on the other side of the mountain range, as far as the mountains of Jaca.

It is evident to me that men come from Castile, from Navarre and from other regions to Jaca in order to learn its good customs and rights and take them to their own countries. First of all, I approve and confirm that the men of Jaca may dispose freely of the goods and property that God has given them, whether they have children or not, without let or hindrance. If they die intestate, let their nearest relatives inherit their goods, and if they have no close relatives, then let all these things be given to the poor. If any stranger should die in Jaca, or in the region of the mountain range above it, if he has a will, then let it be executed. But if he leaves no will, let his goods be kept for thirty days, and if his relatives come, and prove their kinship, let them be given two thirds of his property, and let the third part be

122

spent for the good of his soul in such manner as shall be decided by the good men and the bishop of Jaca. If no relatives appear, then let everything be spent for the good of his soul, as the same gentlemen shall decide. Let the men of Jaca and its region take care when giving surety in business affairs; and if they buy something, or give sureties for payment on a fixed date, let them pay the merchant stranger on the day, because if they do not do so, their farms will be seized and sold to pay the traders; therefore let no one give sureties or guarantees for more than he can pay.

With regard to thieves, this is what we decree; in each town or village there will be three or four good men who will swear not to conceal thefts, but to tell what they know to the king's steward; but on no account will the steward tell the thief who has denounced him and so he will come into the king's power. If anyone dares to oppose the king's steward when he is arresting a thief, then let the steward inform the lord king, who will execute justice on the whole town and will punish those who helped the thief exactly as he himself would have been punished.

If anyone should steal oxen, sheep or goats, he will return nine for each one. No creditor shall seize an ox, a sheep or a goat, if there is anything else he can take; but if there is nothing, he can take his surety in sheep and oxen for the steward to mediate. If any animal should die when taken as a surety, the creditor must not return the skin or hide of another animal, but return the same skin or hide of the one that died. He who does the contrary shall be adjudged a thief.

When the herds are being driven down into Spain, they must not be kept on private land for more than one day, without payment. All may make full and free use of the lord king's pastures and waters. With regard to the call to arms, this is what we decree; when the men in the towns and villages, and those who are in the mountains with their herds shall hear the call, let them take up arms and obey the summons, leaving their herds and all their occupations.

And if those who were the most distant come upon a place nearer to the call, whose men have not turned out, the place which was dilatory shall pay a cow to its lord. And every man who arrives late, allowing himself to be passed by others coming from a greater distance, shall pay three sueldos, one to the lord king, one to the lord of his town or village, and the other for his comrades in arms. Notwithstanding, in Jaca and in the other towns and villages there shall be a certain number of men chosen by the Council, who shall remain behind to guard and defend them. In the lawsuits, once the case has been judged and decided, let the documents be handed to the mayor, who will destroy them. If anyone makes a false accusation, then all his property shall be transferred to the lord king. When the herds come down to Spain, let none dare to exact, steal or impound any of the animals for any reason whatsoever. In the water courses there shall be certain places where the herds may drink without damaging them. If it is proved that someone has knowingly given false evidence, or committed perjury to deprive another of his property, let him be judged and his property given to the lord king. No one shall impound the goods of merchants, either of Jaca, or elsewhere, or make claims upon them unless they are their guarantors or creditors. If anyone deposits goods in Jaca, let them be safe and sure, and no one, not even the steward, must dare to take or impound them, provided always that their owner promises to defend his title in court, should anyone make a claim against him; but if the owner is a robber or a thief, who has no rights in law, and if anyone makes a claim against him, the steward may impound the goods. You may hold fairs every year during the feast of the Holy Cross. We receive all those who attend these fairs under our protection and safeguard, whosoever they may be and from wheresoever they may come.

Given in Jaca in the presence of me, Alfonso, King of Aragon, ruler of Barcelona and lord of Provenza. [Ibid.]

CHAPTER 10
TRADE, MONEY, AND BANKING

MERCHANTS AND SAILORS

Chaucer describes a merchant and a ship-man:

> 118. There was a merchant with a forkéd beard.
> In colored coat, high on his horse he sat,
> Upon his head a Flemish beaver hat.
> His boots were clasped both fair and stylishly.
> He gave his views and thoughts most solemnly,
> Proclaiming all the profits he could gain.
> He would have pirates swept from off the main,
> Twixt Middleburgh and Suffolk's sandy coast.
> He understood exchanges was his boast.
> He spoke to such remarkable effect
> That no-one ever dreamed he was in debt.
> He was a worthy man, I must maintain,
> Though truth to tell, I don't recall his name.
>
> There was a shipman, native of the west,
> From Dartmouth town, if I recall aright.
> He rode an agéd nag as best he might.
> His cloak of fustian reached down to his knee;
> A dagger hanging on a cord had he,
> Slung round his neck, under his arm and down.
> The summer sun had burnt his skin quite brown.
> He was a worthy man, for in his time,
> He'd purloined many a draught of vintage wine
> In Bordeaux town, while all the merchants slept.
> The nicer rules of war he never kept,
> For if he fought and had the upper hand,

He made his captives swim their way to land.
Such was his skill to calculate the tides,
The currents and all other risks besides,
The moon, the harbours and the pilotage,
He had no peer twixt Hull and far Carthàge.
He was full wise in all he undertook.
In tempests wild his grey beard often shook.
He knew well all the havens that there were
From Gotland to the Cape of Finisterre
And ev'ry creek in Brittany and Spain.
His trusty bark was called The Maudelayne.
[*The Canterbury Tales*]

Chaucer does not comment adversely on the fact that the ship-man captures other vessels, only that he throws his prisoners overboard. Most merchant captains combined piracy and privateering with lawful trade. The trade was expected to bring a satisfactory profit, while a prize, if one could be taken, was a welcome bonus.

A French poet sings the praises of merchants:

119. Above all, people should honor merchants
Who cross land and sea
And visit such strange countries to obtain wool and skins.
Others cross the seas to obtain pepper
Or cinnamon or ginger.
God keep from harm all merchants, whom we often revere.
The Holy Church was first established for merchants.
And know that the nobility should esteem the merchants
Who bring it such splendid steeds.
In Lagny, Bar and in Provence

CHAPTER 10. TRADE, MONEY & BANKING

Are merchants of wine, of wheat, salt and herrings
And of silk, gold and silver, and precious stones.
Merchants go all over the world to buy great diversity of goods.
[*Dit des Marchands*, 13th century]

On the other hand, John Gower wrote:

120. Sooth to say, there is a difference betwixt the merchant whose thoughts are set on deceit, and him whose day is spent in honest work; both labour alike for gain, but one would ill sort with the other. There is one merchant in these days whose name is on most men's tongues: Trick is his name, and guile his nature: though thou dost seek from the East to the going out of the West, there is no city or good town where Trick doth not amass his ill-gotten wealth. Trick at Bordeaux, Trick at Seville, Trick at Paris buys and sells. He hath his ships and his crowds of servants, and of the choicest riches, Trick hath ten times more than other folk. Trick at Florence and Venice hath his counting house and his freedom of the city, nor less at Bruges and Ghent; to his rule, too, hath the noble city of the Thames bowed herself, which Brutus founded in old days, but which Trick stands now in the way to confound, fleecing his neighbors of their goods: for all means are alike to him whether before or behind; he followeth straight after his own lucre, and thinketh scorn of the common good. [*Mirour de l'Omme*]

TREATIES AND CONTRACTS

Trade was regulated, after a fashion, by treaties and contracts. The following are two examples of trading agreements made by Castile. The first is in the form of a charter granted to Genoese living in Castile:

121. Be it known to all men who may see this charter, granted by us, Don Alfonso, by the grace of God, king of Castile, Toledo, Leon, Galicia, Seville, Cordoba, Murcia, Jaen, the Algarve and Algeciras, and lord of Molina. For the many and distinguished services that the people of the city of Genoa have given to the kings of our country, and to us

since our accession, and notably in the conquest of Algeciras, which we took by the mercy and aid of God. To honor and assist the aforesaid city we decree that any Genoese who enters our territory to trade, whether by sea or by land, shall be quit and free and shall not pay any duty on whatever they may buy in our territories. And by this our charter, or by any transcript of it signed by a  public scribe, we order whomsoever may in future receive or collect in any way the aforesaid duties in the most noble city of Seville and in all the other towns and places under our rule, that they may not tax the aforesaid people of Genoa, neither the ones now living in the aforesaid city of Seville and in all the other towns and places in our kingdom, nor those who may come into our realms trading as aforesaid, on account of anything they may buy in whatever cities and towns and places in our aforesaid realms, provided that they swear on oath that the goods which they purchased are their own and are for themselves.

And we order this our charter to be issued sealed with our lead seal. Given in Avila, the 26th day of August, 1346. [González Gallego, *El Libro de los Privilegios de la Nación Genovesa*]

These are extracts from a treaty of 1443 made between Castile and the Hanseatic League, a powerful association of north German ports. There had been conflict between the two since 1419:

122. To the glory of the Holy Trinity and for the increase in trade between us, the nations of the Hanseatic League and

Spain, heretofore enemies, due to the machinations of Satan, agree as follows:

1. The said nations agree and ratify a treaty for three years.

2. All the merchants, sailors and subjects of the Hanseatic League may, in complete freedom and security come and go, stay and remain at their convenience in the places, cities and ports which belong to the king of Castile, with their goods, possessions, merchandise and persons. In cases where the Hanseatic merchants enter the ports of the monarch aforesaid, with their own ships and their own goods, they can sell them and then load all the goods purchased with the product of this sale into their own ships and transport them wherever they may wish. On the other hand, if the aforesaid Hanseatic sailors bring in their ships goods other than their own, those goods purchased in exchange should be embarked in Spanish ships, if any are to be found in the ports aforesaid and disposed to sail to the countries or ports to which the merchants wish to despatch their goods.

5. If it should happen that Hanseatic and Spanish ships should meet enemies of the latter on the high seas, whether English or any other, the Hanseatic sailors must unfurl their banner to show clearly that they are not enemies. Then they must retire so that they do not interfere with the Spanish ships in their combat with their enemies.

9. If the merchants and sailors of both nations meet in a port and leave it together, they must commit themselves, either by oaths or by simple promises, to help each other against enemies or pirates. If these appear, and one party refuses to help, it will be severely punished by the nation to which it belongs, as an example to others, in the future.

15. The two parties agree with regard to goods which the Hanseatics acquire in the port of La Rochelle, wines and other products, that they should be embarked, preferably, in Spanish ships, provided that these are present and are going to the ports to which the Hanseatic merchants wish to despatch their

cargo. [There are several clauses of this nature.] [In T. Hirsch, *Danzigs Handels und Gewerbegeschichte*]

This is a contract made in thirteenth-century Spain:

123. Be it known to all men that I, Bernardo Corretger, concede and acknowledge that I have received as a consignment from you, Juan de Banyeres, in the present voyage that I am making to Sicily in the "levy" of Ramon de Cánoves and his partners, a Saracen slave woman valued at seven Barcelona pounds. I promise to sell this slave at the best possible price, and in good faith, and the money that I obtain for her, I will apply to the purchase of cumin or cotton, and these goods I promise, God willing, to deliver to you when I return from my voyage. Also, from the profits made on this transaction, your capital being deducted, I shall take the fourth part, and you will take the remaining three parts, along with the capital. Also, this assignment shall depend on the will of God and be at your own risk.

Done on the nones of October in the year of Our Lord 1238. [In Madurel Marimón et al., *Comandas Maritimas Barcelonesas de la Baja Edad Media*]

Such agreements were often fragile. In 1387 a London fishmonger petitioned the crown:

124. To our most renowned lord the King, your poor servant John Blakeneye, citizen and fishmonger of London, complains that he chartered a ship which belongs to Sir William de Windsor, called *St. Mary Cog*. This ship was to take a cargo of herrings from Yarmouth to Bordeaux and to return to London laden with wines of the said John. For which freight the said John was to have paid the said Sir William 200 marks, of which the said John paid £40. And then the said John caused the ship to be laden with 65 lasts of herrings to the value of 700 marks at Yarmouth. And the ship sailed for Bordeaux, but as she came off Sandwich she could go no further, for she was not seaworthy. Neither would the said Sir William repair her,

but unladed her of the said goods of the said John and would not carry them further.

Whereby the said John lost most of his said goods and the carriage of the said wines from Bordeaux to his damage of £1,000. [*Ancient Petitions*]

Jacques de Vitry, bishop of Acre in the early 13th century, wrote:

125. I have known certain sailors bound for the city of Acre who had hired a ship from a man on condition that, if it perished on the sea, they would be bound to pay naught. When therefore they were within a short distance of the haven, without the knowledge of those pilgrims and merchants who were on board, they pierced the hold and entered into a boat while the ship was sinking. All those passengers were drowned; and the sailors, having laden their boats with the money and goods of the pilgrims, put on feigned faces of sadness when they drew near the haven. Therefore, having drowned the pilgrims and carried away their wealth, they paid not the hire of the ship, saying they were not bound thereunto unless the vessel should come safe and sound to haven. [*Exempla*]

THE FIFTEENTH-CENTURY WOOL TRADE

Trade is as old as civilization, and it became very important in classical times, especially after the Romans imposed their peace on the Mediterranean. The fall of the Empire along with widespread piracy brought disruption, but trade never ceased entirely and it gradually revived, so that it became vital to the medieval economy.

Trade and its routes were complex, and went through so many changes it is impossible to examine the whole subject in this book. What follows is a case study of one particular trade, that in wool, viewed mainly from the English standpoint.

Many peasant women could spin and local weavers could turn their coarse thread into inferior cloth, but producing woolens of high quality required several skills, including not only spinning and weaving, but, for example, fulling, shearing and dyeing. Since it was so specialized, the manufacture of cloth became concentrated in a few areas, the most important of which was the Low Countries, modern Holland and Belgium, and more particularly the provinces of Flanders and Brabant. An English monk wrote:

> 126. And though Flanders is a little land, it is full of many good things, rich pasture, beasts, merchandise, rivers, harbors and fine towns. The men of Flanders be fair, strong and rich; and bring forth many children and be peaceful to their neighbors, true to strangers, noble craftsmen and great makers of cloth, that they send all over Europe. The land is flat and has little wood. Therefore instead of wood, they burn turfs, that smell worse than wood and make worse ashes. Brabant is to the south-east

> of Flanders and is famous for its cloth. They have their wool from England and they make cloth of different colors, which they send to other lands, as Flanders does. The English have the best wool, but do not have so much good water for different colors as Flanders and Brabant have. Nevertheless, at London is a well that makes good scarlet, and so at Lincoln is a certain place in a brook that passes by the town. [Ralph Higden, *Polychronicon*, 14th century]

Raw wool came to the Low Countries from Spain, Burgundy and England. It was one of the ambitions of the Hapsburg monarchs to bring all these states under their control. They acquired the Low Countries, Spain and Burgundy, but England was more elusive. It was in pursuit of her that Philip II of Spain wed the plain, dour, Mary Tudor, courted her more attractive, but cross-grained, half-sister Elizabeth, and, in the end, sent the Armada to secure by conquest what he had failed to obtain by marriage.

CHAPTER 10. TRADE, MONEY & BANKING

English wool had to be transported from a multitude of producers, some large, but some quite small, to another multitude of Flemish craftsmen, most of them working in their own homes. Middlemen were essential. First, dealers toured  the farms and brought the wool to centers like Northleach in Gloucestershire. Here, it came into the hands of the aristocrats of the wool trade, the members of the English Company of the Merchants of the Staple. Many of these men made fortunes. One of them, John Barton of Holme, had a stained glass window in his house inscribed:

127. I thank God and ever shall,
It is the sheep hath paid for all.

A merchant, Richard Cely, describes his purchases of wool in 1480:

128. I greet you well and I have received a letter from you writ at Calais the 13th day of May, the which letter I have well understood of your being at the marts and of the sale of my middle wool, desired by John Destermer and John Underbay. Wherefore by the grace of God, I am busied for to ship this foresaid 29 sarplers, the which I bought of William Midwinter of Northleach, 26 sarplers, the which is fair wool, as the wool packer Will Breten saith to me, and also the 3 sarplers of the rector's is fair wool, much finer wool nor was the year before, the which I shipped afore Easter last past. The shipping is begun at London, but I have none shipped as yet, but I will after these holy days, for the which I will ye order for the freight and other costs. [*Cely Papers*, 30-31]

The English crown drew much of its revenue from taxes on wool, so it regulated the trade. Exports could only be made through certain ports, and all had to go to Calais, which was known as the staple town. Here, royal officials inspected the bales to make sure they contained no foreign bodies as make-weights, and to check that the wool was of the right quality. They also collected the export duties.

The choice of Calais as the staple town had been a compromise. The crown wanted all woollen exports to go through one port, to avoid employing officials in many places along the coast. But had this port been in England, it would have enjoyed such an advantage over its rivals that there would have been discontent. Calais, therefore, was a good choice, for it was then an English possession, but on the other side of the Channel.

One of Cely's men reports on his master's exports. It is autumn, so, instead of shorn wool, there are fells, or the skins of sheep with the wool attached, many of the animals having been slaughtered at the approach of winter:

129. Right worshipful sir, after due recommendation I lowly recommend unto you, letting you understand that my master hath shipped his fells at the port of London now at this shipping in October, which fells ye must receive and pay the freight. First by the grace of God, in the *Mary* of London, William Sordyvale master, 7 packs, sum 2,800, lying be aft the mast, one pack lieth up rest and some of that pack is summer fells marked with an O, and then lieth 3 packs fells of William Daltons and under them lieth the other 6 packs of my masters. Item in the Christopher of Rainham, Harry Wylkyns master, 7 packs and a half Cotswold fells, sum 3000 pelt, lying be aft the mast, and under them lieth a 200 fells of Welther Fyldes, William Lyndys man of Northampton, and the partition is made with small cords. Item in the *Thomas* of Maidstone, Harry Lawson master, 6 pokes, sum 2,400 pelt, whereof lieth 5 packs next before the mast under hatches, no man above them, and one pack lieth in the stern sheet; of the six packs fells be some summer fells marked with an O likewise. Item in the *Mary Grace* of London, John Lokyngton master 6 packs sum 2,400 pelt, lying be aft under the fells of Thomas Graunger, the partition between them is made with red; sum of the fells my master hath shipped at this time 26 packs and a half whereof be winter fells of the country 561 fells and they be marked with a C, and of summer fells there should be 600 and more, but part of them be left behind, for we have two packs we

could have no appointment for them, and all the summer fells be marked with an O. Item, sir, ye shall receive of the *Mary* of Rainham, John Danyell master, your trunk with your gear and a Essex cheese marked with my master's mark. [*Cely Papers*, 71-72]

The voyage to the Low Countries, short though it was, could be exciting. In 1482 Richard Cely reported, "Robert Eryke was chased with Scots between Calais and Dover. They scaped narrow." The safe arrival of a cargo was a cause for rejoicing. Thomas Betson wrote to his colleague:

130. Thanked be the good Lord, I understand for certain that our wool shipped be come in to Calais. I would have kept the

tidings till I had comen myself, because it is good, but I durst not be so bold, for your mastership now against this good time may be glad and joyful of these tidings, for in truth I am glad and heartily thank God of it. [*Stonor Letters* 2, 2]

At Calais, royal officials checked the quality of the wool, inspecting bales at random. If a carrier knew that a bale chosen for examination was faulty, he had to act quickly. William Cely describes how, in 1487, he switched the contents of two packages:

131. Sir, I cannot have your wool yet awarded, for I have to cast out a sarpler, the which is appointed by the lieutenant to be casten out toward the sort by, as the ordinance now is made that the lieutenant shall appoint the awarding sarplers of every man's wool, the which sarpler that I have casten out is number 24, and therein is found by William Smith, packer, a 60 middle fleeces and it is very gruff wool; and so I have caused William Smith privily to cast out another sarpler number 8, and packed up the wool of the first sarpler in the sarpler of number 8, for this last sarpler is fair wool enough. [*Cely Papers*, 160]

Later, he reports:

132. Item, sir, your wool is awarded by the sarpler that I cast
out last. Item, sir, this same day your mastership is elected and
appointed here by the court, one of the 28, the which shall
assist the Master of the Staple now at this parliament time.
[Ibid., 162]

The next stage was to sell the wool to foreign merchants. Some
came to Calais, but the English went themselves to fairs and markets
all over Flanders and Brabant. Thomas Betson wrote in a letter to a
colleague:

133. Liketh it you to wit that on Trinity even I came to Calais
and, thanked be the good Lord, I had a full fair passage, and,
Sir, with God's might I intend on Friday next to depart to the
mart-wards. I beseech the good Lord be my speed and help
me in all my works. And, Sir, I trust to God's mercy, if the
world be merry here, to do somewhat that shall be both to
your profit and mine. As yet there cometh but few merchants
here; hereafter with God's grace there will come more. I shall
lose no time when the season shall come I promise you. And,
sir, when I come from the mart I shall send you word of all
matters by the mercy of the Lord. [Stonor Letters 2, 48]

The English had a high opinion of their contribution to the fairs:

134. But they of Holland at Calais buy our fells,
And our wools, that English men him sells.
And we to martis of Brabant loaded been
With English cloth, full good and fair to seen,
We been again chargéd with mercery
Haberdashery ware and with grocery,
To which martis, that Englishmen call fairs
Each nation often maketh here repairs,
English and French, Lombards and Genoese,
Catalans, thither take their ways,
Scots, Spaniards, Irishmen there abides,
With great plenty bringing of salt hides,
And I here say that we in Brabant lie,

CHAPTER 10. TRADE, MONEY & BANKING

Flanders and Zeeland, we buy more marchandie
In common use, than done all other nations;
This have I heard of merchants' relations,
And if the English be not in the marts,
They be feeble and as naught been here parts;
For they buy more and from purse put out
More marchaundy than all the other rout.

[*Libelle of Englysshe Polycye*]

MONEY AND BANKING

The wool trade had a sophisticated system of credit, one feature of it being that purchasers usually paid by bills of exchange that fell due, as a rule, in six months. But sooner or later – as the intense activity of the fairs shows – merchants had to collect payment in coin. It was an arithmetical nightmare, for numerous currencies were involved, which were in various stages of debasement, and whose rates of exchange were fluid. William Cely wrote home describing the complex system of international exchange that by the 14th century had given rise to the first great banking houses:

135. Please your masterships to understand that I have received of John Delowppys upon payment of the bill, the which is sent me by Adlington but £300 fleming, whereof I have paid to Gynott Strabant £84-6s-6d fleming. Item, I have made you over by exchange with Benynge Decasonn, Lombard, 180 nobles sterling, payable at usance. I delivered it at 11s-2½d fleming the noble, it amounteth to £100-17s-6d fleming. Item, I have made you over by exchange in like wise with Jacob van de Base 89 nobles and 6s sterling, payable at London in like wise; I delivered it at 11s-2d fleming for every noble sterling; £50 fleming and the rest of your £300 remains still by me, for I can make you over no more at this season, for here is no more that will take any money as yet. And money goeth now upon the bourse at 11s-3½d the noble and none other money but Nimuegen groats, crowns, Andrew guilders and Rhenish guilders, and the exchange goeth ever the longer and worse and worse. Item, sir, I send you enclosed in this said letter, the two first letters

of the payment of the exchange above written. Benynge
Decasonn's letter is directed to Gabriel Defuye and Peter
Sanly, Genoese, and Jacob van de Base's is directed to Anthony
Carsy and Marcy Strossy, Spaniards; in Lombard Street ye shall
hear of them. [*Cely Papers,* 159]

Finished cloth returned to England, again passing through several
hands, so that every pound of wool that had gone out had increased
enormously in cost by the time it returned. The English complained
that the Flemings bought the fox's skin from them for a groat, and
then sold them the tail for a guilder. The remedy was for the English
to develop their own woollen industry which, eventually, they did. In
the sixteenth century their exports of finished cloth increased twenty
fold, while their exports of raw wool declined dramatically.

Meanwhile, even
more dramatic forces
had been at work for
some time. By the mid-
14th century, the system
of financial exchange,
first developed at the
fairs and used primarily
to evaluate goods
against different curren-
cies, had taken on a life
of its own. The church
had long held the lending of money at interest in abhorrence. Scripture, the Councils of Arles (314), Nicaea (325), Lateran III (1179), and
the Second Council of Lyon (1274) all condemned the lending of
money at interest. The Fourth Lateran Council in 1215 had allowed
such activities only to Jews. Yet, by the late tenth century money-
lenders were beginning to accumulate enough "capital" to make large-
scale commercial ventures – including the transport of the Crusades
– possible. Christian, not Jewish, financiers, especially in northern
and Central Italy, began to flourish. Eventually the Italians replaced even
such orders as the Hospitallers in safeguarding specie, especially after
they became the chief agents for collecting the pope's taxes all across

CHAPTER 10. TRADE, MONEY & BANKING

Europe, and his chief bankers. The word "Lombard" became synonymous with banker, so that London's financial district still boasts its Lombard Street. The following document from Provence, in southern France, is a statute against the crime of usury from the year 1235:

> 136. It is decreed and established that if anyone should take greater usury than 4 for 5 at the beginning of the year he shall be punished according to the wishes of the court. Nor can usury be demanded on the basis of a concession made by the court. Likewise, it is decreed and established that no usury shall be taken in the sale of any good; and should anyone presume to do this, he shall be punished at the discretion of the court. Likewise it is decreed that the satisfaction of any debt bearing interest shall not be pressed upon any debtor from now until the feast of St. Michael. What is said here of the crime holds with special emphasis with respect to the sale of bread. [From C. Giraud, *Essai sur l'histoire du droit français au moyen-âge*]

Money lent was, of course, money put to work in the emerging capital economy. In the Mediterranean the practice of "depositing" goods or money had been common since Roman times. A contract of *depositum* or *accomendatio* involved one party giving a moneychanger, banker or any commecial concern use of "capital" *(commenda)* for a set time. In return for the use of the money or goods the depository returned the full amount along with a premium – a share in the successful venture – at the end of the period. Thus the payment of "interest" was avoided, church law satisfied, and everyone the richer. The following is one such deposit contract drawn up at Genoa on November 7, 1200:

> 137. I, Oberto, banker, of Pollanexi, acknowledge that I have received from you, Maria, wife of Rolando Generificio, £50

Genoese in *accomendacio*, which belong to your husband, the aforesaid Rolando. I am to keep them in the bank and to employ [them] in trade in Genoa as long as it shall be your pleasure; and I promise to give you the profit according to what seems to me ought to come to you. Moreover, I promise to return and to restore the aforesaid £50 or just as much instead of them, myself or through my messenger, to you or to your husband or to your accredited messenger, within eight days after you tell me and make the request, and similarly [to give you] the profit; otherwise the penalty of the double and the seizure of my goods as security. Done in the house of the late Baldovino de Arato. Witnesses: Rufo de Arato and Aimerico, cooper. In the year of the Nativity of the Lord 1200, third indiction, the seventh day of November. [From Lopez & Raymond, *Medieval Trade in the Mediterranean World*, p. 214]

As banking houses and their widespread network of contacts and agents became a part of European life, it became standard practice not to actually transfer the specie or coinage in payment for goods, debt, or investment, but to issue a simple "order of payment," the predecessor of modern checks and fund transfers. While most commercial contracts involved the formal drawing of documents by notaries – the medieval equivalent of commercial lawyers – many such orders could be drawn up privately by any business person or concern. The following is from Savona, near Genoa, dated September 21, 1392:

138. On September 21, in Savona.

Please pay from my account at the time of the next Kalends of October to Ser Gregorio Squarzafico £134 s.17 d.8, that is, one hundred thirty four pounds seventeen solidi eight deniers. And they are for his share of the profit from grain of Sicily, in which he was a participant.

Niccolò Lomellini.

CHAPTER 10. TRADE, MONEY & BANKING

[Address on the outside:] To be given to Ser Federico de Promontorio, Genoa. [Mark of Niccolò Lomellini] [Ibid., p. 235]

Having put their capital to work by *commendatio*, medieval investors looked carefully after the success of their *commenda* or *societas*, loosely translated as "business venture." Investors contributed capital for shares of the return upon completion of the venture – very often a trading voyage – plus any profit above that. This example of a *commenda* comes from Genoa and is dated September 29, 1163. It spells out the division of profits for investment in a ship:

> 139. Witnesses: Simone Bucuccio, Ogerio Peloso, Ribaldo di Sauro, and Genoardo Tasca. Stabile and Ansaldo Garraton have formed a *societas* in which, as they mutually declared, Stabile contributed £88 [Genoese] and Ansaldo £44. Ansaldo carries this *societas*, in order to put it to work, to Tunis or to wherever goes the ship in which he shall go – namely, [the ship] of Baldizzone Grasso and Girardo. On his return [he will place the proceeds] in the power of Stabile or of his messenger for [the purpose of] division. After deducting the capital, they shall divide the profits in half. Done in the chapter house, September 29, 1163, eleventh indiction.
>
> In addition, Stabile gave his permission to send that money to Genoa by whatever ship seems most convenient to him [to Ansaldo]. [Ibid., p. 179]

THE EMERGENCE OF PORTUGAL

It was not only Europeans who were trading. Others, notably Arabs, were busy in the Indian Ocean. Among their most valuable cargoes were spices that they brought from the East Indies and then carried overland, through the Middle East, to the Mediterranean. Spices were important in medieval cooking, so they commanded high prices, and the middlemen who handled them on their long journey made large profits. European traders longed to deal directly with the spice growers, but powerful Muslim states in the Middle East barred their way. Then, in the 15th century, improvements to shipping made it possible to look for a sea route. The Mediterranean traffic in spices had long been a Venetian monopoly, but the Portuguese were better placed, and had more incentives, to make voyages of discovery. Under the guidance and encouragement of their Prince Henry, known as the "Navigator," they began to feel their way along the west coast of Africa until, in 1487, Bartholomew Diaz rounded the Cape of Good Hope. The following year, Vasco da Gama reached India.

Hitherto, the civilizations of the world had developed, each in its own sphere, and, though there was contact between some of them, it was tenuous. Sooner or later, though, it was inevitable that one of them would burst its bounds and flood the rest. The Portuguese ensured that it was the Europeans who did so before any of the others.

Contemporaries, less aware of the importance of what was happening, were more bemused by the curiosities that the Portuguese brought to Europe. A German visitor wrote:

140. In Evora we saw in the church of San Blas, the skin of a snake brought from Ethiopia, which snake was thirty spans long and as far round as a man, and was killed with flaming arrows. They flayed it from head to tail, and this piece of skin is of many different and beautiful colors, and covered with marks like stars and golden spots, which give cause for great admiration. The skin measured 22 spans and they assured us that the snake would devour two men at a time, overcoming them in its coils, and that it would fight with elephants. This I can well believe, because Pliny spoke of the animals of India and Ethiopia, which today are brought from Ethiopia and the adjacent islands.

We also saw a young, beautiful camel in the royal courtyard, which had been brought from Africa, where they abound.

CHAPTER 10. TRADE, MONEY & BANKING

King John II also shows great skill in acquiring riches by trade and in other ways. He sends to Genoa woolen cloth of different colors, as well as Tunisian carpets; also fabrics, horses, miscellaneous merchandise from Nuremberg, many copper cauldrons, brass basins, scarlet and yellow cloths, cloaks from England and Ireland, and an infinity of other things. They bring to him gold, slaves, pepper, numerous elephant tusks, etc. [Jeronimus Münzer, *Journey through Spain and Portugal,* c. 1494]

CHAPTER 11
FAMILIES 1. THE LEGAL AND
RELIGIOUS FRAMEWORK

FAMILY LAW

Tacitus describes the customs of the Germans of his day:

> 141. The marriage tie with them is strict. You will find noth-
> ing in their character to praise more highly; they are al-
> most the only barbarians who are content with one wife
> apiece. The very few exceptions have nothing to do with
> passion, but consist of those with whom polygamous mar-
> riage is sought for the sake of their high birth.
>
> As for the dower, it is not the wife who brings it to the
> husband, but the husband to the wife. The parents and re-
> lations are present to approve these gifts, which gifts are
> not intended to satisfy female fancies, nor to adorn the
> bride, but oxen, a horse and bridle, a shield and spear or
> sword. It is to share these things that the wife is taken by
> the husband, and she, herself, brings some piece of armor
> to her husband. Here is the gist of the bond between them,
> here in their eyes is the mysterious sacrament, the divinity
> which hedges it. That the wife may not imagine herself re-
> leased from the practice of heroism, released from the
> chances of war, she is thus warned by the very rites with
> which her marriage begins that she comes to share hard
> work and peril; that her fate will be the same as his in peace
> and in panic, her risks are the same. The things she takes
> she is to hand over inviolate to her children, fit to be taken
> by her daughters-in-law and passed on again to her grand-
> children.

So their life is one of fenced-in chastity. There is no arena with its seductions, no dinner-tables with their provocations to corrupt them. Of the exchange of secret letters men and women alike are innocent; adulteries are very few. Punishment is prompt and is the husband's prerogative: her hair close-cropped, stripped of her clothes, her husband drives her from his house in the presence of his relatives and pursues her with blows through the length of the village. For prostituted chastity there is no pardon; not beauty nor youth nor wealth will find her a husband. No one laughs at vice there; no one calls seduction, suffered or wrought, the "spirit of the age." Better still are those tribes where only maids marry, and where a woman makes an end, once for all, with the hopes and vows of a wife; so they take one husband only, just as one body and one life, in order that there may be no second thoughts, no belated fancies. [*Germania*]

When the Germanic tribes came into contact with Rome, some of their members, at least, became literate so they were able to codify their laws and set them down in writing. The following are some of the laws of the Salian Franks of the sixth century. They show much the same concern for female honor, which Tacitus noted:

142. If three men abduct a girl who is free born, let these three be compelled to pay 1,200 denarii. If there are more than three, let each one of them be held liable for 200 denarii.

But if the girl who is carried off is under the king's protection, then the fine demanded shall be 2,500 denarii.

For a rapist, let him be held liable for 2,500 denarii.

If anyone is united in an incestuous marriage with his sister or his brother's daughter, or with a cousin of the nearest degree, or with his brother's or uncle's wife, let them be subjected to punishment so that their union will be dissolved. And if they have children, they are not legitimate heirs, but are marked with infamy.

If anyone abducts another's fiancée and unites himself with her in marriage, let him be liable for 2,500 denarii.

If anyone follows a betrothed girl in a wedding procession who is on her way to be married and assaults her on the road and forces her to engage in sex, let him be liable for 8,000 denarii.

If a freeman touches a free woman's or any woman's hand, arm, or finger, and it can be proved that he did this, let him be held liable for 600 denarii.

If he presses her arm, let him be held liable for 1,200 denarii.

If he places his hand above her elbow, and it can be proved that he did this, let him be held liable for 1,400 denarii.

If anyone touches a woman's breast, or cuts it so that blood comes forth, let him be held liable for 1,800 denarii.

[*The Laws of the Salian and Ripuarian Franks,* Theodore John Rivers, trans.]

There is also special protection for female servants, since, if one of them became pregnant, her employer was deprived of her services, for a time:

143. If anyone abducts another's maidservant, let him be held liable for 1,200 denarii.

If anyone seduces a maidservant worth fifteen or twenty-five solidi, if he is a swineherd, a vinedresser, a blacksmith, a miller, a carpenter, a groom or any overseer worth twenty-five solidi, let him be held liable, if it can be proved he did this, for 2,880 denarii, in addition to her value. [Ibid.]

The laws also sought to preserve the distinctions between slaves and the free:

144. If a woman unites in marriage with her slave, let the public treasury acquire all her property and let her be outlawed.

If any one of her relatives kills her, let nothing at all be required from either her relatives or the public treasury for this death. Let that slave endure the worst death by torture, that is, let him be broken on the wheel. If any one of the relatives gives food or shelter to this woman, let him be liable for fifteen solidi. [Ibid.]

During the Middle Ages, there were even more laws to protect the honor of women, but, as societies grew richer, there was an increasing obsession with money and property. This was particularly true of the nobility, where marriages could involve the transfer of huge estates. But the middle classes were also affected. These laws were in force in Magdeburg in the thirteenth century:

145. If a man dies leaving a wife, she shall have no share in his property, except what he has given her in court, or has appointed for her dower. She must have six witnesses, male or female, to prove her dower. If the man made no provision for her, her children must support her as long as she does not remarry. If her husband had sheep, the widow shall take them.

No one, whether a man or woman, shall, on his sick bed, give away more than three shillings' worth of his property without the consent of his heirs, and the woman must have the consent of her husband.

When a man dies, his wife shall give to his heirs his sword, his horse and saddle, and his best coat of mail. She shall also give a bed, a pillow, a sheet, a table-cloth, two dishes and a towel. Some say she should give other things also, but that is not necessary. If she does not have these things, she shall not give them, but she shall give proof for each article that she does not have it.

After giving the above articles the widow shall take her dower and all that belongs to her; that is, all the sheep, geese, chests, yarn, beds, pillows, cushions, table linen, bed linen, towels, cups, candlesticks, linen, women's clothing, finger rings, bracelets, headdresses, Psalters, and all prayer books, chairs, drawers, bureaux, carpets, curtains etc., and there are many other trinkets which belong to her, such as brushes, scissors, and mirrors, but I do not mention them. But uncut cloth, and unworked gold and silver do not belong to her. [In Oliver J. Thatcher and Edgar H. McNeal, *A Source Book for Medieval History*]

THE CHURCH'S VIEW OF MARRIAGE

The orthodox medieval view of marriage was derived from St. Paul and the early fathers of the Christian church. St. Paul's opinions can be studied in 1 Corinthians 7. This is what St. Jerome wrote in AD 393:

> 146. There is a golden book current, written by the philosopher Theophrastus; it is called *On Marriage* and examines the question whether a wise man would take a wife. The author concludes that a wise man would do so if the lady were fair to see, well bred, and of honorable parents, and if he himself were healthy and wealthy. But he adds, "These things are seldom found together in a marriage; the wise man, therefore, should not wed."
>
> First, it impedes the study of philosophy, for no man can serve his books and his wife with equal zeal. A married woman has many needs; precious robes, gold and gems, great expenses, handmaidens, furniture of all kinds, litters and a gilded carriage. Then he must listen all night long to her interminable complaints. "This woman goes about better clad than I; that other is admired everywhere; I, poor wretch, cannot hold up my head among my fellows. Why did you make eyes at that woman over the way? What were you saying to the maidservant?

What was that you brought home from the market." We may not have a friend or a companion, for then our wife suspects our love for others, our hate for herself. However learned a teacher there may be in the city, we may not leave our wife, nor can we burden ourselves with her at his lectures. If poor, she is hard to feed; if rich she is unbearable.

Moreover, we have no choice of wives, but must take what we can find. Whether she be ill-tempered, foolish, deformed, proud, unsavory, whatever her faults, we only discover them after we have married her. A horse or an ass, an ox or a dog, or even the commonest slaves, are tried before we choose to buy them; so are clothes, and kettles, chairs and cups and earthen pipkins; a wife alone is not to be had on approval, lest she be found wanting when we marry her. We must study her face from hour to hour, and praise her beauty, lest, if we do but look at some other woman, the wife should feel herself neglected. You must call her My Lady, remember her birthday, swear by her health, and wish that she may survive you. You must honor her nurse and nursemaid, her slave, her pupil, her comely follower and the curled manager of her affairs, names which simply conceal adulterers. Whoever she has chosen to love, these must have your unwilling affection.

If you have given over your house for her to rule, you are her servant. If you keep any part of it for yourself, she thinks you distrust her. From this comes hatred and quarrels, and unless you see to it quickly, she will brew poison for you.

If you open your doors to her old women and fortune-tellers, to her jewelers and silk-merchants, there is another danger to her chastity. For what use is even the strictest watchfulness, when a wanton woman cannot be kept, and a chaste one ought not? For necessity is a poor guardian of chastity; she alone can be called truly chaste who, if she had wished, might have sinned. A fair woman is easily loved, a foul woman easily falls into desire. It is hard to keep what many men desire; it is burdensome to possess what no man wants. Yet it is less misery to possess the unshapely wife than to guard the shapely;

for nothing is safe when all men sigh after it. One man woos with his comely person, another with his understanding, a third with his wit, a fourth with his generosity. In one way or another, when a fortress is wholly besieged, it must at last be taken by storm.

If, however, a man marries for the sake of a well-kept house, or for comfort in sickness, or to escape loneliness, yet shall a faithful bondsman keep house far better and more obediently than a wife. For she feels she is truly mistress only when she goes against her husband's will, following not his commands, but her own fancy. In sickness, again, we have far more help from friends and grateful servants than from a wife who blames us for every tear she sheds: whose eyes water at the hope of a legacy; and who, by flaunting her anxiety, drives a sick man to desperation. If she, for her part, be sick, we must be sick with her and never leave her bedside. [*Against Jovinian*]

In AD 423 St. Augustine of Hippo wrote:

147. It is one thing for married persons to have intercourse only for the wish to beget children, which is not sinful. It is another thing for them to desire the pleasures of the flesh, even with the spouse only, which is a venial sin. For although propagation of the offspring is not the motive of the intercourse, there is still no attempt to prevent such propagation, either by wrong desire or evil appliance. Those who resort to these, although called by the name of spouses, are really not such; they retain no trace

of true matrimony, but use the honorable name as a cloak for evil behavior. Having gone so far, they are betrayed into exposing their children, which are born against their will.

Sometimes, indeed, the lustful cruelty, or, if you please, this cruel lust, resorts to such outlandish methods as to use poisonous drugs to avoid pregnancies; or else, if this is not successful, to destroy the conceived seed before birth, preferring that the offspring should die rather than live; or, if it was growing in the womb, that it should be killed before it was born. Well, if both parties are so wicked, they are not husband and wife; and if they were so from the beginning, they have not been joined in marriage, but in debauchery. If the two are not both guilty of such sin, then I do not hesitate to say that the woman is, so to speak, the husband's whore; or the man, the wife's adulterer.

Carnal lust is no part of marriage; it is only to be tolerated in marriage. It is not a good which is an essential part of marriage, but an evil which is the result of original sin. [*On Marriage and Lust*]

The following resolution was passed by the Spanish bishops in AD 589. It supports the reasons which St. Augustine gave when he condemned sexual intercourse undertaken for pleasure rather than procreation:

148. Let the bishops, in conjunction with the judges, severely punish those who kill their children.

Among the many complaints considered by the council, there is one which embraces such great cruelty that the assembled bishops could hardly bear to hear of it. It appears that in certain regions of Spain, the parents, anxious to fornicate, and ignoring all piety, put their own children to death. If it does not suit them to increase the number of their children, let them abstain from all carnal relationships, because, marriage having been instituted for the procreation of children, they are guilty of parricide and fornication who murder their own offspring, and who come together, not to produce children, but to gratify their lust. This horrible crime having been brought to the notice of our glorious overlord, King Recaredo, he has, accordingly, ordered the judges in such places to investigate these atrocities in conjunction with the bishops, and to forbid it with all severity. In consequence, this holy council urges the bishops of the aforesaid territories, even more earnestly, to investigate the aforesaid crime with the greatest diligence, and visit it with the severest punishments, saving only sentence of death. [*Third Council of Toledo*]

The views of the early fathers echoed down the Middle Ages. An anonymous [woman?] author of the thirteenth century wrote:

149. Now thou art wedded, and from so high estate alighted so low, into the filth of the flesh, into the manner of a beast, into the thraldom of a man, and into the sorrows of the world. See now, what fruit it has, and for what purpose it chiefly is: all for that, or partly for that, be now well assured, to cool thy lust with filth of the body, to have delight in thy fleshly will from man's intercourse; before God, it is a nauseous thing to think thereon, and to speak thereof is yet more nauseous.

"Nay," thou wilt say, "as for that filth, it is nought; but a man's vigor is worth much, and I need his help for maintenance and food; of a woman's and man's copulation, worldly welfare arises, and a progeny of fair children, that give much joy to their parents." Now thus hast thou said, and thinkest that thou sayest the truth. But I will show thee that this is all made smooth with falsehood. But first of all now, whatsoever welfare or joy come out of it, it is too expensively bought, for which thou soilest thyself, and surrenderest thine own dear body to be given up to ill usage, and dealt with so shamefully, with so irrevocable a loss as the grace of maidenhood is.

Thou sayest that a wife hath much comfort of her husband, when they are well consorted, and each is well content with the other. Yea. But 'tis rarely seen on earth. But suppose it is so: wherein is their comfort and delight for the most part, but in the filth of the flesh or worldly vanity, which turns all to sorrow and care in the end? Not only in the end, but ever and anon; for many things shall anger and vex them, and make them worry, and sorrow and sigh for each other's ills. Many things shall separate and divide them, which annoy loving persons; and the dint of death at the end sever one from another. So it cannot be but that vigor must end in misery; and the greater their satisfaction together was, the worse is the sorrow at parting.

Thus, woman, if thou hast a husband, yet shallt thou be in need. And what if things be lacking to thee, so that thou hast neither thy will with him, nor prosperity either, and must groan without goods within waste walls, and in want must breed thy offspring; and still further, lie under the most hateful man, who, though thou hadst all wealth, will turn it to sorrow; for, suppose now, that riches were rife with thee, and thy wide walls were proud and well supplied, and suppose that thou hadst many under thee, domestics in thy hall, and thy husband were angry with thee, and should become hateful to thee, so that each of you two shall be exasperated against the other; what worldly goods can be joy to thee? When he is out, thou shalt await his home coming with all sorrow, care, and dread. While he is at home, all thy wide dwelling seems too narrow for thee; his looking on thee makes thee aghast; his loathsome mirth and his rude behavior fill thee with horror. He chideth and jaweth thee, as a lecher does his whore; he beateth thee and mauleth thee as his bought thrall and patrimonial slave. Thy bones ache, and thy flesh smarteth, thy heart within thee swelleth of sore rage, and thy face outwardly burneth with vexation. What shall be the copulation between you in bed? But those who best love one another often quarrel there, though they make no show thereof in the morning; and often from many a slight, though they love each other ever so much, they each bitterly grieve by themselves. She, much against her will, must suffer his will, often with great misery, though she loves him well. All his foulness and his indecent playings, be they accompanied with filthiness, especially in bed, she shall, whether she wishes to or not, suffer them all. May Christ shield every maiden from enquiring or wishing to know what these be, for they that try them most, find them most odious. [*Holy Maidenhood*]

The same author describes other sorrows of married life:

150. Little knoweth a maiden of all this same trouble of wives' woe, in her relation to her husband; nor of their work so nauseous that they in common work; nor of the pain, nor of the sorrow and the filth in the bearing and birth of a child; nor of a nurse's watches, nor of her sad trials in the child's fostering: how much she must at once put into its mouth, neither too much, nor too little; though these things be unworthy to be spoken of, yet they show all the more in what slavery wives be, that must endure the like, and in what freedom maidens be, that are free from them all. And what if I ask besides, though it may seem silly, how the wife stands, that heareth, when she cometh in, her child scream, sees the cat at the meat, and the hound at the hide? Her cake is burning on the stone and her calf is sucking all the milk up, the pot is running into the fire, and the churl is scolding. Though it be a silly tale, it ought, maiden, to deter thee more strongly from marriage, for it seems not silly to her that trieth it. [Ibid.]

The famed fifteenth-century Italian priest and preacher, San Bernardino, took a more positive view of marriage. The following are extracts from a sermon he preached at Siena in 1427:

151. And so I bid you all, men and women, follow virtue, that your love may be founded on these three things, Profit, Pleasure and Honesty; then shall true friendship reign among you. And when you have these three things, hear what David says of you: "Thy wife shall be as a fruitful vine, on the sides of thine house." Lo! all these three things are here. First, Honesty; your wife – your own wedded wife. Secondly, Pleasure; as a vine – how delightful a thing is a vine at the door of a house! Thirdly, Profit, a fruitful vine, rich in grapes and

profitable; from which three things grow and endure true love between man and woman conjoined by the sacrament of Holy Matrimony....

Some men say, "What need have I to take a wife? I have no labor; I have no children to break my sleep at night; I have less expense by far. Why should I undertake this burden? If I fall ill, my servants will care for me better than she would." Thus you say, and I say the contrary; for a woman cares better for her husband than any other in the world. And not him alone, but the whole house and all that needs her care. Hear what Solomon says: "He that possesseth a good wife, beginneth a possession."

"Well," says another, "I will not take a wife, but rather keep a mistress: then at least I shall be cared for, and my house and my household." No, I tell you: for such a woman will be concerned only to make provision for herself; she will be set on stealing; and, when things go badly, she does not care, but says to herself, "Why should I take the trouble to worry about every little thing? When I am old, I shall no longer be welcome in this house." Therefore, I say, it is better to take a wife, and when you have taken her, take care to live as every good Christian should. Do you know who best knows this? That man knows it who has a good wife, who looks after the household well. She sees to the granary, she keeps it clean, so that no dirt may defile it. She keeps the jars of oil, and notes them well: this jar is to use, and that jar to keep. She guards it, so that nothing falls in it, and that neither dog nor any other beast comes near it. She takes every care that the jars are not spilt. She attends to the salt meats, first in the salting and afterwards in the keeping. She cleans them, and sorts them: This is to sell, and that is to keep. She sees to the spinning and then to the making of linen cloth from the yarn. She sells the yarn, and with the money she buys yet more cloth. She pays heed to the wine casks, lest their hoops should break, or the wine leak at any point. She does not do as the hired servant, who steals from everything that passes through her hands, and who is not troubled by waste, for the goods are not her own, so she is slow to trouble herself and does not care about them.

If a man has neither wife nor anyone else to look after his household, how is it with him? I know, and I will tell you. If he is rich, and has plenty of grain, the sparrows and the moles eat their fill of it. It is not kept in its place, but scattered so widely that the whole house is littered with it. If he has oil, it is all neglected and spilled. When the jars break and the oil is spilled, he throws a little earth on it, and leaves it at that! And his wine? When he comes to draw the wine, he thinks of nothing else, but perhaps the cask has a small split at its back, and the wine is leaking. Or again, a hoop or two may be loose, or the wine may turn to vinegar, and go completely bad. In his bed, do you know how he sleeps? He sleeps in a pit, just as the sheets have fallen on the bed, for they are never changed until they are torn. Even so is his dining hall; here on the ground are melon rinds, bones, peelings of salad, everything left lying on the ground, with no attempt to sweep it. Do you know how it is with his table? The cloth is laid with so little care that no one ever removes it until it is covered with filth. The trenchers are but carelessly wiped, the dogs lick and wash them. His pipkins are all foul with grease: go and look at them! Do you know how such a man lives? Just like a brute beast. I say it cannot be good for a man to live thus alone. Ladies, make your curtsey to me! [*Le Prediche Volgari di San Bernardino da Siena*]

Churchmen wrote and spoke a great deal, but it is harder to discover what ordinary people thought and did. There are, though, some indications. In the first place it is clear that kings and nobles, in general, made little or no effort to control their sexual desires, and it is unlikely that humble folk behaved differently. Secondly, there are certain literary works which, though fictional, give, one must suppose, an accurate picture of society. Those who will take the trouble to read Boccaccio's *Decameron*, Chaucer's *Canterbury Tales*, or Langland's *Vision of Piers the Ploughman*, may draw their own conclusions.

CHAPTER 12
FAMILIES 2. HUSBANDS, WIVES AND CHILDREN

HUSBANDS

In the sermon quoted in the last chapter, San Bernardino had this to say to husbands:

152. Marriage is love. What says St. Paul in the fifth chapter of his Epistle to the Ephesians? "Husbands, love your wives as Christ also loved the church."

Do you want a faithful wife? Then keep faith with her. Many a man would take a wife, but can find none. Do you know why? The man says, I must have a wife full of wisdom, and you, yourself, are a fool. The two do not go together. He-fool goes well with she-fool. How would you like your wife to be? I would like her tall, and you are a mere willow-wren. The two do not go together. There is a country where women are bought by the yard. It so happened that one of these people wanted a wife and asked to see her first. So the girl's brothers brought him to see her, and she was shown to him without shoes or head-gear; and measuring her, he found her tallest among the maidens, and he himself was one of those puny weaklings! Then they asked him, "Does she please you?"

"Yes, indeed, she pleases me very well."

But she, seeing what a miserable little creature he was, said, "But you do not please me."

Was that not right? But to my point again. How do you want your wife to be? I want an honest woman, and you are dishonest. That again, is not well. Once more, how would you have her? I would have her temperate – and you are never out of the tavern. You shall not have her! O, how would you have this wife of yours? I would not have her gluttonous, and you are ever at the fegatelli: that is not well. I would have her active – and you are a veritable sluggard. Peaceful – and you would storm at a straw if it crossed your feet. Obedient – and you obey neither your father nor your mother nor any man. You do not deserve her. I would have her good and fair and wise and bred in all the virtues. I answer, if you would have her so, it is fitting that you should be the same; even as you are seeking a virtuous, fair and good spouse, so think likewise that she would like a husband who is prudent, discreet, good, and full of all the virtues. [*Le Prediche Volgari di San Bernardino da Siena*]

Later, San Bernardino adds:

153. There are men who have more patience with a hen, which lays a fresh egg daily, than with their own wedded wife: and sometimes the hen may break a pipkin or a cup, and the man will not strike her, all for the love of her egg, and the fear that he might lose it. O madman, thrice worthy of chains! that cannot bear with a word from his wife, who bears such fair fruit, but if she speaks one word more than he thinks fit, at once he takes the staff and beats her; and the hen, cackling all day long without end, you have patience with her for her paltry egg's sake; yet the hen may, perhaps, do you more harm in broken vessels than she is worth; and yet you bear with her for her egg's sake! Many a cross-grained fellow, seeing perhaps his wife less clean and delicate than he would like, smites her without more ado; meanwhile, the hen may foul the table, and he will suffer it. Do you not consider your duty in this matter? Do you not see that pig, squeaking and squealing all day long, and always fouling your house? Yet you bear with him, until he is ready for slaughter. You have patience with him, only for the sake of his flesh, so that you may eat it. Consider now,

wicked fellow, consider the noble fruit of the woman, and have patience. It is not right to beat her for every cause. [Ibid.]

San Bernardino was unusual in that he had so much to say to men. The usual pattern was for the moralist to inform the husband, in a few brief sentences, that it was his duty to love and cherish his wife, and then deliver a lengthy homily on the woman's duties. Being the daughter of Eve, and the weaker vessel, she was, it was supposed, in much more need of guidance.

WIVES

Women in the lower ranks of society were expected to work. We have already seen San Bernardino's praise for the conscientious housekeeper, but more than that was expected. Fitzherbert, author of a sixteenth-century manual on agriculture, wrote:

154. In the beginning of March, or a little before, it is time for a wife to tend her garden, and to get as many good seeds and herbs as she can, and especially such as are good to eat.

Let your distaff be always ready for use, so that you are not idle. Though a woman cannot earn her living by spinning with the distaff, it fills a need, and must be done.

It may sometimes happen that you have so many things to do, that you do not know where to begin.

It is good for a husband to have sheep of his own, for then the wife may have some of the wool to make her husband and herself clothes, blankets and coverlets. And if she has no wool of her own, she may spin for clothiers, so earning a little money, and, at the same time, perform other tasks.

It is the wife's duty to winnow all manner of corn, to make
malt, to wash and wring, to make hay, reap corn, and, in time
of need, to help her husband fill the dung cart, drive the plough,
load hay, and all such other tasks. And she must go to market,
to sell butter, cheese, milk, eggs, chickens, capons, hens, pigs,
geese and all manner of corn. And also to buy things needed
by the household, and to give her husband a true account of
what she has spent. And if the husband should go to market
to buy or sell, than he, too, must account to his wife in the
same way. For if they deceive each other, they deceive themselves, and are unlikely to prosper. I could, perhaps, show husbands some of the ways in which their wives deceive them,
and, in like manner, how husbands deceive their wives. But
were I to do so, I would teach them both more tricks than they
know already, so it is better for me to hold my peace. [*Boke of
Husbandrie*]

In about 1394, an elderly Parisian wrote a manual of advice for his
young wife. He accepted that she would marry again after his death,
and advised her how to behave towards her new husband:

155. Fair sister, if you have another husband after me, know
that you should think much of his comfort. Therefore cherish
the person of your husband carefully, and, I pray you, keep
him in clean linen, for it is your duty. And because the care of
outside affairs is the responsibility of men, so must a husband
take heed, and go and come, and journey hither and thither, in
rain and wind, in snow and hail, now drenched, now dry, now
sweating, now shivering, ill-fed, ill-lodged, ill-warmed and ill-
bedded; and nothing harms him, because he is sustained by
the hope that he has of his wife's care of him on his return,
and of the ease, the joys and the pleasures she will do to him,
or cause to be done to him in her presence; to have his shoes
removed before a good fire, his feet washed and to have fresh
shoes and stockings, to be given good food and drink, to be
well served and well looked after, well bedded in white sheets
and night-caps, well covered with good furs, and comforted

with other joys and amusements, privities, loves and secrets, about which I am silent; and on the next day fresh shirts and garments. Certain it is, fair sister, that such service makes a man love and desire to return to his home and to see his good wife and to be distant with other women. [*Le Ménagier de Paris*]

In 1371, a French knight, Geoffrey de la Tour Landry, wrote a book for the guidance of his daughters. It was very popular, and went through seven editions in French, German and English. The following is an extract from an English edition of the fifteenth century:

156. Nowadays, if a woman hears of a new fashion, she will never be in peace until she has the same. And the wife says to to her husband every day, "Sir, such a wife has such goodly clothes that suit her well, and I pray that I may have the same." And if her husband says, "Wife, if such a woman has such clothes, others wiser than her do not," she will reply, "No force! It does not become them, but if I have it you will see how well it will suit me." And so her husband must let her have her way, otherwise she will never leave him in peace, for she will find so many arguments that she cannot be dissuaded. But the woman who acts like this is not the wisest, nor does she know what is best for her, since she thinks more of the pleasures of this world than of her husband's pocket.

And there is now a fashion common among serving women of low estate to wear fur collars hanging down to the middle of the back, and fur heels, which are soon daubed with filth, and unlined bodices over their breasts. I think this is unsuitable for both winter and summer. In winter, a woman would do better to put the fur on her heels about her stomach, for that has more need of warmth, and in summer, she should leave it off altogether, for flies hide in it. [*Knight of La Tour Landry*]

The Parisian already quoted advises his young wife on dress:

157. Take care that you are honestly clad, without too new fashions and without too much or too little adornment. And before you leave your bedroom or the house, take care that

163

the collars of your shift and your outer garments do not hang over each other, as happens with some drunken, foolish or senseless women, who care nothing for their honor, nor for their own positions or that of their husbands, and who walk with wandering eyes, and heads disgustingly reared up, like a lion's, their hair straggling out of their wimples, and the collars of their shifts and their coats crumpled one on the other, and who walk like men and behave themselves in front of other people in an undignified and shameless way. Therefore, dear sister, see that your hair, wimple, kerchief and hood and all the rest of your clothes are carefully arranged and tidy, so that none who see you may ridicule you, but that all may find you a model of good, simple, decent clothing. [*Le Ménagier de Paris*]

This is one of Geoffrey de la Tour Landry's moral tales:

158. There was a gentlewoman married to a squire, who loved him so much that she was jealous of every woman he spoke to. He often chided her for this, but she never improved. And among others, she was jealous of a woman of excellent character; and one day, she accused this woman of having designs on her husband. This she denied and the wife called her a liar. Then they ran together, and each tore off the other's hat and pulled her hair viciously. And she that was accused took a staff, and gave the wife such a blow on the nose that she broke it, and for ever afterwards, her nose was all crooked. This disfigured her badly, for the nose is the most important part of the face, sitting as it does, in the middle. And so the wife was maimed for the rest of her days, and her husband often said to her that it would have been better if she had controlled her jealousy, rather than be damaged in this way. And because of her deformity, her husband could never find it in his heart to love her as he had done before, and he took other women, and so she lost his affection through her jealousy and folly. [*Knight of La Tour Landry*]

CHAPTER 12. HUSBANDS, WIVES & CHILDREN

The Parisian provides his wife with an example he feels she should follow:

159. You know how a greyhound, or a mastiff, or a little dog, whether on the road, or at table, or in bed, always stays near the person who feeds him, and is timid or fierce towards others. Even if the dog is a long way off, his heart is always with his master, and his eyes are on him. Even if his master beats him, or throws stones at him, the dog will follow, wagging his tail, and lying down in front of his master, trying to placate him, and he will follow him through woods, robbers and battles. Therefore it is even more right that women, whom God has endowed with sense and reason, should love their husbands perfectly. [*Le Ménagier de Paris*]

There was an anecdote which ran as follows:

160. A certain woman complained to a witch of her husband that he ill-treated her. The witch said, "I will give you a remedy. Take cheese, wine and a penny, and go and lie down in yonder forest, saying:

'So wist I the broom
That is for me to do'n!
I have the worst husband
That is in the land.'"

Whereupon the witch, hid among the thorn bushes, answered:

"If thy husband be ill,
Hold thy tongue still!"
[Wright, *Latin Stories*]

CHILDREN

This is an early sixteenth-century translation of an extract from a fifteenth-century manual of behavior:

161. Of the little chylde
The new born child's flesh is tender, soft and flabby, so special care is needed. New born babies should be swathed in roses

ground in salt, so that their limbs may be comforted and cleansed of clammy moisture. Then the roof of the mouth and the gums should be rubbed with a finger dipped in honey, to cleanse and comfort the inner part of the mouth, and also to excite the child's appetite with the sweetness of the honey. And he should often be bathed and anointed with oil of roses, and all his limbs should be rubbed with oil, and mainly the limbs of males which, because of the work they will have to do, need to be firmer than the limbs of females. And they should be put to sleep in dark places, until their eyes are stronger; for a place that is too bright harms vision and hurts small eyes, that are still immature, causing children to squint. And above all, you should beware of bad milk and corrupt food. From dirty wet-nurses and sucking clammy milk like glue, come many sores and illnesses, such as pimples in the mouth, sickness, fevers, cramp, flux, and so on. And if the child is sick, medicines should be given to the wet-nurse, and not to the child. And she should be careful of her diet, so that her own well-being may make up any deficiencies in the child. For good milk ensures the good health of the child. And the contrary.

And because the child's limbs are tender, they may easily bow and bend and take different shapes. And therefore the child's limbs should be bound with bandages, so that they do not become crooked, or assume any evil shape. [*Trevisa's Batholomew*]

The same author describes children:

162. Children have soft flesh, lithe, supple bodies, are quick to move and quick to learn. They lead their lives without thought or care. They do just whatever pleases them, and fear nothing more than a beating with a rod; and they love an apple more than gold.

Whether they are praised, or shamed, or blamed, they think little of it. They have sudden changes of mood, being soon angry, soon pleased, and very quick to forgive. And because their bodies are so tender, they are easily hurt. And they cannot tolerate hard work. Hot humors dominate them, so they move quickly and are unstable. For the same reason, they eat a great deal. This excess of food and drink means that they are often ill. [Ibid.]

When the baby grew into a child, the ominous figure of the father appeared in its life:

163. A man loves his child, and feeds and nourishes it, and sets it at his own table when it is weaned. And teaches him with words, when he is young, and chastises him with beating, and ap-

points tutors to teach him. And the father shows him no great affection, lest he should grow proud; and he loves most the son that is most like him, and often looks at him. And he gives his children clothes, food and drink, as their age requires, and buys lands and inheritances for his children, and does not cease to make it more and more.

The more a father loves his child, the more he teaches, chastises and disciplines him, and when the child is most loved by his father, it seems that he loves him not; for he beats and grieves him often, lest he should acquire wicked habits, and the more the child is like the father, the more the father loves him. The father is ashamed, if he hears his children speak evil. The father's heart is sore grieved, if his children rebel against him. [Ibid.]

A mother advises her daughter:

164. And if thy children be rebel and will not bow low,
If any of them misdo, neither curse them nor blow [scold],
But take a smart rod and beat them in a row,
Till they cry mercy and their guilt well know.

Dear child by this lore
They will love thee ever more, my lief child.
[*The Babee's Book,* c. 1475]

The Flemish chronicler Froissart describes his childhood:

165. In my boyhood I was one that liked too well to have a
good time. When I was only twelve I was very eager for dances
and carols, to hear minstrels and lively talk. And I always liked
those who loved dogs and birds. And when they sent me to

school, there were little girls there of
my own age, and I gave them pins or
an apple or a pear or a little glass ring,
and it seemed wonderful when they
were pleased.

I was never tired of playing the
games children play when they are
under twelve. For one thing, in a brook
I made a little dam with a tile. And I
took a small saucer and made it float
down. We got our coats and hats and
shirts wet in the brook. Sometimes we
made a feather fly down the wind, and
I have often sifted earth with a shell
onto my coat. I was very good at chasing butterflies. When I
caught them, I tied threads to them; then when I let them go,
I could make them fly as I pleased. Dice, chess, tables and other
grown-up games I did not care about, but I liked to make mud
pies, round loaves, cakes and tarts. I had an oven of four tiles
where I put this stuff.

We played games called "Follow the Leader," and "Trot-
trot Merlot," and "Heads or Tails." And when we were all together, we all ran and played "Robber Enguerrard" and
"Brimtells." And I have often made from a stick a horse called
Grisel. We used to make helmets of our caps and often, before
the girls, we beat one another with our caps. Sometimes we
played at "The King Who Doesn't Lie," at bars, and "I Tell on
Who Strikes Me," at charades, at "Strike the Ball," at "Who

Can Jump Highest," at "Hare and Hounds," at "Cows Horn in the Salt," and throwing pebbles against a fence. And then we rolled nuts; the boy who missed, lost his temper. I amused myself night and morning with a spinning top. I've often made soap bubbles in a little pipe, two, three, four or five. I loved to watch them.

When I was a little wiser, I had to control myself, for they made me learn Latin. If I made mistakes in saying my lesson, I was beaten. When I was beaten, or afraid of being beaten, I did better. Nevertheless, away from my master, I could never rest till I fought with other boys; I was beaten and I beat, and I was so knocked about that often my clothes were torn. I went home and there I was scolded and beaten again, but, to be sure, one gets used to all that. [*L'Espinette Amoureuse*]

An Italian who visited England in about 1500 reported:

166. The want of affection in the English is strongly manifested towards their children; for after having kept them at home till they arrive at the age of seven or nine years at the most, they put them out, both males and females, to hard service in the houses of other people, binding them generally for another seven or nine years. And these are called apprentices, and during that time they perform all the most menial offices; and few are born who are exempted from this fate, for every one, however rich he may be, sends away his children into the houses of others, whilst he, in return, receives those of strangers into his own. And on inquiring their reason for this severity, they answered that they did it in order that their children might learn better manners. But I, for my part, believe that they do it because they like to enjoy all their comforts themselves, and that they are better served by strangers than they would be by their own children. Besides which the English being great epicures, and very avaricious by nature, indulge in the most delicate fare themselves and give their household the coarsest bread and beer, and cold meat baked on Sunday for the week, which, however, they allow them in great abundance.

That if they had their own children at home, they would be obliged to give them the same food they made use of for themselves. That if the English sent their children away from home to learn virtue and good manners, and took them back again when their apprenticeship was over, they might, perhaps, be excused; but they never return, for the girls are settled by their patrons, and the boys make the best marriages they can, and, assisted by their patrons, not by their father, they also open a house and strive diligently by this means to make some fortune for themselves; whence it proceeds that, having no hope of their paternal inheritance, they all become so greedy of gain that they feel no shame in asking, almost "for the love of God," for the smallest sums of money; and to this it may be attributed that there is no injury that can be committed against the lower orders of the English, that may not be atoned for by money. [Camden Society, *Italian Relation of England*]

CHAPTER 13
FOOD AND DRINK

FOOD OF THE POOR

A French inventory of 1291 describes the food given to a peasant when performing his labor services:

167. He owes three ploughing services every year, and for the ploughing of every acre he has half a loaf. And he ploughs half an acre of fallow land, and for this he shall have bread and stew once a day. And he owes a man and a horse for harrowing twice a year, and for each day that he harrows he shall have a quarter of a loaf in the morning and half a loaf in the evening and a measure of oats. And he owes a man to work for one day in the ploughlands and for this he shall have bread three times a day, and a pennyworth of cheese, and a loaf when he leaves in the evening. [*Records of the Monastery of St. Ouen*]

The poor, then, lived mainly on bread, and what they baked themselves was made from the mixture of flours ground from any crops they had harvested, including peas and beans. If the cereals ran out before harvest, as often happened, the poor had to subsist on what they could find. Langland's Piers the Ploughman addresses Hunger:

168. "I have no penny," quoth Piers, "to buy pullets, and neither geese nor pigs, but two green cheeses, a few curds, and cream and an oaten cake, and two loaves of beans and bran baked for my children. And yet I say by my soul, I have no salt bacon, nor any eggs, by Christ, to make eggs and bacon. But I have parsley and leeks and many coleworts, and a cow and a calf and a cart-mare to draw my dung afield, while the drought lasts. And by these few things we must live till Lammas

171

tide; and by then I hope to have a harvest in my barn and then I may serve you the dinner that I would like."

Then the poor people brought peas and beans and baked apples, and spring onions and hundreds of ripe cherries and gave them to Piers, so that he might appease Hunger. But Hunger soon devoured it all and demanded more, at which the poor people were afraid, and quickly brought leeks and peas and would have been glad to poison him. [*Vision of Piers the Ploughman*]

This sounds like a pleasant, healthy diet, but there were no bulk foods in it, so people went hungry. Everything changed after the harvest:

169. So the people were comforted and, and, and fed Hunger right royally. Even Glutton couldn't have wished for better ale. Then they put him to sleep.

Then Waster refused to work any more and set off as a tramp. Beggars refused bread that had bean flour in it, but demanded milk loaves and the best wheaten bread. And they would not drink cheap beer on any account, but only the best brown ale that could be had in the towns.

And the laborers who have no land to live on, but only their spades, would not condescend to eat yesterday's vegetables. Cheap ale would not do for them, or a hunk of bacon. They demanded fresh meat or fish, baked, and warm into the bargain for fear they would catch a chill in their bellies. [Ibid.]

FOOD OF THE WEALTHIER CLASSES

The following is an "ordinance of the cooks, ordered by the mayor and aldermen [of London] as to divers flesh-meats and poultry, as well roasts as baked in pasties":

170. Ordinance of Cooks

Best roast lamb	7d
Best roast pig	8d
Best roast goose	7d
Best roast capon	6d
Best roast hen	4d
Best roast pullet	2½d
Best roast rabbit	4d
Best roast river mallard	4½d
Best roast dunghill [domestic] mallard	3½d
Best roast teal	2½d
Best roast snipe	1½d
Five roast larks	1½d
Best roast woodcock	2½d
Best roast partridge	3½d
Best roast plover	2½d
Best roast pheasant	13d
Best roast curlew	6½d
Three roast thrushes	2d
Ten roast finches	1d
Best roast heron	18d
Best roast bittern	20d
Three roast pigeons	2½d
The best capon baked in a pasty	8d
The best hen baked in a pasty	5d
Cooking a customer's capon	1½d
Cooking a customer's goose	2d
Ten eggs	1d

[*London Letter Book H*, fol. XCIX]

Chaucer's host says to Roger the cook:

171. Now tell on Roger, look that it be good.
From many pasties hast thou drained the blood [gravy],
And numerous Jacks of Dover hast thou sold,
That have been heated twice and twice gone cold.
Many a pilgrim has called down Christ's curse;
Your parsley stuffing made them sick or worse,
That they had eaten with your straw fed goose.
For in your shop, full many a fly is loose.
[*The Canterbury Tales: The Cook's Prologue*]

These are extracts from the accounts of travelers in Castile in 1352:

172. At Nájera

Bread	4 maravedis
Wine	12 maravedis
Meat	8 maravedis
Garlic, pepper and grape juice	1 maravedi
Almonds for Gil Garcia	6 dineros
Apples	2 dineros

At Logroño

Bread	6 maravedis
Wine	12 maravedis
Rabbits	3 maravedis
Eggs	15 dineros
Vinegar and onions	5 dineros
Pears and apples	2 maravedis

[*Desde Estella a Sevilla; Cuentas de un Viaje*]

Substantial English freeholders were known as "franklins." They came highest in the social scale, outside the knightly classes. An anonymous poet describes a franklin's feast:

173. A franklin may make a feast improberabille;
Brawn with mustard is concordable.
    Bacon served with peas;

Beef or mutton stewed serviceable;
Boiled chicken or capon agreeable,
   Convenient for the season;
Roasted goose and pig full probable;
Capon bakemeat or custard costable,
   When eggs and cream be plentiful.
Therefore stuff of house is behoveable;
Mortrewes or Jussel are delectable
   For the second course by reason,
Then veal, lamb, kid or coney,
Chicken or pigeon roasted tenderly,
   Bakemeat or sweet tarts with all,
Then following fritters and a leche lovely,
Such service in season is full seemly
   To serve with both chamber and hall.
Then apples and pears with spices delicately,
After the term of the year full daintily,
   With bread and cheer to all.
[*The Babee's Book*]

The same author advised young people on their table manners:

174. Let good manners and silence dwell with you, and tell no foul tales to each other.

Say you are pleased with the food and drink set before you. Praise your food, whether it be good or bad.

Whether you spit near or far, hold your hand before your mouth to hide it. Keep from picking your nose, your teeth and your nails at mealtime.

Do not hang your head over your dish, or drink with your mouth full. When you drink, wipe your mouth clean with a cloth, and your hands also. Then your companions will be willing to drink with you.

Take care not to put so much food in your mouth that you cannot answer when men speak to you. Do not dip your food in the salt cellar, but lay salt on your trencher.

Keep your knife clean and sharp. Clean it on a piece of bread, and not on the cloth. Do not put your spoon in the dish, or on the edge of it. Do not make a noise when you eat, like animals do. Do not carry your food to your mouth with your knife. Do not put food from your trencher back into the dish, but get a voider, and empty it into that.

Do not cut your food like farm workers. They have such an appetite that they do not care how, where or when they hack at their food.

Do not scratch at table, or men will call you a jackdaw. Do not wipe your nose, or men will call you a peasant. Feed neither the cat nor the dog when you are at table.

In your feeding look you appear goodly and keep your tongue from jangling. When the end of the meal is come, clean your knives and put them where they ought to be. Keep your seat until you have washed.

If good food be brought to you, share it with others. It is not polite, when others be eating with you, to keep all that is brought to you and give none to others. [Ibid.]

CHAPTER 13. FOOD & DRINK

The following are English recipes of the early fifteenth century:

175. Strawberries

Take strawberries and wash them in good red wine. Then strain through a cloth, and put them in a pot with good almond milk; cover it with wheat flour or rice flour, and make it thick, and let it boil, and add currants, saffron, pepper, sugar, powdered ginger, cinnamon, galingale; make it acid with vinegar and add a little white grease; color it with alkanet and mix it together, sprinkle it with the grains of pomegranate, and then serve it up.

Pork pie

Take fresh pork, cut it and grind it in a mortar, and put it in a fair vessel. Take the white and the yolks of eggs, and strain into a vessel through a strainer, and mix with the pork. Then take pine seeds and currants and fry them in fresh grease, and powdered pepper, ginger, cinnamon, sugar, saffron and salt; and put all in a pie crust, and set on the crust lid above it, pine seeds, cut dates, raisins, and small birds, or hard yolks of eggs; and if you use birds, fry them in a little grease before you put them on the pie crust, and gild with yolks of eggs and saffron. Bake the pie until it is done, and then serve.

Roasted peacock

Take a peacock and cut its throat, and flay it, skin and feathers together, with the head still attached to the skin of the neck, and keep the skin and the feathers whole together. Draw the bird like a hen, and keep the bone to the neck whole, and roast it. And set the bone of the neck above the spit, as the bird was wont to sit when it was alive, and bend the legs to the body, is it was wont to sit when it was alive. And when it is roasted enough, take it off and let it cool, and then wind the skin with the feathers and the tail about the body, and serve as if the bird were still alive; or else pick it clean and roast it and serve it as you do a hen.

Biscuit of pike

Take the belly of a full-grown pike and seethe it well,
and put it in a mortar, and put cheese thereto; grind them
together; then take flour and white of eggs and beat together; then take sugar and powder of ginger, and put all
together, and look that thine eggs be hot, and lay thereon
of thine paste, and then make thin wafers and serve. [*British
Museum, Harleian* MSS 279 & 4016]

176. How to make white wine into red at table

Take in spring the flowers that grow in wheat, which are
called darnel or passerose, and dry them until they can be powdered. Put some of this, without being observed, into the wine
glass, and the wine will turn red. [*British Museum, Sloane MS* 1313]

DRINK

Wine was drunk throughout the Roman Empire, and there were
connoisseurs then, just as there are today. Pliny wrote somewhat
condescendingly of Spanish wines:

177. In Dyrrachium they praise the balisca, which in Spain
they call coccolobis; it withstands well the heat and the
winds of the south; its wine is bad for the head; its produc-
tion is abundant. The provinces of Spain produce two kinds
of the grape, one oval and the other round. It is the latter
that they harvest. The sweeter coccolobis is, the better it is,
but it can be given a dry taste, if allowed to mature. Then, it
can compete with the wines of Alba. They say that this wine, when
drunk, is good for diseases of the bladder.

The wines of Letania in Spain are famous for their abundance, but those of Tarragona and Lauron for their quality,
while those of the Balearics will bear comparison with the
best in Italy. [*Natural History,* 14, 29-30; 17]

In medieval times, not everyone approved of alcohol. A fifteenth-century English cleric wrote:

178. Where is it expressed by word or by any person in Holy
Scripture that men should make ale or beer, of which so

much horrible sin cometh, much more than setting up of images? And the faults done about images are much lighter and more easily amended than the faults that come by making ale and beer. And also herewith, it is true that without ale and beer, and without cider and wine and mead, men and women might live full long, and longer than they do now, when they have little jollity and cheer of heart and fall into horrible great sins. [*Pecock's Repressor*]

But teetotalers were rare. It is probably significant that in a typical English telephone directory with 150,000 names, there are only nine Drinkwaters. A problem which all total abstainers face is that there is plenty of scriptural authority for drinking alcohol, including St. Paul's advice to Timothy, "Drink no longer water, but use a little wine for thy stomach's sake and thine often infirmities." Pecock evades the difficulty by saying

quite rightly, that the Scriptures do not approve beer or ale, which were North European in origin, and then slipping wine, almost surreptitiously, into the list of drinks he would like to prohibit. In fact, many people enjoyed wine, including churchmen. An English friar wrote:

179. If Bacchus were alive, he would praise wine as it deserves. For among all the liquors and juices of trees, wine bears away the prize; better than all other liquors, wine, drunk moderately, most comforts the body, gladdens the heart, and heals and salves wounds and illnesses. As Isaac says, wine nourishes the body and restores lost health, and comforts and increases the natural heat, better than any other food or drink. And so wine purifies the blood and

cleanses troubled, thick blood, and opens and cleans the
mouths of veins and comes inwards in a subtle way to
cleanse and purge the inner parts. [*Trevisa's Bartholomew*]

A practical problem was that the only common alternative to
alcoholic drinks was water:

180. And water in springtime is unwholesome to drink; for
it is made thick with vapours that contaminate it. Also it is
infected with frogs and worms and other things that breed
in it. And therefore, if it is necessary to drink water at that
time, Constantine advises that you should seeth it first, so
that it may be cleansed and purged by boiling. [Ibid.]

The church, though, did not encourage drunkenness. Salimbene
da Adam, a thirteenth-century Italian friar, wrote:

181. French and English drink full goblets. As a result the
French have bloodshot eyes; for from drinking too much
their eyes become red-rimmed, bleary and bloodshot. And
in the early morning, after they have slept off their wine,
they go with such eyes to the priest who has celebrated Mass,
and beg him to drop into their eyes the water in which he has
washed his hands. But one priest of whom I heard, used to
say, "Put the water in the wine when you drink it and not in

your eyes."
The English
delight in drink
and drain full
goblets. For an
Englishman
will take a cup
of wine and
drain it, saying,
"Drink as much
as I drink." He
thinks this is

very polite and will take it ill, if his guest does not follow his example. Yet we must forgive the English if they are glad to drink good wine when they can, for they have but little wine in their own country. The French have less excuse, for they have much more. [*Monumenta Germaniae*]

Ordinary folk had few inhibitions about alcohol. This is a fifteenth-century drinking song:

182. Bring us in no brown bread, for that is made of bran,
Nor bring us in no white bread, for therein is no game.
But bring us in good ale, and bring us in good ale;
For our blessed Lady's sake, bring us in good ale.

Bring us in no beef, for there is many bones,
But bring us in good ale, that goeth down at once.
And bring us in good ale, etc.

Bring us in no bacon, for that is passing fat,
But bring us in good ale, and give us enough of that
And bring us in, good ale etc.

Bring us in no mutton, for that is often lean,
And bring us in no tripes, for they be seldom clean;
But bring us in good ale, etc.

Bring us in no butter, for therein are many hairs;
Nor bring us in no pigges flesh, for that will make us boars;
But bring us in good ale, etc.

Bring us in no capon's flesh, for that is often dear;
Nor bring us in no ducks' flesh, for they slobber in the mere;
But bring us in good ale, etc.

[Percy Society MS]

MUSLIM SPAIN

The following are thirteenth-century recipes:

183. Pigeon
Take a fat pigeon, clean it and put it in the stew pan and add a little salt, pepper, coriander and oil. Allow to heat for

a while and then cover with water, throw in a quarter of a pound of sugar, and finish cooking. Cover with four eggs, beaten with saffron and cloves. Fry with egg yolk and leave on the embers for a while; then drain off the liquids, sprinkle with sugar, lavender and cloves, and serve.

Hare

Cut the hare into small pieces and wash in boiling water. Put in a stew pan and add salt, pepper, coriander, much cumin seed, three spoonfuls of oil and as many of strong vinegar. Then take three or four onions and pound them a great deal in a wooden mortar, squeeze out the juice and put it in the stew pan with all the rest. Heat it, and when the meat is cooked and falls apart, place it on the embers and cover it with four or five eggs. When it is finished, take it off and leave it to cool.

Lamtuniya

This is made in el-Andalus and in Garb with all kinds of birds, like hens, geese, capons, pigeons and others. Take whatever fowl you have, clean and half bake it, like the tafaya of eggs. Then take it out of the oven and put it on the spit and baste it with the sauce used for roasts. Turn it on the spit in front of a charcoal fire of moderate heat, little at a time, until it is done and leave it on one side. There are some who fry it and afterwards submerge it in a sauce with crushed garlic, almonds and nuts. Then they bake a loaf with white flour, from which they make many crumbs the size of a diner. Then pour off the sauce from the fowl and return the stew pan to the heat and add much oil, pepper and cumin. When the pan boils, take it off and add crushed garlic, with nuts, almonds and hard grated cheese. Throw in the crumbs and then take the fowl and place it on the dish, after breaking it up in the sauce. Crown it with eggs, olives and almonds, sprinkle it with grated cheese and cinnamon and cover it with the leaf of isfiriya done with egg.

[*Anonymous manuscript from Granada*]

CHAPTER 13. FOOD & DRINK

These extracts from a fifteenth-century almanac throw light on several aspects of Moorish life, including diet:

184. January

In this month pituita increases [i.e., your nose runs]. It is good to eat garlic every morning and afterwards to drink hot water. It is also good to eat meat, fat and fish. You should beware of eating brains and of drinking fresh or curdled milk. This month, sugar cane is harvested. If there is an eclipse of the moon, there will be hunger in the east and in the west. If there is thunder this month, no good will come to you in the year. If there is an earthquake, it will be a year of great mortality. And you will say your prayers when your shadow is ten feet long, and your al'asr when your shadow is seventeen feet long. This month, the sun enters the sign of Aquarius.

[For every month, the author states the consequences of natural phenomena, like eclipses, but, from now on, they are only given here when they are of special interest.]

February

At the beginning of February, wind, rain and snow all increase. Blood flows in man's body, and the desire to eat and drink decreases. This month, the bees have their young. This month, apples and pear trees are grafted, and sap rises in the trees.

If there is thunder, it will be good for sheep and cattle and others. Milk will be abundant, and so will honey.

March

When March comes in, the land is verdant and the pituita disappears, and blood flows in man. You should beware of eating salted food, like fish, and onions and beef, though you may purge yourself and be bled and apply cupping glasses.

This month, sugar cane and cotton are planted. The silk worms are born.

April

When April comes in, men grow strong. It is good to eat capon. Man anoints himself with medicinal oil, and this is beneficial, if Allah is willing. It is good to mingle with young girls and go to the baths.

You should abstain from eating radishes and all cold, salted food and things like it, which cause heart disease. It is good to be bled and apply cupping glasses. You should abstain from eating rice, and roots which grow beneath the ground.

Roses and violets appear. Palm trees are planted, and so are water melons.

If there is thunder, there will be wheat in abundance and barley and other cereals.

May

When May comes in, you must not sleep much, or go to the baths simply to pass time, for that causes illness. Going to sea is allowed.

This month the olive sets, and early apples, plums, apricots, cucumbers and gherkins appear. Beans and poppies are gathered and barley is reaped. Flax is pulled and guinea fowl have their young. Vines sprout and bees make their honey.

If there is an earthquake, a sultan will die.

August

When August comes in, eat only cold food. One should keep out of the baths.

At the end of the month, grapes and peaches ripen and walnuts are gathered. Plants that have been transplanted and evergreen oaks sprout. Rape, beans and beet are sown.

It is said that if a tree is planted at the end of this month, it grows by the will of Allah, and that timber cut from it will never be attacked by worms.

September

When September comes in, you must avoid eating melons, beef and goat meat. This month it is good to eat fish. Grapes, pomegranates and quinces ripen. Olives blacken and the new oil appears. The myrtle sheds its seeds.

This month, there are diseases of the eye.

October

When October comes in, it is good to eat fish and lemons. It is also good to mingle with young girls and go to the baths, but not to stay there a long time. This month it is good to take purgatives. White and other roses appear, and lettuce and onion seeds are collected.

December

When December comes in, cold and rain become more intense. It rains for the entire month. You should abstain from drinking cold water during the night, after going to bed.

This month the almonds flower, the narcissus appears and water collects in the dams. Palm trees are uprooted and pumpkins and poppies are sown. If there is thunder, there will be an abundance of wheat and barley. [*Anonymous calendar from Granada*, 15th century]

CHAPTER 14
PASTIMES

WILLIAM FITZ STEPHEN describes the pastimes of the citizens of London in the late twelfth century. His quotations are from the classics, Virgil, Horace and Ovid:

185. Each year upon the day called Carnival – to begin with the sports of boys (for we were all boys once) – boys from the schools bring fighting-cocks to their master, and the whole forenoon is given up to boyish sport; for they have a holiday in the schools that they may watch their cocks do battle. After dinner all the youth of the city goes out into the fields to a much-frequented game of ball. The scholars of each school have their own ball, and almost all the workers of each trade have theirs also in their hands. Elder men and fathers and rich citizens come on horse-back to watch the contests of their juniors, and after their fashion are young again with the young; and it seems that the motion of their natural heat is kindled by the contemplation of such violent motion and by their partaking in the joys of untrammeled youth.

Every Sunday in Lent after dinner a "fresh swarm of young gentles" goes forth on war horses, "steeds skilled in the contest," of which each is "apt and schooled to wheel in circles round." From the gates burst forth in throngs the lay sons of citizens, armed with lance and shield, the younger with shafts forked at the end, but with steel points removed. "They make war's semblance" and in mimic contest exercise their skill at arms. Many courtiers come too, when the king is in residence; and from the households of earls and barons come young men not yet invested with the belt of knighthood, that they may there contend together. Each one of them is on fire with hope

of victory. The fierce horses neigh, "their limbs tremble; they champ the bit; impatient of delay they cannot stand still." When at length "the hoof of trampling steeds careers along," the youthful riders divide their hosts; some pursue those that fly before, and cannot overtake them; others unhorse their comrades and speed by.

At the feast of Easter they make sport with naval tourneys, as it were. For a shield being strongly bound to a stout pole in mid-stream, a small vessel, swiftly carried on by many an oar and by the river's flow, carries a youth standing at the prow, who is to strike the shield with his lance. If he break the lance by striking the shield and keep his feet unshaken, he has achieved his purpose and fulfilled his desire. If, however, he strike it strongly with splintering his lance, he is thrown into the rushing river, and the boat of its own speed passes him by. But there are on each side of the shield two vessels moored, and in them are many youths to snatch up the striker who has been sucked down by the stream, as soon as he emerges into sight or "once more bubbles on the topmost wave." On the bridge and the galleries above the river are spectators of the sport "ready to laugh their fill." [The Thames at London is tidal, and the huge piers of old London Bridge concentrated the flow so much that taking a boat under one of the arches was akin to shooting the rapids.]

On feast-days throughout the summer the youths exercise themselves in leaping, archery and wrestling, putting the stone, and throwing the thonged javelin beyond a mark, and fighting with sword and buckler. "Cytheria leads the dance of maidens and the earth is smitten with free foot at moonrise."

In winter on almost every feast-day before dinner either foaming boars and hogs, armed with "tusks lightning swift," themselves soon to be bacon, fight for their lives, or fat bulls with butting horns, or huge bears, do combat to the death against hounds let loose upon them.

When the great marsh that washes the Northern walls of the city is frozen, dense throngs of youths go forth to disport themselves upon the ice. Some gathering speed by a run, glide sidelong, with feet set well apart, over a vast space of ice. Others make themselves seats of ice like millstones and are dragged along by a number who run before them, holding hands. Sometimes they slip owing to the greatness of their speed, and fall, every one of them upon their faces. Others there are, more skilled to sport upon the ice, who fit to their feet the shin-bones of beasts, lashing them beneath their ankles, and with iron-shod poles in their hands they strike ever and anon against the ice and are borne along swift as a bird in flight or a bolt shot from a mangonel. But sometimes two by agreement run one against the other from a great distance and, raising their poles strike one another. One or both fall, not without bodily hurt, since on falling they are borne a long way in opposite directions by the force of their own motion; and wherever the ice touches the head, it scrapes and skins it entirely. Often he that falls breaks shin or arm, if he fall upon it. But youth is an age greedy of renown, yearning for victory, and exercises itself in mimic battles that it may bear itself more boldly in true combats.

Many of the citizens delight in taking their sport with birds
of the air, merlins and falcons and the like, and with dogs that
wage warfare in the woods. The citizens have the special privi-
lege of hunting in Middlesex, Hertfordshire and all Chiltern,
and in Kent as far as the river Cray. [*A Description of London*]

PASTIMES OF WOMEN AND GIRLS

Modern books devoted to medieval women are reticent about the
ways ordinary women and girls enjoyed themselves. There may be
several reasons for this, but certainly the sources are not very helpful.
Fitz Stephen mentions only one pastime in which females could join,
which was dancing. This was frowned on by many churchmen. A
French Dominican friar said:

186. We should specially avoid places wherein dances take place,
and the dances themselves. The devil is the inventor and dis-
poser of dances and dancers. I have heard how a certain holy
man saw the devil, under the form of a little Ethiopian, standing over a woman who led the dance, and leading her round at
his will, and leaping upon her head.

The inventor of these things is Satan, leading vain folk who
are like unto thistledown wafted on the blast or the dust which
the wind lifteth from the face of the earth, or clouds without
water, which are carried about by winds.

Moreover, God suffereth him sometimes to vex men with a
sudden tempest for this sin of dancing, and to wreak the fury
of his wrath upon them. I have heard from Brother Philip,
first prior of our convent at Rheims, of a certain church within
the diocese of Soissons wherein dances had been made. While
the priest sang mass one morning in that church, there arose
suddenly a great whirlwind and uproar, and a thunderbolt fell
upon the church, consuming the altar-cloth and slaying many
of the congregation, but leaving the priest and his host un-
touched; moreover, it overthrew a mill that was there and killed
four men. One who fled thence saw many demons springing
and leaping after the fashion of dancers over a certain ditch;

by whom he was beaten almost to death and scarce escaped by making the sign of the cross, whereat they fled in indignation and terror. One of the demons in his wrath bit a mighty stone in the wall and carried away a great part in his mouth, leaving the marks of his teeth on the stone. [Etienne de Bourbon, *Anecdotes Historiques,* c. 1250]

These are the opinions of a priest from Brabant, on the same topic:

187. There is a kind of game called dancing. How harmful this is, St. Augustine teaches in his book of *The City of God,* wherein he relates how Scipio Nasica, the most noble general of the Romans, removed all benches from the theater lest the citizens, who had recently triumphed over Carthage, should give themselves over to dances and the sports of Venus, whereby they would become effeminate and envious one of the other, and be moved to civil war, even when all outward wars were at an end. This is a most plain and evident token among dancers, that they circle round towards the left, on which side the accursed goats will be set, and will therefore lose that Kingdom which shall be bestowed by the Judge upon the blessed who are set at His right hand. But if it be better, as St. Augustine truly says, to plough on a Sunday or holy day than to dance; and if servile works, such as ploughing, are a mortal sin upon holy days, therefore it is far more sinful to dance than to plough. Yet these dances which are held at weddings of the faithful may be partly, if not wholly excused; since it is right for those folk to have the con-solation of a moderate joy, who have joined together in the laborious life of matrimony. For, according to the vulgar proverb, that man is worthy to have a little bell hung with

a golden chain around his neck, who has not repented of
taking a wife before the year is out. [Thomas Cantimpratanus,
Bonum Universale de Apibus, c. 1260]

This is a fifteenth-century poem:

188. Now gossip mine, gossip mine,
When will ye go to the wine?

I will you tell a full good sport,
How gossips gather them on a sort,
Their sick bodies for to comfort,
    When they meet, in a lane or street.

But I dare not, for their displeasance,
Tell of these matters half the substance;
But yet somewhat of their governance,
    As far as I dare, I will declare.

"Good gossip mine, where have ye be?
It is so long sith I you see,
Where is the best wine? Tell you me.
    Can you ought tell, then say full well."

"I know a draught of merry-go-down,
The best it is in all this town;
But yet would I not, for my gown,
    My husband it wist, ye may me trist!

Call forth your gossips by and by,
Elinor, Joan and Margery,
Margaret, Alice and Cecily;
    For they will come both all and some.

And each of them will somewhat bring,
Goosë, pig, or capon's wing,
Pasties of pigeons, or some other thing;
    For a gallon of wine they will not wring."

CHAPTER 14. PASTIMES

"Go before by twain and twain,
Wisely that ye be not seen;
For I must home and come again,
    To wit ywis where my husband is.

A stripe or two God might send me,
If my husband might here see me,
She that is afearëd, let her flee."
    Quoth Alice then, "I dread no man."

"Now we be in tavern set,
A draught of the best let him go fet,
To bring our husbands out of debt;
    For we will spend, till God more send."

Each of them brought forth their dish;
Some brought flesh and some brought fish.
Quoth Margaret meek, "Now with a wish,
    I would Anne were here, she would make us cheer."

"How say you, gossips, is this wine good?"
"That it is, "quoth Elinor, "by the rood;
It cherisheth the heart and comforteth the blood;
    Such junkets among shall make us live long!

"Anne, bid fill a pot of muscadel;
For of all wines I love it well,
Sweet winës keep my body in heal;
    If I had of it nought, I should take great thought."

"Now look ye, gossip, at the board's end?
Not merry gossip? God it amend.
All shall be well, else God it forfend;
    Be merry and glad, and sit not so sad."

"Would God I had done after your counsel!
For my husband is so fell,
He beateth me like the devil of hell;
    And the more I cry, the less mercy!"

Alice with a loud voice spake then,
"Ywis," she said, "little good he can,
That beateth or striketh a woman,
    And specially his wife; God give him short life!"

Margaret meek said, "So mot I thrive,
I know no man that is alive,
That gives me two strokes, but he shall have five;
    I am not afeard, though I have no beard!"

"Now reckon our shot, and go we hence,
What? cost it each of us but three pence?
Pardé, this is but a small expense,
    For such a sort, and all but sport."

Some be at the tavern once in a week;
And so be some every day eke;
Or else they will groan and make them sick.
    For thingës used will not be refused.

Now fill the cup and drink to me;
And then shall we good fellows be.
And of this talking leave will we,
    And speakë then of good women.
[15th-century MS in T. Wright, *Songs and Carols*]

THE THEATER

Religion dominated the theater. The following is an account of the
Paternoster Guild at York, founded in about 1390:

189. Once on a time a play setting forth the goodness of the
Lord's Prayer was played in the City of York. In this play all
manner of vices and sins were held up to scorn, and the virtues were held up to praise. This play met with such favor that
many said, "Would that this play could be kept up in this city,
for the health of souls and for the comfort of citizens and neighbors." Hence the keeping up of that play was the beginning of
this brotherhood. And so the main charge of the guild is to
keep up this play, to the glory of God and for the holding up of
sins and vices to scorn. The brethren keep a table showing the

whole meaning and use of the Lord's Prayer, hanging against a pillar in the cathedral church. Also, when the said Play of the Lord's Prayer is played, they ride through the chief streets of the City of York, all clad in

one suit. And to ensure good order during the said play, some of the brethren ride or walk with the players until the play is wholly ended. [*Chancery Miscellanea, Guild Certificate*]

This was the program at Beverley, Yorkshire, in 1467:

190. The players: Pride, Envy, Anger, Avarice, Sloth, Gluttony, Luxury, Vice.

Craftsmen and mysteries are assigned to perform the said play.

For the pageant of Vice: gentlemen, merchants, clerks and yeomen.

For the pageant of Pride: shoemakers, goldsmiths, glovers, glaziers, skinners and fishers.

For the pageant of Luxury: listers, walkers, weavers, pinners, cardmakers, wire drawers.

For the pageant of Sloth: watermen, husbandmen, laborers, saddlers, ropers, creelers, milkers and furbishers.

For the pageant of Gluttony: baxters, vintners, brewers, cooks, tilers.

For the pageant of Envy: butchers, wrights, coopers, fletchers, patteners.

For the pageant of Avarice: tailors, masons, brewers, plumbers and cutlers.

For the pageant of Anger: tanners, barbers, smiths and painters.

[MSS of the Corporation of Beverley]

In 1536, the people of Bourges, in central France, were treated to the Mystery of the Holy Acts of the Apostles, which lasted forty days. The spectacle began with a procession of the 494 actors who were to take part. The parade included "a Hell fourteen feet long by eight feet broad, in fashion of a rock crowned with a tower ever burning and belching flames, wherein Lucifer's head and body appeared vomiting flames of fire unceasingly, and holding in his hands certain kinds of serpents or vipers which writhed and belched fire."

The following is the producer's notes for just one episode, the Virgin Mary's death, funeral and assumption:

> 191. We must have a palm sent from Paradise for Gabriel to bring to Mary. There must be a thunder-clap in Paradise; and then we need a white cloud to come, fetch and ravish St. John preaching at Ephesus, and to bring him before the door of the Virgin Mary's abode. We must have another cloud to catch up all the Apostles from their divers countries and bring them all before the aforesaid house. We must have a white robe for the Virgin Mary to die in. We must have a little truckle bed and several torches of white wax which the virgins will hold at the said Lady's death. Jesus Christ must come down from Paradise to the death of the Virgin Mary, accompanied by a great multitude of angels, and take away her soul with Him. At the moment He cometh into the said Virgin's chamber, we must make great fragrance of divers odors. We must have the holy soul ready. We must have a crown encircled with twelve stars to crown the aforesaid soul in Paradise. We must have a bier to bear the said Lady's body to the tomb. We must have a tomb. There must be sent down from Paradise to the tomb aforesaid a round cloud shaped like a crown, wherein are several holy angels with naked swords and javelins in their hands; and, if it may be, we must have these living, that they may sing. Belzeray, prince of the Jews, and others set off to go and prevent lest the body of the said Lady be laid in the

tomb. The Jews strive to lay hands on the Virgin Mary's body to tear her from the Apostles; and forthwith their hands are withered and they are blinded with fire thrown by the angels. Belzeray laying hands on the litter whereon the Virgin Mary is borne, his hands remain fixed to the said litter, and much fire is cast down like unto thunderbolts, and the Jews must fall blinded to the earth. Belzeray's hands must be severed and joined again to his arms; then he is given a palm which he beareth to the rest, whereby such as would believe were enlightened. Then he brings back the said palm. We need a tomb wherein to lay the said Lady's body. Such as would not be converted are tormented by devils; some must be borne to hell. God purposeth to send to Our Lady's tomb, to raise her and bring her up to Paradise, body and soul. St. Michael should present the soul to Jesus Christ. This done, they come down accompanied by all the orders of angels in Paradise; as so soon as Jesus Christ is come to the tomb, a great light must be made, whereat the Apostles are amazed. Gabriel must raise the tombstone and the soul laid therein, so that it be no more seen. The soul is reunited to the body, and Mary riseth, having her face clearer than the sun; then she must humble herself before Jesus Christ. Jesus, Mary and the angels must mount up; and in mounting they must stay awhile here and there, even as the Orders shall speak. Mary, for the doubt that St. Thomas had, casteth him her girdle. A cloud must cover the Apostles; then let each depart underground and go unto his own region. [Baron de Girardot, in Didron's *Annales Archaeolgiques*, vol. 13]

The following is an extract from a play in the Chester cycle, *Noah's Wife*. Noah builds the ark, and his sons bring two of every kind of beast. Mrs. Noah delays:

192. *Noah's Wife*
Noah: Wife, come in! Why standest thou there?
Thou art ever forward, that dare I swear.

Come in for God's sake! Time it were,
For fear lest we should drown.
Wife: Oh yes, sir, now set up your sail,
And row forth hence with evil haile,
For without the slightest fail.
I will not leave this town,
Unless I bring my gossips on,
A single foot I will not gone,
They shall not drown, by good St. John,
If I can save their life.
They love me well, by our Lord,
And thou must let them now on board,
Or row now of your own accord,
And get thee a new wife!
Noah: Shem, son, now look, thy mother's wraw
Forsooth another such I do not know.
Shem: Father, I shall fetch her in I trow,
Without a risk of fail.
Mother, my father to you does send,
And bids thee to that ship to wend,
Look up at once and see the wind,
For we're about to sail.
Wife: Son, go to him and say
I will not come therein today!
Noah: Come in, wife, in twenty devils' way,
Or else stand there without!
Ham: Shall we all fetch her inside?
Noah: Yes, sons, with my grace and Christ's beside;
I would betimes you to her hied,
For of this flood I am in doubt.

The good Gossip's song

The flood comes fleeting in full fast,
On every side that spreads full far;
For fear of drowning I am aghast.
Good gossip, meet me at the bar,

And let us drink ere we depart,
For oftentimes we have done so.
For at a draught thou drink'st a quart,
And so will I do, ere I go.

Japhet: Mother, we pray you altogether,
For we are all here your own childer,
Come aboard for fear of the weather,
For His love who thee has bought.
Wife: I will not do that for your call
Unless I have my gossips all.
Shem: In faith, good mother, yet you shall
Whether thou wilt or not.

The three sons carry Noah's wife, kicking and screaming, into
the ark.

Noah: Welcome, wife, into this boat.
Wife: And take thou that for thine own note.

She boxes him on the ear.

PASTIMES AT HOME

We know little of the ways humble folk amused themselves at home, but one pastime seems to have been asking riddles:

> 193. Demaunde: What thynge is it that never was nor never shall be?
>
> Response: Never mouse made her nest in a cattes ear.
>
> Demaunde: Why dryve men dogges out of chyrche?
>
> Response: Because they come not up and offre.
>
> Demaunde: Why doth a dogge tourne hym thryse about or that he lyeth hym downe?
>
> Response: Bycause he knoweth not his beddes hede from the fete.
>
> Demaunde: Why do men make an oven in the towne?
>
> Response: For bycause they can not make the towne in the oven.
>
> Demaunde: What alms is worst bestowed that men gyve?
>
> Response: That is to a blynde man, for as he hathe onythynge gyven hym, he wolde with good wyll se hym hanged by the necke that gave it to hym.
>
> Demaunde: What thyng is it that hath none ende?
>
> Response: A bowle.
>
> Demaunde: What is it that freseth never?
>
> Response: That is hote water.
>
> Demaunde: What thyng is it, the lesse it is the more it is dredde?
>
> Response: A brydge.
>
> Demaunde: What is it that is a wryte [builder], and is no man, and he dothe that no man can, and yet it serveth both God and man?
>
> Response: That is a be.
>
> Demaunde: Howe many strawes go to a goose nest?
>
> Response: None, for lack of fete.
>
> Demaunde: What became of the asse that Our Lady rode upon?
>
> Response: Adams moder dede ete her.

CHAPTER 14. PASTIMES

Demaunde: Who was Adams moder?
Response: The erthe.
Demaunde: What space is from the hyest space of the se to
the depest?
Response: But a stones cast.

[*Reliquiae Antiquae, The Demaundes Joyous,* 15th century]

A sixteenth-century writer on agriculture had this advice for people who were inclined to spend their winter evenings by the fire:

194. One thinge I wyl advise the to remembre, and specially in wynter-tyme, when thou syteste by the fyre, and hast supped, to consyder in thy mynde, whether the warkes that thou, thy wyfe, and thy servantes shall do, be more avauntage to thee than the fyre, and candell-lyghte, meate and drynke that they shall spende, and if it be more avauntage, than syt styll; and if it be not, than go to thy bede and slepe, and be uppe betyme, and breake thy faste before day, that thou mayste be all the shorte wynters day about thy busynes. [Fitzherbert, *The Boke of Husbandry*]

It should be noted that the reason for sitting by the fire in the evening was not pleasure, but "warkes."

CHAPTER 15
THE POOR

POVERTY AND ITS CAUSES

William Langland describes the miseries of poor housewives:

195. The poorest folk are our neighbors, if we look about us, overburdened with children and rack-rented by landlords. For whatever they save by spinning they spend on rent, or on milk and oatmeal to make gruel and fill the bellies of their children who clamor for food. And they themselves are often famished with hunger, and wretched with the miseries of winter, cold, sleepless nights, when they get up to rock the cradle cramped in a corner, and rise before dawn to card and comb the wool, to wash and scrub and mend, and wind yarn and peel rushes for their rushlights. The miseries of these women who dwell in hovels are too pitiful to read, or describe in verse. [*Vision of Piers the Ploughman*]

Rutebeuf, a thirteenth-century French poet, describes his own poverty:

196. I know not where to begin, I have so much to say about my poverty. I beg you, for God's sake, king of France, give me some goods! Great king, I am without food, and have been without for long; no man offers, nor gives to me. I cough with the cold, I gape with the hunger that consumes me. I have no bed, I have no mattress. From Paris to Senlis, there is none so poor as I. Sire, I know not where to turn. My ribs know well the taste of horse litter; a bed of straw is no bed, and there is nothing but straw in mine. [*Lay of the Poverty of Rutebeuf*]

There was a great deal of poverty in medieval Europe, and the reasons for this were many and complex, but the most important was that the economy was not strong enough to produce sufficient wealth to allow more than a minority of people to live in comparative comfort. Further, while normal times were hard enough for many, bad times meant disaster:

197. 1315 There were portents which showed that God had turned his face against us. For example, last year, there was so much rain that men could hardly reap their corn or carry it to their barns.

This year was even worse. Torrents of rain destroyed nearly all the seed, so that Isaiah's prophecy seemed to come to pass that "ten acres of vineyard should yield but one small measure of wine and that thirty bushels of wheat should yield but three." In many fields, the grass was so deep under water that it could not be mown. Sheep and other animals died of a plague.

1316 After Easter, corn was in even shorter supply. We had never seen such a dearth in our lives, and nothing like it had been known for a hundred years. A bushel of wheat cost forty pence in London and its neighborhood, while in less populous places it was commonly thirty pence.

At this time of want there was a great famine, followed by a scourging pestilence, from which thousands died. It was even reported that in Northumberland folk ate dogs, horses and other unclean meat. For in that county, work is difficult, on account of the many raids by the Scots. Those accursed Scots rob the people of their food almost daily. [*Anonymous Life of Edward II*]

VIEWS OF POVERTY

While we will treat the issue of the "voluntary poverty" of the mendicant orders of the later Middle Ages in *Those Who Prayed*, suffice it to say here that the poor themselves were sometimes portrayed unfavorably. This song was current in Flanders during the early fourteenth century:

CHAPTER 15. THE POOR

198. All the Karls have long beards. They wear ragged clothes. Their hats sit strangely on their heads. Their shoes are in shreds.

Sour milk, bread and cheese, that's what Karl eats every day, and if he had anything better his wits would be fuddled.

A hunk of rye bread is all he needs. He holds it in his hand as he goes forth to plough. His ragged wife follows him, munching bran and plying her distaff until it is time for her to cook the porridge for supper. [*Kereslied*]

Desiderius Erasmus [c. 1469-1536] tells of a beautiful girl who, like Titania, fell in love, inexplicably, with a hideous creature. The fellow is not only poor and ugly, but evil:

199. Pamphilus: He had a peaked head, thin hair, and that torn and unkempt, full of scurf and lice. The mange had laid bare most of his scalp. He was cross-eyed, had flat, wide-opened nostrils like an ape's, thin mouth, rotten teeth, a stuttering tongue, pocky chin; he was hunchbacked, pot-bellied, and had crooked shanks. What's more, they said he had only one ear.
Maria: Perhaps he lost the other in war.
Pamphilus: Oh, no, in peace.
Maria: Who dared to do that to him?
Pamphilus: Denis the hangman.
Maria: Maybe a large family fortune made up for his ugliness.
Pamphilus: Not at all; he was bankrupt and head over heels in debt. With this husband, so exceptional a girl now spends her life and is often beaten. [*Colloquies*, 1523]

There were, though, alternative views of the poor, for the Bible is studded with references to the virtues of poverty, and with dire warnings for the rich:

200. He hath shewed strength with his arm: He hath scattered the proud in the imagination of their hearts.
He hath put down the mighty from their seat: and hath exalted the humble and meek.

He hath filled the hungry with good things: and the rich he
hath sent empty away.
[*Magnificat*, Luke 1:51-53]

Texts like this, and the example of Christ, led some, who could
have enjoyed comfortable lives, to seek poverty. St. Francis of Assisi
is the best known of these and he and his kind are described in
the next volume in this series. Such people attracted a great deal
of adulation, but there was respect, too, for the poor in general.
Alan of Lille wrote:

> 201. Christ cannot live in the palace of the bishop, for there
> is simony. He cannot live in the castle of the knight, for
> there is plunder. He cannot live with the burghers, for they
> practice usury. He cannot live with the merchants, for they
> are cheats. He cannot live with the common folk, for they
> are thieves. Where, then, can Christ live? Only among His
> paupers, of whom He said, "Blessed are the poor in spirit."
> [*Sermon of the Cross*, 1189]

THE RELIEF OF POVERTY

There was no question of medieval people trying to eradicate
poverty. In the first place, it would have been an impossible task,
for there were not nearly enough resources to accomplish it. Secondly, it was obviously the will of God that some should be poor,
for had not Christ himself said, "The poor ye have always with
you"? Thirdly, the poor had a role to play; they could ensure the
salvation of the rich by accepting their charity. On the other hand,
helping the poor was an essential part of Christian duty.

One of the most famous stories in hagiography shows the rewards of giving charity:

> 202. So it came about one day when he had nothing on him
> but his weapons and his uniform, in the middle of a winter
> which had been fearfully hard beyond the ordinary, so that
> many were dying of the intense cold, he met at the city
> gate of Amiens a coatless beggar. This beggar had been asking

the passers-by to take pity on him, but all had gone past the unfortunate creature. Then the God-filled man understood, from the fact that no one else had had pity, that this beggar had been reserved for him. But what was he to do? He had nothing with him but the cape he had on, for he had already used up what else he had, in similar good works. So he took the sword he was wearing and cut the cape in two and gave one half to the beggar, putting on the rest himself again.

This raised a laugh from some of the bystanders, for he looked grotesque in the mutilated garment; but many had more sense, and sighed to think that they had not done something of the kind; indeed, having more to give, they could have clothed the beggar without stripping themselves. And that night, in his sleep, Martin saw Christ wearing the half  of his cape with which he had clothed the beggar. He was told to look carefully at Our Lord and take note that it was the garment he had given away. Then he heard Jesus say aloud to the throng of angels that surrounded Him, "Martin is still only a catechumen, but he has clothed Me with this garment." [Sulpicius Severus, *Life of Martin of Tours*, c. AD 400]

Kings and nobles being, on the whole, wealthy, were expected to give generously to the poor, and some of them did:

203. The country on the borders of Anjou and Maine was suffering from lack of bread, and Henry II found sufficient food for ten thousand people every day from 1 April until there was enough of the new grain. Whatever had been reserved in England for the king's use, whether in barns,

wine cellars and storehouses, was all given out on the royal command to our pious colleagues and to the poor. [Ralph of Diceto, *Images of History*, 1176]

204. Not unmindful that the justice of Christians ought to surpass the justice of the Pharisees, when all his produce had been rightly tithed, he ordered a ninth part to be set aside so that it might be used to buy various necessaries for the poor, and from this, as occasion demanded, clothes were also bought for the needy who presented themselves from time to time. In addition, he always carried money with him, of which he secretly gave as much as he could to poor people whom he met. [Odo of Cluny, *Life of Saint Count Gerald of Aurillac*, c. 920]

For a long time, it was the Church that assumed most of the burden of helping the poor. An unknown chronicler describes the work of Bishop Massona of Mérida, in western Spain:

205. It is only God who knows how generous he was in giving alms to the poor; none the less, we can give just one small example. He was so concerned at the tribulations of the unfortunate that he entrusted a deacon of the church of St. Eulalia with 2,000 solidi. From this, anyone who was in dire need was to receive what he needed, without delay or difficulty, and, moreover be given comfort and consolation for his penury.

Later, he built a hospice, and endowed it with broad estates. He appointed doctors and servants to care for strangers and the sick. He ordered them to hunt high and low in the town, and if they found anyone who was sick, be he slave or free, Christian or Jew, they were to carry him in their arms to the hospice. Here, they were to lay him on a bed of clean straw and give him clean, delicate food until, with God's help, they had restored him to health. And although the endowments yielded much wealth for the hospice, it seemed little enough to the saintly man. Accordingly, he added to all these benefits others, even greater, and so that the doctors should work with easy minds, he ordered them to receive half of all the offerings brought to his palace by all the administrators of church property, so that it might be given to the sick.

And if any one of the city or the countryside should come to his palace in need, he might ask the dispenser for a measure of wine, oil or honey. He was to be shown a small jar in which to take it, and the holy man was to see him. And if the suppliant's expression remained agreeable and his face happy, the bishop at once ordered that the small jar should be broken and replaced with a bigger one. [*Vitae Sanctorum Patrum Emeritensium*, 6th century]

Monasteries, in particular, became centers for the distribution of alms, each with its *eleemosynarius*, or almoner, who was responsible for the work. There was quite a ritual. First, the almoner selected the poor who were to receive help and led them into the church, where mass was said. Next, the paupers' feet were given a preliminary, and, one would hope, thorough, washing in hot water. A monk now stood in front of each pauper and, when the abbot made a sign, he gave his pauper's feet a ritual washing, dried them and kissed them. The paupers then received food, drink and a little money.

Adelard, abbot of Corbie, made these rules for his monastery early in the ninth century:

206. We decree that the hospice of the poor shall receive daily 45 maslin loaves, each weighing 3½ pounds, and five wheaten or spelt loaves, which will make 50 loaves in all.

Each of the twelve paupers who shall spend the night here will be given a loaf, and then a further half loaf for his journey. The five wheaten loaves must be shared between any churchmen who are traveling, and the sick who are fed here.

Those who come and leave on the same day usually receive a quarter of a loaf, or whatever the almoner shall think right, according to their circumstances.

A half a muid of beer shall be provided daily, which is eight setiers. The twelve paupers aforesaid shall share four setiers, so that each one receives two cups. Churchmen who are traveling shall also receive a cup. The almoner may divide the surplus between the poor and the sick, at his discretion.

To go with the bread of the poor there will be up to thirty portions of cheese or bacon and 30 muids of beans. Further, we add to that a fifth of the eels which the porter receives from the cellarer, and a fifth of the fresh cheese which the shepherds deliver. Moreover we add a fifth of the tithe in cattle, calves and sheep which is received by the porter.

As is the custom, the porter will give the poor wood, and everything that is customary, but not set down in writing, like sheets and beds. Also, the chamberer shall give the almoner the monks' cast-off clothes and shoes, so that he can distribute them to the poor. [*Inventory of Abbot Irminon*]

A German monk told this anecdote:

207. In the days when that most terrible famine of the year 1197 was raging and destroying wholesale, our monastery, poor and new though it was, gave help to many. It has been told me by those who had seen the poor flocking round the

gate, that sometimes fifteen hundred doles were given in a single day. Our then abbot, the lord Gerard, on every flesh-eating day before harvest, had a whole ox sodden in three caldrons, together with herbs gathered from all sides, whereof he dealt out a portion with bread to every one of the poor. Thus also he did with the sheep and other food-stuffs; so that, by God's grace, all the poor who came to us were kept alive until harvest time. And (as I have heard from the mouth of the aforesaid Abbot Gerard) he feared lest this store for the poor should fail before harvest time, where-fore he rebuked our baker for making his loaves too great; but the man replied, "Of a truth, my lord, they are very small in the dough and grow great in the oven; we put them in small, and draw out great loaves." This same baker, Brother Redhead, who lives to this day, has told me that not only did these loaves grow in the oven, but even the meal in the bags and vessels, to the wonder of all the bak-ers and of the poor who ate thereof; for they said, "Lord God! Whence cometh all this store?" Moreover, that same year the Lord of all plenty rewarded an hundredfold, even in this life, the charity of His servants. For Master Andreas of Speyer, with the money he had gathered together at the court of the emperor Frederick, and again in Greece, bought a great estate at Plittersdorf, which he freely gave unto us; who then could have put this into his heart but God? [Caesarius of Heisterbach, *Dialogus Miraculorum*, early 13th century]

During the later Middle Ages, monastic charity remained impor-tant, but there were other agencies at work. There was a certain amount of self-help. The merchant guilds had always looked after their members who fell on hard times, but now guilds were formed whose main purpose was to provide welfare. They obtained their funds from members' subscriptions and from endowments. These are some of the rules of the Guild of the Holy Trinity, King's Lynn:

208. If any of the brethren shall die, the aldermen shall or-der a mass to be celebrated for him, at which every brother

of the guild shall make his offering. And the aldermen shall cause every chaplain of the guild to say thirty masses for the deceased.

The aldermen of the guild must visit four times a year all the infirm, all that are in want, need or poverty, and to minister to and relieve all such out of the alms of the guild.

If any brother shall become poor and needy, he shall be supported in food and clothing out of the profits of the lands and tenements, goods and chattels of the guild. [*Records of King's Lynn,* 14th century]

The following are summaries of fourteenth-century guild certificates:

209. The Guild of St. George, Norwich Cathedral, gave each of its members who fell into poverty eightpence a week. Every member of the guild paid a farthing a week into the fund. Surplus funds paid for the making of an effigy of St. George.

The Guild of the Conception of the Blessed Virgin Mary, London, kept a common box into which every brother and sister paid threepence a quarter. Members stricken with infirmity, imprisoned, or suffering from any other misfortune, received sevenpence a week.

The Guild of the Holy Cross, King's Lynn, sent a gallon of ale to any brother who was sick or going on a pilgrimage. [*Chancery Miscellanea*]

The growing wealth of the merchants meant they could take an increasing share of the burden of caring for the poor, and the fact that they had more access to ready money than most people, meant it was easy for them to do so. William Langland wrote:

210. Truth sent the merchants a letter under his secret seal, telling them to buy up boldly all the best goods they could get, then sell them again, and use the profits to repair hospitals and to help folk in trouble, to get the bad roads mended quickly and rebuild the broken bridges, to enable

poor girls to marry or enter nunneries, to feed the poor and men in prisons, to send boys to school or apprentice them to a trade, and to assist religious orders and give them better endowments. "And if you will do these things," said Truth, "I myself will send you St. Michael, my Archangel when you die, so that no devil shall harm your souls or make you afraid; and he will ward off despair, and lead your souls in safety in Heaven."

The merchants were pleased with this, and many of them wept for joy, praising Piers for gaining them such an indulgence. [*Vision of Piers the Ploughman*]

The London merchants relieved a famine in 1399:

211. The pinch of hunger was felt most sharply in the county of Leicester and in the central parts of the kingdom. Eleven ships loaded with an abundance of provisions were sent to different parts of the country for the relief of people. The citizens of London contributed two thousand marks to purchase provisions for a common box for orphans. And the twenty-four aldermen added twenty pounds for similar purchases on account of the fear of famine about to come

to the city, and they located at different places suitable conveniences for the people, so that the needy could come and buy at a fixed price what would suffice for maintaining themselves and their families. Those that did not at the time have any money would make payment in the following year. And thus they were relieved so that no one perished because of the famine. [Henry Knighton, *Chronicle*]

The following are extracts from merchants' wills:

212. John, son of Adam de Salisbury, pepperer, to be buried in the church of St. Mary Bothaw. An ironbound chest is to be deposited in the aforesaid church, and in it are to be placed forty pounds sterling, to be lent to poor parishioners upon certain securities to be repaid at a fixed time so that no loan exceed sixty shillings, and the security must be greater than the loan. Three parishioners are to have each a key to the said chest, so that it might be opened and closed, with the consent of all three. [*Records of the Parishes of St. Swithin and St. Mary Bothaw, London*, 1349]

213. Will of Peter of Briklesworth, citizen and draper of London, who dwelt within the close of the Hospital of St. Thomas the Martyr, Southwark.

Item, I bequeath to be divided among the lepers and the poor bedridden, as my executors shall ordain, 100 shillings. Item, to every sister of the Hospital of the Blessed Mary without Bishopsgate, 3s 4d. Item, to the Master of the Hospital of St. Thomas the Martyr of Southwark, for my tithes and oblations and all things else by me of right to him belonging, 10s 0d. Item, to every brother there, 20d., and to every chaplain celebrating divine service in the said hospital to pray for my soul, 12d. [*Prerogative Court of Canterbury*, 1411]

214. Will of Richard Baret, burgess of Gloucester.

Item, I bequeath for constructing beds in the Hospital of St. Bartholomew, Gloucester, especially for the poor, sick and feeble, 100 shillings. [*Ibid.*, 1401]

CHAPTER 15. THE POOR

Often, large numbers of paupers came to funerals. They provided prayers and holy water, while the executors of the will distributed largesse:

215. The coroner was informed that a certain Alice de Lincoln, and three other women and Henry le Dumbe and four other men, poor persons and beggars, lay dead of other than their rightful deaths in the entrance of the rent of John Paulin in the parish of St. Andrew. Having heard this, the coroner and sheriffs proceeded thither, when they called together the good men of the same ward diligently to inquire what had happened. The jurors say that whereas on the preceding Tuesday Walter de Frysney and Robert de Waleby, executors of the will of Robert de Retford, caused a distribution of money to be made for the soul of the testator, according to custom, in the said rent, there assembled a great multitude of poor beggars and, for greed of receiving the money, they entered running swiftly into the said entry, among whom were the deceased; and because they were weaker than the others, they fell and were immediately trampled under the feet of the said poor people and crushed to death. [*London Coroners' Rolls*, 1322]

CHAPTER 16
CARE OF THE SICK

MEDICAL THEORY

Medical theory was based on the idea, inherited from the ancient Greeks, that there were four bodily humors, blood, phlegm, yellow bile and black bile, and that they had the four qualities, heat, cold, dry and wet. It was important that the four humors should be kept in balance, for sickness resulted if there was an excess of any of them.

Chaucer wrote of the doctor in his *Canterbury Tales:*

216. He knew the cause of ev'ry malady,
Whether 'twere hot or cold or moist or dry,
And where engendered and of what humor.
He was a quite perfect practitioner.

A book by an Italian woman practitioner gives some examples of the practical application of this theory:

217. God created [the human race] male and female, so that through their fertile propagation, offspring would never cease to appear. Making a pleasing mixture of their embraces, he caused the man's nature to be hot and dry, and the woman's cold and wet, so that the opposition of their qualities would control each other's excesses. The man's nature being hot and dry might comfort the woman's coldness and wetness, while her nature being cold and wet, soothes the man's heat and dryness....

Since there is not enough heat in women to dry up the moistures that gather in them, they cannot discharge their moisture into the air, as men do. On account of this lack of heat, Nature has given them a purgation of their own, the menses, commonly known as flowers.

217

This purgation usually starts in women when they are about thirteen or fourteen, or a little earlier or later, depending on whether they have an excess of cold or heat. It lasts until about the age of fifty, if the woman is lean, and sometimes up to sixty or sixty-five, if she is moist.

If these purgations are normal and regular, Nature relieves women of excess moisture. But if the menstruation is too copious, certain illnesses result. Those afflicted have little appetite for food and drink, sometimes they vomit. and sometimes they want to eat earth, coal, chalk and such-like things. For the same reason, they may have pains in the neck, the back and the head. Alternatively, they may have a high temperature, stabbing pains to the heart, dropsy and dysentery, and these problems arise, either because they only menstruate at long intervals, or do not menstruate at all. They may suffer not only from dropsy, dysentery and heart disease, but from other serious illnesses as well. [*The Diseases of Women*, n.d., but probably 11th century]

PHYSICIANS

There were two kinds of physician, the popular and the professional. The popular physician had no formal training, dealt only with humble folk and charged modest fees, if any at all. The professional physician was expensively educated, dealt mainly with the rich and charged considerable fees.

Popular medicine was largely in the hands of women. Every housewife was her family's doctor. She had inherited from her own mother a store of experience, superstition and folklore, while, if she had a garden, its most important plants were the herbs from which she made her medicines. Many a village also had its "wise woman," whose resources were similar, but more extensive. As like as not, the wise woman was also the midwife. Many such people had considerable experience, and, had they been guided by that alone, might have been more useful than they were. Unfortunately, they were influenced as well by the inevitable superstition and folklore. Finally, there were a very few women who specialized in the diseases of their own sex. Trotula of Salerno explained how she began to practice:

> 218. Since women are by nature weaker than men, sicknesses are more common with them, especially in the organs that involve the work of nature. As well as being fragile and delicate, these organs are concealed, so women, being modest, are unwilling to reveal them to men. Therefore I, pitying their misfortune, and encouraged by a certain lady, began to study the illnesses that afflict the female sex. [*The Diseases of Women*]

Trotula is as enigmatic as she is interesting. No one knows when she lived; while some scholars have cast doubts on her very existence, saying her works were those of a man. What is certain, however, is that in the eleventh century women were admitted to the medical faculty at Salerno. The "women of Salerno" were famous all over Europe, and it is perfectly possible that Trotula was one of them. But what was the position of these women within the faculty? They must have been valued for their empirical knowledge, but there is no evidence at all that they emerged into the world as qualified physicians, competing on equal terms with men.

The University of Salerno was unique in according any real status to women since, in general, professional medicine was the preserve of men, and any woman who seemed to be trespassing in it was likely to be in trouble. For example, in 1322 Jacqueline Felicie of Paris was excommunicated for practicing medicine, even though she used the same arguments as Trotula. Jacqueline's accusers made much of her lack of qualifications, but her main crime seems to have been that, though she charged very little herself, she was depriving professional doctors of their fees by taking their patients.

Professional doctors, then, were all men. Such a one was university trained. He took an Arts degree and then specialized in medicine, which he might well study at one of Europe's more famous faculties, Paris, Montpellier, Salerno, or Bologna. He could qualify to practice after four or five years, but it took as long again to become a Master. There was little practical work in the training, most of it being the study of the Graeco-Roman authorities, such as Hippocrates and Galen.

Both the professional physicians and governments tried to prevent practice by amateurs, the former, as we have seen, to protect their fees, and the latter to protect their subjects. The Emperor Frederick II included this clause in the code of laws he made for his kingdom of Sicily:

> 219. We consider it especially important to care for the safety of our subjects. Therefore, since we are mindful of the considerable expense and irredeemable harm that inexperienced physicians can cause, we order that, in future, none may practice medicine, claiming to be a physician, unless he has been examined in public and approved by the Masters of Salerno. Anyone disobeying this edict shall suffer the penalty of the confiscation of all his goods and a year in prison. [*Constitutions of Melfi*, Title LXV]

Presumably, anyone could still practice medicine; the crime was to masquerade as a qualified physician.

It was recognized that doctors needed more than paper qualifications. John Aderne, a fourteenth-century English physician, wrote as follows. The spelling has been modernized, but the language is close to the original:

> 220. First it behoveth him that will profit in this craft that he set God afore evermore in all his works, and evermore

call meekly with heart and mouth His help; and sometimes visit of his earnings poor men, according to his means, that they by their prayers may get him grace of the Holy Ghost. And that he be nought found bold or boastful in his sayings, or in his deeds; and abstain he from much speech, most of all among great men. Also, be a leech not much laughing nor much playing. And as much as he may without harm, flee he the fellowship of knaves and dishonest persons. And be he evermore occupied in things that pertain to his craft; other read he, or study he, or write or pray he; for the exercise of books honors a leech. For why? He shall both be honored and he shall be more wise. And above all these it profits to him that he be found evermore sober; for drunkenness destroys all virtue and brings it to naught. Be content in strange places of food and drink there found, using moderation in all things.

If there be made speech to him of any leech, neither set he him at nought, nor praise him too much, or commend him, but thus he may courteously answer, "I have not much knowledge of him, but I have naught heard of him but good and honest."

Consider he not over openly the lady or the daughters or other fair women in great men's houses, nor proffer them not to kiss, that he run not into the indignation of the lord, nor none of his.

When sick men come to the leech for help, be he not with them over stern, nor over homely, but moderate in his bearing, according to the needs of the person, to some reverently, to some commonly. For, according to wise men, over much homeliness breeds despising.

Also it is expedient that he have suitable excuses, when he is not inclined to their askings. Or feign him hurt, or for to be sick, or some other reasonable cause by which he may likely be excused. Therefore, if he will favor any man's asking, make he covenant for his travail, and take it beforehand. But advise the leech himself well that he give no certain answer in any cause, but he see first the sickness and the manner of it; and when he has seen and assayed it, though it may seem to him that the sick may be healed, nevertheless, he shall make prognostication to the patient of the perils to come, if the cure be deferred. And if he see the patient pursues busily the cure, then, according to the means of the patient, let him ask boldly more or less; but ever be he wary of scarce askings, for over scarce askings set at naught both the market and the thing. Therefore for the cure of fistula, ask he of a worthy man and a great an hundred marks or forty pounds, with robes and fees of an hundred shillings, term of life, by year. Of lesser men, forty pounds or forty marks ask he without fees; and take he not less than an hundred shillings; for never in all my life took I less than an hundred shillings for cure of that sickness.

And if the patient asks by how much time he hopes to heal it, let the leech state the double that he supposes, for it is better that the term be lengthened than the cure. For prolongation of the cure gives cause of despairing to the patient, when trust in the leech is the most hope of health. And if the patient asks why he put him so long a time of curing, since he cured him by the half, answer he that it was for that the patient was strong hearted, and suffered well sharp things and that he was of good complexion, and had able flesh to heal; and feign he other causes plausible to the patient, for patients of such words are proud and delighted.

CHAPTER 16. CARE OF THE SICK

Have the leech also clean hands and well shaped nails, and cleansed from all blackness and filth.

Beware that there be never found double words in his mouth, for if he be found true in his words, few or none shall doubt his deeds.

Learn also the young leech good proverbs pertaining to his craft in comfort of patients. Also is speedeth that a leech can talk of good tales and of honest that may make the patients to laugh, as well of the Bible and of other tragedies; and any other things that are no trouble, whilst they induce a light heart to the patient or sick man.

If the patient stands steadfastly to be cured, then say the leech thus, "I doubt not, with God's help, and your good patience following, if you will make satisfaction to me, as such a cure requires, supposing that all things are kept that should be kept, and all left that should be left, I shall be able to bring this cure to a lovable end and healthful. And then agree your covenant, of which covenant, all excuses put aback, take he the half beforehand. And then assign a day to the patient when he will begin. [*Treatise on Fistula*]

SURGEONS

In the absence of anesthetics and antiseptics, complicated surgery was out of the question, and since most of the surgeons' work was relatively simple, they were considered inferior to physicians. They were, in fact, craftsmen rather than professional men, and they learnt their trade, like other craftsmen, through apprenticeship. Bologna was the only university to have a faculty of surgery. Many surgeons were also barbers, since both trades required the use of sharp instruments on the human body.

An Austrian knight, Ulrich von Lichtenstein [our heart-sick friend from *Those Who Fought*, reading 125], describes an operation he underwent. He had been rejected by a lady who told him she could never love him because of his hare lip, so he decided to have it removed:

221. I rode to Gratz, where I found my Master. He took me in hand at once, and arranged to cut me on a Monday morning. He wanted to bind me, but I would not allow it. He said, "You may easily be harmed, for if you stir as much as a hair's breadth, then the damage is done, I tell no lie!"

"No," said I, "I will have none of it. I rode here of my own free will, and whatever you do to me, even if it should kill me, no man shall see me flinch." Yet in truth, I was much afraid, and sat down on a bench in front of him. Then he took a knife and cut my mouth clean through above my teeth. I bore this so stoically, that, when all the cutting was done, I had not stirred in the slightest. He cut me like a master, and I bore it like a man. At once my mouth swelled until it was far bigger than a tennis ball, and he dressed my wound.

I had to stay in my sickbed for five and a half weeks and more. I was in much pain and woe, woe for the wound to my body, but glad at heart. Love constrained me, so that I was both sad and merry. I was glad for my pain, though much troubled by hunger and thirst. I could take nothing, because of the soreness of my teeth and lips, so my mouth was anointed with an ointment that was greener than grass and more foul smelling than any dog. This ointment came into my stomach with whatever I took, so all food and drink disgusted me. So I lived like those who can eat nothing on account of sickness, and became very weak. I stayed at Gratz until I was cured. [*Frauendienst*]

Ulrich's trouble was all in vain, because the lady still rejected him.

TREATMENT

Trotula of Salerno gives her advice on contraception:

222. If a woman, through fear of death, does not want to conceive, she should wear next to her skin the womb of a goat that has never given birth. There is a stone to be found at Galgates, which, if it is worn round the neck, or tasted,

will prevent conception. Also, take a weasel's testicles, but be sure the creature does not die. The woman should carry these testicles on her bosom, wrapped in the skin of a goose. [*The Diseases of Women*]

These are Trotula's views on helping women who have difficulty in giving birth:

223. When a woman has difficulty in giving birth, the most essential thing is to appeal to God. As to what we can do ourselves, let the woman be bathed in water in which mallow, chick peas, flax seed and barley have been cooked. She should be rubbed vigorously, and given vinegar and sugar to drink, along with powdered mint and a measure of absinthe. Make her sneeze, by placing the dust of incense or pepper in her nose. If the child does not come out as it should, that is, if the arms and legs come out first, the midwife should moisten her hands with the essence of flax seed and chick peas, and put the child back in its correct position. If the child is dead, crush rue, mugwort, absinthe and black pepper and administer them in the liquor in which lupins have been boiled. Also, place the woman on a linen cloth, and have it stretched by four men, one on each corner. She will then give birth at once, God willing. If the afterbirth remains, make her sneeze with the mouth and nostrils closed. Or give her lye made from the ash of the ash tree, mixed with powdered mallow seed. When she drinks this, she will immediately vomit. Also, she should be fumigated from below with smoke from burning fish bones or horses hooves or the dung of cats or lambs. [Ibid.]

This is a Welsh cure for toothache, which, it was thought, was caused by worms in the teeth gnawing them:

224. Take a candle of mutton fat, mixed with the seed of sea holly. Burn this candle as close as possible to the tooth, holding a basin of cold water beneath it. The worms will fall into the water to escape the heat of the candle. [*Meddygon Myddven*, 14th century]

This is a fourteenth-century cure for tonsillitis:

225. For he that has quinsy, take a fat cat, and flay it well, and clean it and draw out the guts, and take the grease of a hedgehog and the fat of a bear, and resins, and sage and gum of woodbine, and virgin wax; crumble this small, and stuff the cat with it, as you would a goose, roast it whole and collect the grease and use as an ointment. [In Wright, *Reliquiae Antiquae*]

This was how to diagnose whether a wound was fatal:

226. Take pimpernel and pound it, and mix it with water, and give it him to drink, and if it comes out of the wound, he shall live.

Give him to drink lettuce with water, and if he spews, he shall be dead.

Give him ice to drink, and if he spews it, he shall be dead.

Give him mensore [unknown term] to drink with ale, and if he holds it until the next day at the same time, he shall live.

To cure a wound, take red nettle and salt and pound together, and drink the juice fasting. [In Henslow, *Medical Works of the Fourteenth Century*]

The following is a twelfth-century incantation:

227. Holy Goddess Earth, parent of Nature, who dost generate all things, and regenerate the earth: thou guardian of heaven and sea, and arbiter of all the gods, by whose influence Nature is wrapped in silence and slumber, thou art she who restoreth

the day and puttest darkness to flight, who governest the shades of night in all security, restraining at thy will the mighty chaos, winds and rain and storms, or again letting them loose. Thou churnest the deep to foam and puttest the sun to flight, and arousest the tempests; or again at thy pleasure thou sendest forth the glad daylight. Thou givest us food in safety by a perpetual covenant; and, when our soul fleeth away, it is in thy bosom that we find our haven of rest. Thou too art called, by the loving kindness of the gods, the Great Mother, who has conquered the god of mighty name. Thou art the force of the nations and the mother of the gods, without whom nothing can be born or come to maturity. Mighty art thou, Queen of the Gods! Thee, O Goddess, I adore in thy godhead, and on thy name do I call; vouchsafe now to fulfill my prayer, and I will give thee thanks, O Goddess, with the faith that thou hast deserved. Hear, I beseech thee, and favor my prayers; vouchsafe to me, O Goddess, that for which I now pray; grant freely to all nations upon earth all herbs that thy majesty bringeth to life, and suffer me thus to gather this thy medicine. Come to me with thy healing powers; grant a favorable issue to whatsoever I shall make from these herbs, and may those thrive to whom I shall administer the same. Prosper thou all thy gifts to us, for to thee all things return. Let men take these herbs rightly at my hand; I beseech thee now, O Goddess, may thy gifts make them whole; suppliant I beseech thee that thy majesty may vouchsafe me this boon. [*British Museum,* MS *Harl.* 1585, fol. 12a]

This, of course, is undiluted paganism. Indeed, the line between medicine and magic was never clear.

CHAPTER 17
PLAGUE AND REBELLION

THE BLACK DEATH

"Black Death" was a name given in later centuries to the bubonic plague and the closely related pneumonic plague. Medieval people knew it simply as "the plague," as they did most epidemic diseases.

Bubonic plague is caused by the microbe *pasteurella pestis*, which infects a flea carried by the black rat. Normally, the flea bites only its host, but when suffering from the plague, it will bite any animals, including humans. In the Middle Ages, some 70 percent of those infected died, and within a week. Pneumonic plague is spread directly from human to human, when a patient suffering from bubonic plague coughs, and another breaths in droplets of his sputum. Formerly, all victims of pneumonic plague died, usually within two days.

The plague had long been endemic in parts of Asia when, in about 1340, there was a pandemic that spread along the trade routes of the world. It reached western Europe in 1348. Henry Knighton wrote:

> 228. There was a general mortality throughout the world. It began first in India, then spread to Tharsis, thence to the Saracens and at last to the Christians and Jews, so that in the space of one year, eight thousand legions of men, according to rumors in the Court of Rome, died in those remote regions, besides Christians. The king of Tharsis, seeing such a sudden and unheard of mortality among his people, set out with a great multitude of nobles, intending to seek out the Pope at Avignon and have himself baptized as a Christian, believing the vengeance of God to have overtaken his people because of their sinful disbelief. But when

he had traveled twenty days, he heard that the plague had
invaded the ranks of the Christians as well as other nations,
and therefore he turned to go back to his own country. But
the Christians, following the Tharsians, attacked them from
the rear and slew two thousand of them.

Then the dreadful pestilence penetrated through the
coastal regions from Southampton and came to Bristol, and
almost the whole strength of the town perished, as if over-
come by sudden death; for few there were who kept their
beds for more than two or three days, or even half a day.
Then this cruel death spread everywhere, following the
course of the sun. At Leicester, in the small parish of St.
Leonard's, there perished more than 380 people, in the parish of Holy Cross, 400, in the parish of St. Margaret's, 700;
and so in every parish a great multitude. Then the bishop
of Lincoln sent a message throughout his diocese, and gave
general power to all priests, religious as well as secular, to
hear confessions and give absolutions to all men with full
episcopal authority, excepting only in cases of debt. And in
such a case, the debtor was to pay the debt, if he were able
to do so while he lived; or others were to be appointed to
do so from his property after his death. Similarly, the pope
granted plenary remission of all sins to all receiving abso-
lution at the point of death, and granted that this power

should last until the following Easter, and that everyone might choose his own confessor at will.

In the same year there was a great murrain of sheep everywhere in the realm, so that in one place more than 5,000 sheep died in a single pasture; and they rotted so much that neither beast nor bird would approach them. And there was a great cheapness of all things for fear of death, for very few took any account of riches or of possessions of any kind. Sheep and oxen strayed through the fields and among the crops, and there was none to drive them off or collect them, but they perished in uncounted numbers throughout all districts for lack of shepherds, because there was such a shortage of servants and laborers. For there was no recollection of such a severe mortality since the time of Vortigern, King of the Romans, in whose day, as Bede testifies, the living did not suffice to bury the dead.

The Scots, hearing of the cruel pestilence in England, imagined that it had come about at the hand of an avenging God, and they adopted it as an oath, according to the common report, under the form, when they wished to swear, "by the foul death of England." And thus believing that a terrible vengeance of God had overtaken the English, they gathered in Selkirk Forest with the intention of invading the kingdom of England. There, the horrible death overtook them, and their ranks were thinned by sudden and terrible mortality, so that in a short time about 5,000 had perished. And as the rest, some strong, some feeble, were preparing to return to their own country, they were surprised by pursuing Englishmen, who killed a very great number of them. [*Chronicle*]

Boccaccio described the plague in Florence:

229. In the year of Our Lord 1348, Florence, doyenne of all the cities of Italy, fell victim to a deadly pestilence. This was visited upon us to chastise us, either by the direction of the heavenly bodies, or by God in His just wrath, because

of our evil deeds. It had held sway in the east for several years, where it had devoured numerous lives and whence it pursued its devastating course, remorselessly and spreading constantly, towards the west.

Numerous workmen cleansed the city, those suffering from the disease were excluded, much advice was given on preserving health, and several times a day humble supplications were made to God, by processions and other forms of piety, but all to no avail.

This dreadful pestilence first appeared during the spring of the year mentioned. But it did not manifest itself as in the east, where bleeding from the nose was a sure sign of death. Instead, at the onset of the disease in both women and men, there appeared in the groin and in the armpits, swellings which grew to the size of an apple or an egg. The common people called these swellings "boils." And, in a short time, these deadly eruptions covered all parts of the body. Then, other symptoms appeared, livid marks on the arms and thighs, sometimes large and far apart, sometimes small and close together. Thus, the original boil became an unmistakable sign of death, as did the marks.

Neither any advice from doctors nor any medicine could cure this sickness, partly because its nature was not understood, and partly because no-one knew its cause, or how to treat it. Thus, not only were very few cured, but nearly all those affected died on the third day after the appearance of the symptoms, or soon afterwards. The spread of the disease was all the more rapid, because it was transmitted from the sick to the healthy by contagion, as fire does, when things that are dry or greasy are brought near to it. But the disease was even worse than this. Not only did contact with the sick spread the illness and even lead to death, it was sufficient just to touch the clothes or anything else that the afflicted had touched or used.

It was not enough that men avoided each other, and that no-one took thought for his neighbor. Even relatives visited but seldom, and if they did, they kept their distance. The disaster had struck such horror into the hearts of men and women that brother abandoned brother, while uncles, sisters and wives left those dear to them to perish. What is even more incredible is that parents refused to visit or care for their own children, as if they were not of their flesh.

The plight of the common people was wretched, as was that of most of the middle classes. Either hoping to preserve themselves, or because of poverty, they confined themselves to their houses, where, in their isolation, they succumbed in their thousands. Many perished in the streets, both by day and by night. Many perished in their homes, and only the stench from their rotting bodies announced their death to their neighbors. The city was full of corpses. More from fear than from any consideration for the dead, people would drag the corpses from their homes and heap them at their doors, where, any morning, numberless bodies could be seen. When there were no biers to be had, the corpses were carried two and three together on planks. It was common to see the one bier carrying the bodies of a husband and wife, two or three brothers, a father and a son, and several others. [Boccaccio, *Decameron, Introduction to the First Day*]

Many people believed, like Boccaccio, that the plague was a punishment from heaven for man's sins, so they did penance, something which a sect called the Flagellants carried to extremes. The movement had been in existence since 1260, but now it gathered new strength. A German chronicler wrote:

> 230. As the plague spread in Germany, people began traveling the country, flagellating themselves.
>
> In June, seven hundred came to Strasbourg from Swabia, under three masters, whom they all obeyed implicitly. At dawn, they crossed the Rhine, and people gathered to see them. When they had made a large circle, they removed their clothes and shoes and piled them in the center. Wearing only shifts that came from their waists to their ankles, they walked round and then, one at a time, they threw themselves on their faces in the circle in the shape of a cross. Each in turn stepped over the others, and struck each one with scourges as they did so. At length, they all stood and began scourging themselves with whips that had knotted thongs and iron spikes, all the while singing hymns to God. The three leaders stood in the middle, flogging themselves and leading the singing in loud voices. This went on for some time and then, with one accord, they fell on their knees and again threw themselves on their faces in the form of a cross.
>
> The masters went among them, telling them to pray to God, so that he would have mercy on all people, all sinners and all in purgatory. Then the Flagellants stood, raised their hands to heaven, knelt once more and sang. Then, rising to their feet, they flagellated themselves for a long time, exactly as before. At last, they dressed, and those who had been looking after their clothes, stripped and did the same.
>
> Then one of them stood, and read aloud a letter, very like the one which an angel had delivered to the Church of St. Peter in Jerusalem. In it, the angel said that Christ was angry at the sins of the world, naming profanation of the Sabbath, failing to fast on Fridays, blasphemy, usury and fornication. The letter also said that the Virgin Mary and

the angels had interceded with Christ, who had said that a man might obtain mercy if he went willingly into exile and flagellated himself for thirty-three and a half days.

The people of Strasbourg were so moved by the Flagellants that they gladly offered them hospitality, so that they all had lodgings. The Flagellants would not take alms, but their masters allowed them to accept hospitality, if it was offered. They behaved in the same way, whether with rich or poor. Twice a day, they performed their rites in public, and some did so secretly again, at night. They would have no converse with women, neither would they sleep on feather beds.

Some thousand men of Strasbourg joined the Flagellants, and promised to obey the masters for the time decreed. None was accepted unless he promised to go through the rites for the days decreed, had with him four pennies for every day, so that he would not have to beg, and swore that he had confessed all his sins and repented, had forgiven his enemies for the wrongs they had done him, and had his wife's agreement. [Matthew of Neuenberg, *Chronicle*]

Another reaction to the plague, also particularly common in Germany, was to blame the Jews for it and massacre them.

THE ENGLISH PEASANTS' REVOLT OF 1381

There were numerous popular risings during the Middle Ages, but the English peasants' revolt of 1381 is of special interest, partly because it was one of the more spectacular and partly because it was a sequel to the Black Death.

As has been shown in a previous chapter, the plague killed so many people that there was a chronic shortage of labor. Accordingly, the lords enforced their manorial dues as strictly as possible; and these dues fell on families which were, on the whole, much smaller than they had been, making them particularly irksome. Many villeins had been more or less indifferent to their semi-servile status, but now they resented it. Laborers were also unhappy because of the government's attempts to hold wages to the levels they had been before the plague. Demagogues played on this discontent, one of them being a priest called John Ball:

231. For twenty years and more this man had been preach-
ing things which he knew were pleasing to the common
people, speaking evil of both ecclesiastics and secular lords,
and had won the admiration of the common people, rather
than merit in the sight of the Lord. For he taught that tithes
should not be paid, unless he who gave them was richer
than the vicar or rector who received them; and that tithes
should be withheld if the parishioner was known to be a
better man than his priest, and also that none are fit for the
Kingdom of Heaven who are not born in matrimony. He
taught, moreover, the perverse doctrines of the wicked John
Wycliffe, his ideas and his follies. At last, having been excommunicated because he would not desist, he was imprisoned, whereupon he predicted that he would be freed by
twenty thousand of his friends, which happened in the great
disturbances, when the commons broke open all the prisons and set the prisoners free.

And to corrupt the more, at Blackheath, where twenty thousand commons were gathered, he began a speech in this wise:

"When Adam delved and Eve span,
Who then was the gentleman?"

And continuing, he strove to prove that from the beginning all men were created equal by nature and that servitude had been introduced by the unjust oppressions of evil
men, against the will of God. Let them consider, therefore,
that a time was now given them by God, a time in which
they might lay aside the yoke of long servitude and enjoy
their liberty. Wherefore they should be prudent men, and,
with the love of a good husbandman tilling his fields and
uprooting the tares that destroy the grain, they should first
kill the great lords of the kingdom, then slay the lawyers
and justices, and finally root out all who might be harmful
to the community in the future. Thus they would obtain
peace and security, dignity and power. [Walsingham, *Historia
Anglicana*]

CHAPTER 17. PLAGUE & REBELLION

There had been discontent for thirty years when, in 1379, the government of the young Richard II levied a poll tax, something that had no precedent. Many people who, formerly, had escaped tax entirely, now had to pay, which was a novel experience for them. The tax was levied again in 1380. It was levied yet again in 1381, when the government not only demanded the tax, but tried to enforce payment. This was too much. An army of peasants assembled in Essex, another in Kent, and they advanced on London. The leader of the men from Kent was Wat Tyler.

The rebels reached London on Thursday, 13 June. They terrorized the guards into opening the gates for them and poured into the city:

232. In Fleet Street the commons broke open the Fleet prison and released all the prisoners. Then they set fire to the shop of a certain chandler and another shop of a certain blacksmith, in the middle of the said street. There shall never again be houses, it is said, to deface the beauty of the street. And after that, they went to the Temple, and they cast down the house to the ground and tore off the tiles. And they went into the Temple Church and took all the books and rolls and remembrances which were in the cupboards of the apprentices at law in the Temple, and carried them into the highway and burnt them. And then they destroyed all the buildings belonging to the Master of the Hospital of St. John. And they went to the house of the Bishop of Chester and they rolled barrels of wine out of his cellar and drank their fill, and departed without doing further damage. At last they came to the Savoy [palace of the unpopular John of Gaunt, Duke of Lancaster]. They broke open the gates and entered the palace and came to the wardrobe, and they took torches and set fire to the sheets and coverlets and beds and headboards of great worth, for their whole value amounted, it was said, to 1,000 marks. And all the napery and other things which they could find they carried into the hall and set it on fire with their torches. And

they burnt the hall and chambers and all the buildings belonging to the said palace. And they found three barrels of gunpowder which they took to be gold or silver, and they threw them on the fire, and this powder blew up high and set the hall in a greater blaze than before, to the great loss and damage of the Duke of Lancaster.

The same Thursday the commons went to St. Martin-le-Grand and tore away from the high altar a certain Roger Legett, a notorious tax gatherer, and took him to Cheapside and beheaded him. On the same day eighteen others were beheaded in various parts of the town. [*The Anonimalle Chronicle*]

Richard II, then a boy of fourteen, hurried to London, where he took refuge in the Tower. From the battlements he could see fires burning in different parts of the city. His counselors had no advice to give him, so he sent word to the rebels, agreeing to accept their demands and ordering them to meet him the following day at Mile End, outside the city:

233. Next day, the Friday, the commons of the countryside and the commons of London assembled in fearful strength to the number of 100,000 or more, to await the coming of the king. And the king advised the archbishop of Canterbury and the others who were in the Tower to go down to the Little Water Gate and take a boat and save themselves. And the archbishop did so, but a wicked woman raised a cry against him and he had to return to the Tower.

And by seven o'clock the king came to Mile End. And when he was come the commons all knelt down to him, saying, "Welcome, our lord, King Richard, we will have no other king but you." And Wat Tyghler, their leader and chief, prayed to him that he would suffer them to take and hold all the traitors who were against him and the law; and the king granted that they should take at their wish those who were traitors and could be proved traitors by the law. And they required that no man should be a serf, nor do homage or any manner of service to any lord, but should give fourpence rent for an acre of land, and that no one should serve any man but at his own will, and on terms of regular covenant. And the king caused a proclamation to be made that he would confirm and grant their freedom and all their wishes generally, and that they should go through the realm of England and catch all traitors and bring them to him and that he would deal with them as the law required. Under color of this grant Wat Tyghler and the commons took their way to the Tower.

At this time the archbishop was chanting his mass devoutly in the Tower, and when he was at the words, "All saints, pray for us" the commons burst in and dragged him out of the chapel of the Tower and struck and hustled him villainously, as they did the others who were with him and dragged them to Tower Hill. There they cut off the heads of Master Simon Sudbury, Archbishop of Canterbury, of Sir Robert Hales, Treasurer of England, of Brother William Appleton, a great physician and surgeon, and of John Legge, the king's sergeant-at-arms. And at the same time the commons proclaimed that anyone who could catch a Fleming or other alien of any nation might cut off his head. Then they set the head of the archbishop above London Bridge, and the eight other heads of those who were murdered. And when this was done, they went to the church of St. Martin's in the Vintry and found therein 35 Flemings, whom they dragged out and beheaded in the street. On that day were beheaded in all some 140 or 160 persons. [Ibid.]

The rebels killed the archbishop and the treasurer because they blamed them for the poll tax. They killed William Appleton because he was physician to the hated John of Gaunt. John Legge had been busy collecting the poll tax. The attacks on the Flemings were probably the work of the Londoners, who hated the aliens because of the privileges they had won in the city and were jealous of them because of their wealth.

In his *Chronicles*, Froissart states that at Mile End, the king gave royal banners to various contingents of peasants and set thirty clerks to work, writing letters patent for the peasants from the different districts, granting them their freedom. He also states that this persuaded many of the peasants to go home.

On the following day, Saturday, the murders continued until, in the afternoon, the king again met the rebels, this time at Smithfield. Whether the meeting was by accident or appointment is not clear. Froissart describes what happened. Some of the detail in his account is probably apocryphal, but other chroniclers agree on the essentials:

> 234. On Saturday, Wat Tyler, John Ball and Jack Straw had gathered their men together in a place called Smithfield. They had with them the king's banners which had been given them and they were planning to overrun and rob London the same day. And the king came the same way, unaware of them, and he had with him some 40 horsemen. When he saw all the people he stopped, wondering what to do. Wat Tyler said to his people, "There is the king. I will go and speak with him. Do not move until I make the sign.

Then, come and slay them all, except the king. He is young. We shall do with him what we want, We shall take him with us all over England, and so we shall be lords of the realm without any doubt."

With that, Wat Tyler left his men and rode to the king. He said, "Sir king, do you see all those people?"

"Yes," said the king, "Why do you ask?"

"Because," said Tyler, "they are all under my orders and have been sworn to be faithful to me."

"Very well," said the king.

Then Wat Tyler said, "Do you think, king, that all those people will go away before they have had your letters?"

"No," said the king. "You shall have them. They are being written and shall be given to you, as I promised."

Then Wat Tyler saw a squire who was bearing the king's sword. Wat Tyler hated this squire because of an argument they had had. "Are you there?" said Tyler. "Give me your dagger."

"No," said the squire. "I will not. Why should I give it to you?"

The king said to the squire, "Give it to him. Let him have it." And so the squire took it to him much against his will. When Wat Tyler had it, he began to play with it, and spoke again to the squire, saying, "Give me also that sword."

"No," said the squire, "it is the king's sword. You are not worthy to have it, for you are but a knave. And if you and I were here on our own you would not dare to speak to me like this."

"By my faith," said Wat Tyler, "I shall not eat again, until I have your head."

At this moment, the Mayor of London came by, being with twelve horsemen, well armed. He heard what Tyler was saying and said to him, "You knave. How dare you say such things in the presence of the king?"

"In God's name," said Tyler, "have I said aught to displease you?"

"Yes, truly," said the mayor. "You are a false and stinking knave. Shall you use such words in the presence of my lord the king? I would rather die than let you go unpunished." With these words, the mayor drew his sword and hit Tyler so great a blow on his head that he fell down at the feet of his horse. As soon as he had fallen, they surrounded him, so that his men could not see him. Then one of the king's squires, John Standish, thrust his sword into Wat Tyler's belly, and so he died. At this, the peasants said, "Our captain is slain. Let us go and kill them all." And they prepared for battle.

Then the king did something very brave. Leaving his company he rode alone to the peasants and said to them, "Sirs, what is the matter? You shall have no captain but me. I am your king. Let there be peace between us." Most of the people who heard the king speak and saw he was among them were shamed, and began to leave. But some who were evil, would not go.

In the meantime, the news spread in London that the peasants were going to kill the king and mayor in Smithfield. At once the king's supporters came well armed to Smithfield, and soon there were seven or eight thousand of them. As they arrived, they lined up in order of battle. Then the king made three knights, Sir Nicholas Walworth, Mayor of London, Sir John Standish and Sir Nicholas Bramber. Then the lords said, "What shall we do? Here are our enemies who would gladly slay us, if they could."

Sir Robert Knolles said they should fight with them and kill them all, but the king did not agree. "No," he said, "I will order them to return my banners, and then we shall see what they will do."

The three new knights were sent to the peasants, and said to them, "Sirs, the king orders you to return his banners. If you do so, he will have mercy on you." And so they handed over the banners and sent them to the king. Also, they were ordered, on pain of death, to hand over any letters they had from the king. Many of them did so and the king had the letters torn up in their presence. Then this unhappy people threw down their bows and departed. Sir Robert Knolles was angry that he was not allowed to go and slay them all. But the king said he would be well revenged, and so he was, soon after. [*Chronicles*]

Richard's approach to the rebels, furious at the loss of their leader, was an act of great courage. It was also amazing that a boy of fourteen took exactly the right action when older and much more experienced men were at a loss. Richard gained enormous prestige, but, as is shown in the first volume of this series, it inflated the dangerously high opinion he already had of himself, which was to lead, eventually, to his downfall.

There had been troubles in other parts of England, mainly East Anglia, where the rebels burnt houses, murdered "traitors" like justices and royal officials and released prisoners. These risings were put down, the bishop of Norwich taking the leading part in his area. Then, there was a special assize, the judges touring the counties that had been affected by the rebellions and condemning the leaders to death.

The peasants had failed to win their freedom at a stroke, but, as we have seen, the piecemeal commutation of manorial services continued, so that by the sixteenth century villeinage in England was all but dead.

GLOSSARY

ANSANGE: measure of land
ARPENT: acre
ARROBA: measure of weight
AUMBRY: cupboard or dresser

BALISCA: kind of grape
BANKER: cover for a seat
BONNIER: measure of land, perhaps between 2-3 acres
BRENN: hissing

CARTAGE: duty to cart goods
CHARGER: flat dish
CHEVAGE: permission given to a bondsman to live away from his village
CIVET: type of perfume
COSCET: bondsman of low status
COSTARD: apple
COTTAR: bondsman of low status
CREELER: maker of creels, large baskets used by fishermen
CUPPING GLASS: glass vessel used to draw blood by suction from small cuts in the skin
CWT: abbreviation for "hundredweight"

DESTRIER: war-horse
DISSEISIN: wrongful ejection of occupant from house or land
DORSER: cover for a chairback
DYKER: ten

FLETCHER: maker of arrows
FOREGRATER: one who tries to rig the market. *Compare* Regrater
FRIARS MINOR: Franciscans

HERIOT: payment due to lord on death of a tenant
HIDE: measure of land, variable, but thought to be the amount needed to support a family and its dependants

INDICTION: fifteen-year cycle used to date legal documents, often associated with imperial Roman and papal reigns

JUSSEL: kind of soup, containing bread, eggs and spices

LAWN: kind of linen cloth
LIEF: darling, dear
LECHE: jelly, containing sliced meat, eggs, fruit and spices

MAINPAST: dependant relative, subordinate member of household
MAZER: silver mounted wooden cup
MERCHET: payment due to lord on marriage of one of his bondswomen
MORTREUSE: type of soup
MUID: measure of capacity, used for liquids and grain

PATTENER: maker of pattens, a type of wooden shoe
PERCH: measure of land, about 30 square yards
POKE: large bag

REGRATER: one who tries to buy up all the goods of one kind in a market, so that he has a monopoly of them and can resell them at a profit
ROD: see Perch

SARPLER: wool pack
SETIER: French measure for grains and liquids, variable according to time and place
STOOK: number of sheaves stacked upright in a field. "Stooking" is to make stooks
STOUNDE: hour
SUELDO: Spanish coin, varying in value, according to time and place

TAILLE: land tax
TESTER: canopy over bed
TURBARY: right to cut turf for fuel

GLOSSARY

Twybylle: Saxon term for mortising chisel

Villein: bondsman, but one with considerable rights
Virgate: measure of land, variable, but often about 30 acres

Walker: fuller of cloth
Withies: long flexible twigs, used for tying bundles
Wraw: angry
Wymbylle: Saxon term for gimlet

Yoke: measure of land, variable, but perhaps the amount that could
be cultivated with a single plough

BIBLIOGRAPHY

PRIMARY SOURCES

Amt, Emilie. *Women's Lives in Medieval Europe: A Sourcebook.* New York: Routledge, 1993.

Cantor, Norman F., and Michael S. Werthman, eds. *Medieval Society 400-1450.* Arlington Heights, IL: Harlan Davidson, 1982.

Chaucer, Geoffrey. *The Canterbury Tales: Done into Modern English Verse by Frank Ernest Hill.* New York: Heritage Press, 1974.

Coulton, G.G., ed. *A Medieval Garner.* Cambridge: Cambridge University Press, 1910.

—. *Medieval Village, Manor and Monastery.* New York: Harper & Row, 1960.

—. *Social Life in England from the Conquest to the Reformation.* Cambridge: Cambridge University Press, 1918.

Duby, Georges. *Rural Economy and Country Life in the Medieval West.* Cynthia Postan, trans. London: Edward Arnold, 1968.

Englander, David, ed. *Culture and Belief in Europe, 1450-1600. An Anthology of Sources.* Oxford: Basil Blackwell, 1990.

Erasmus, Desiderius. *The Colloquies of Erasmus.* Craig R. Thompson, ed. Chicago: University of Chicago Press, 1965.

Fitz Stephen, William. *Norman London.* F. Donald Logan, intro. New York: Italica Press, 1990.

Froissart, Jean. *Chronicles.* J. Joliffe, trans. & ed. New York: Modern Library, 1967.

Hallam, Elizabeth, ed. *Chronicles of the Age of Chivalry.* London: Weidenfeld and Nicolson, 1987.

—. *Plantagenet Chronicles.* London: Weidenfeld and Nicolson, 1986.

Hone, N.J., ed. *The Manor and Manorial Records.* London: Methuen, 1906.

Kempe, Margery. *The Book of Margery Kempe: A Modern Version.* W. Butler Bowdon, ed. Greenwich, CT: Devin-Adaire, 1944.

Langland, William. *Piers the Ploughman*. Margaret Williams, trans. New York: Random House, 1971.

Lopez, Robert S., and Irving W. Raymond, eds. *Medieval Trade in the Mediterranean World*. New York: W.W. Norton, 1967.

Mollat, Michael. *The Poor in the Middle Ages*. Arthur Goldhammer, trans. New Haven: Yale University Press, 1986.

Monkton Jones, H.E., ed. *A Source Book for English Social History*. London: Methuen, 1922.

Mundy, John H., and Peter Riesenberg. *The Medieval Town*. New York: Van Nostrand, 1958.

Musto, Ronald G., ed. *Catholic Peacemakers: A Documentary History*. Vol. 1: *From the Bible to the Era of the Crusades*. New York: Garland Publishing, 1993.

Rickert, Edith, ed. *The Babee's Book: Medieval Manners for the Young*. New York: Cooper Square, 1966.

—. *Chaucer's World*. New York: Columbia University Press, 1948.

Rivers, Theodore John, trans. *The Laws of the Salian and Riparian Franks*. New York: AMS Press, 1986.

Salimbene da Adam, OFM. *The Chronicle of Salimbene da Adam*. Joseph L. Baird, Giuseppe Baglivi, and John Robert Kane, trans. & eds. Binghamton, NY: CMRS, 1986.

Thatcher, Oliver J., and Edgar H. McNeal, eds. *A Source Book for Medieval History*. New York: Charles Scribner's Sons, 1907.

Thiébaux, Marcelle, trans. & ed. *The Writings of Medieval Women*. New York: Garland Publishing, 1987.

Titow, J.Z., ed. *English Rural Society, 1200-1350*. New York: Barnes & Noble, 1972.

Trotula of Salerno. *The Diseases of Women*. Elizabeth Mason-Hohl, trans. Los Angeles: Ward-Ritchie Press, 1940.

Viorst, Milton, ed. *Great Documents of Western Civilization*. Philadelphia: Chilton Books, 1965.

SECONDARY WORKS

GENERAL AND DAILY LIFE

Ariès, Philippe, and Georges Duby, gen. eds. *A History of Private Life*. Arthur Goldhammer, trans. Cambridge, MA: Harvard University Press.

BIBLIOGRAPHY

VOL. 1: *From Pagan Rome to Byzantium*. Paul Veyne, ed., 1987. VOL. 2: *Revelations of the Medieval World*. Georges Duby, ed., 1988.

Artz, Frederick B. *The Mind of the Middle Ages: An Historical Survey A.D. 200-1500*. Chicago: University of Chicago Press, 1980.

Bachrach, Bernard S. and David Nicholas. *Law, Custom and Social Fabric in Medieval Europe*. Toronto: Medieval Institute, 1990.

Bartlett, Robert. *The Making of Europe*. London: Allen Lane, 1993.

Bax, Ernest B. *German Society at the Close of the Middle Ages*. New York: A.M. Kelley, 1967.

Becker, Marvin B. *Civility and Society in Western Europe, 1300-1600*. Bloomington & London: Indiana University Press, 1988.

Bennett, H.S. *Life on the English Manor*. Cambridge: Cambridge University Press, 1969.

—. *The Pastons and Their England*. Cambridge: Cambridge University Press, 1990.

Bloch, Marc. *Feudal Society*. L.A. Manyon, trans. 2 vols. London & New York: Routledge and Kegan Paul, 1961.

Chamberlin, E.R. *Life in Medieval France*. New York: G.P. Putnam, 1967.

Crowder, C.M. *English Society and Government in the Fifteenth Century*. Edinburgh and London: Oliver & Boyd, 1967.

Davies, R.R. *The British Isles, 1100-1500: Comparisons, Contrasts and Connections*. Atlantic Highlands, NJ: Humanities Press, 1988.

DuBoulay, F. *The England of Piers Plowman: William Langland and His Vision of the Fourteenth Century*. Rochester, NY & Woodbridge, Suffolk: Boydell and Brewer, 1991.

—. *Germany in the Later Middle Ages*. Atlantic Highlands, NJ: Humanities Press, 1988.

Duby, Georges, ed. *Revelations of the Medieval World. History of Private Life*. Vol. 2. Philippe Ariès and Georges Duby, gen. eds. Cambridge, MA: Harvard University Press, 1988.

—. *The Three Orders: Feudal Society Imagined*. Chicago: University of Chicago Press, 1980.

—, and Robert Mandrou. *A History of French Civilization*. London: Weidenfeld and Nicolson, 1964.

Duckett, Eleanor S. *Gateway to the Middle Ages: France and Great Britain*. Ann Arbor: University of Michigan Press, 1988.

Fossier, Robert. *Peasant Life in the Medieval West*. Juliet Vale, trans. Oxford: Basil Blackwell, 1988.

Fuhrmann, Horst. *Germany in the High Middle Ages*. Cambridge: Cambridge University Press, 1986.

Furnivall, Frederick James. *Early English Meals and Manners. John Russell's Boke of Nurture*. London: Oxford University Press for the Early English Text Society, 1868.

Hallam, H.E. *Rural England, 1066-1348*. Atlantic Highlands, NJ: Humanities Press, 1981.

Hanawalt, Barbara. *The Ties that Bound: Peasant Families in Medieval England*. Oxford: Oxford University Press, 1989.

Haverkamp, Alfred. *Medieval Germany, 1056-1273*. Helga Braun and Richard Mortimer, trans. Oxford: Oxford University Press, 1988.

Herlihy, David. *Medieval Households*. Cambridge: Harvard University Press, 1985.

Hilton, R.H. *The English Peasantry in the Later Middle Ages*. Oxford: Oxford University Press, 1975.

Hindley, Geoffrey. *England in the Age of Caxton*. London & New York: St. Martin's Press, 1979.

Holmes, Urban Tigner, Jr. *Daily Living in the Twelfth Century*. Madison & London: University of Wisconsin Press, 1966.

Homans, George C. *English Villagers of the Thirteenth Century*. New York: Harper & Row, 1970.

Hoskins, W.G. *The Midland Peasant*. London: Macmillan, 1965.

Huffines, Marion L. *Stricker and Wernher: A View of Chivalry and Peasantry in Germany of the Late Middle Ages*. New York: Gordon Press, 1976.

Huizinga, Johan. *The Autumn of the Middle Ages*. Rodney J. Payton and Ulrich Mammitzsch, trans. Chicago: University of Chicago Press, 1996.

Keen, Maurice. *English Society in the Later Middle Ages, 1348-1500*. New York: Viking Penguin, 1991.

Larner, John. *Italy in the Age of Dante and Petrarch, 1216-1380*. Longman History of Italy. Vol. 2. London & New York: Longman, 1980.

Lewis, P.S. *Late Medieval France*. New York: Macmillan, 1968.

Platt, Colin. *Medieval England: A Social History and Archaeology from the Conquest to A.D. 1600*. New York: Routledge, 1989.

BIBLIOGRAPHY

Power, Eileen, ed. *Medieval People*. London: Methuen, 1963.

Reuter, Timothy. *Germany in the Early Middle Ages*. London & New York: Longman, 1991.

Tuchman, Barbara. *A Distant Mirror: The Calamitous Fourteenth Century*. New York: Alfred A. Knopf, 1978.

Wood, Michael. *Domesday: A Search for the Roots of England*. New York: Facts on File Publications, 1986.

Woods, William. *England in the Age of Chaucer*. New York: Stein & Day, 1976.

FAMILY, WOMEN AND GENDER

Adams, Carol, Paula Bertley, et al. *From Workshop to Warfare: The Lives of Medieval Women*. Cambridge: Cambridge University Press, 1983.

Ariès, Philippe. *Centuries of Childhood: A Social History of Family Life*. Robert Baldick, trans. New York: Alfred A. Knopf, 1962

Baldwin, John W. *The Language of Sex: Five Voices from Northern France around 1200*. Chicago: University of Chicago Press, 1996.

Boswell, John. *Christianity, Social Tolerance and Homosexuality*. Chicago: University of Chicago Press, 1980.

Brooke, Christopher. *The Medieval Idea of Marriage*. Oxford: Oxford University Press, 1989.

Brundage, James A. *Law, Sex, and Christian Society in Medieval Europe*. Chicago: University of Chicago Press, 1987.

Dronke, Peter. *Women Writers of the Middle Ages*. Cambridge: Cambridge University Press, 1984.

Duby, Georges. *Medieval Marriage: Two Models from Twelfth-Century France*. Baltimore: Johns Hopkins University Pres, 1978.

Ennen, Edith. *The Medieval Woman*. Oxford: Basil Blackwell, 1989.

Gies, Frances, and Joseph Gies. *Women in the Middle Ages*. New York: Barnes & Noble, 1978.

Herlihy, David. *Opera Muliebria: Women and Work in Medieval Europe*. Philadelphia: Temple University Press, 1990.

Kirshner, Julius, and Suzanne F. Wemple, eds. *Women of the Medieval World*. Oxford: Basil Blackwell, 1985.

Klapisch-Zuber, Christiane, ed. *Silences of the Middle Ages. A History of Women*. Vol. 2. Georges Duby and Michelle Perrot, gen. eds. Cambridge, MA: Harvard University Press, 1992.

Lucas, Angela M. *Women in the Middle Ages: Religion, Marriage and Letters.* Brighton: Harvester Press, 1984.

Morewedge, Rosemarie Thee. *The Role of Women in the Middle Ages.* Albany: SUNY Press, 1975.

Mundy, John H. *Men and Women at Toulouse in the Age of the Cathars.* Toronto: Pontifical Institute of Mediaeval Studies, 1990.

Otis, Leah L. *Prostitution in Medieval Society.* Chicago: University of Chicago Press, 1985.

Power, Eileen. *Medieval Women.* M. M. Postan, ed. Cambridge: Cambridge University Press, 1975.

Razi, Zvi. *Life, Marriage and Death in a Medieval Parish.* Cambridge: Cambridge University Press, 1980.

Rossiaud, Jacques. *Medieval Prostitution.* Lydia Cochrane, trans. New York: Basil Blackwell, 1988.

Shahar, Shulamith. *Childhood in the Middle Ages.* New York: Routledge, 1990.

—. *The Fourth Estate: A History of Women in the Middle Ages.* London: Methuen, 1983.

Wemple, Suzanne Fonay. *Women in Frankish Society: Marriage and the Cloister, 500-900.* Philadelphia: University of Pennsylvania Press, 1982.

MEDIEVAL URBANISM

Angeli, Marguerite de. *The Door in the Wall: The Story of Medieval London.* New York: Doubleday, 1989.

Beresford, Maurice. *New Towns of the Middle Ages.* New York: Praeger, 1967.

Bonney, Margaret. *Lordship and the Urban Community: Durham and Its Overlords, 1250-1540.* Cambridge: Cambridge University Press, 1990.

Brentano, Robert. *Rome before Avignon. A Social History of Thirteenth-Century Rome.* Berkeley & Los Angeles: University of California Press, 1991.

Epstein, Steven A. *Genoa and the Genoese, 958-1528.* Chapel Hill: University of North Carolina Press, 1996.

Frugoni, Chiara. *A Distant City: Images of Urban Experience in the Medieval World.* William McCuaig, trans. Princeton: Princeton University Press, 1991.

BIBLIOGRAPHY

Gies, Joseph and Frances Gies. *Life in a Medieval City*. New York: Thomas Y. Crowell, 1973.

Hanawalt, Barbara A. *Growing Up in Medieval London*. New York & Oxford: Oxford University Press, 1993.

Holt, Richard, and Gervase Rosser, eds. *The English Medieval Town, 1200-1540*. London: Longman 1990.

Hyde, J.K. *Padua in the Age of Dante*. Manchester: Manchester University Press, 1966.

Krautheimer, Richard. *Rome: Profile of a City, 312-1308*. Princeton: Princeton University Press, 1980.

Lane, Frederic C. *Venice: A Maritime Republic*. Baltimore & London: Johns Hopkins University Press, 1973.

Martines, Lauro. *Power and Imagination: City-States in Renaissance Italy*. New York: Vintage Books, 1980.

Nicholas, David. *The Domestic Life of a Medieval City: Women, Children, and the Family in Fourteenth-Century Ghent*. Lincoln: University of Nebraska Press, 1985.

——. *The Metamorphosis of a Medieval City: Ghent in the Age of the Artveldes, 1302-1390*. Lincoln: University of Nebraska Press, 1987.

Pirenne, Henri. *Early Democracies in the Low Countries*. John H. Mundy, ed. New York: Harper & Row, 1963.

——. *Medieval Cities*. Princeton: Princeton University Press, 1952.

Reynolds, Susan. *English Medieval Towns*. Oxford: Oxford University Press, 1977.

Richardson, H. *The Medieval Fairs and Markets of York*. York: St. Anthony's Press, 1961.

Rosser, Gervase. *Medieval Westminster, 1200-1540*. Oxford: Oxford University Press, 1989.

Rörig, Fritz. *The Medieval Town*. Berkeley & Los Angeles: University of California Press, 1969.

Saalman, Howard. *Medieval Cities*. New York: George Brazillier, 1968.

Schevill, Ferdinand. *Medieval and Renaissance Florence*. 2 vols. New York: Harper & Row, 1963.

Schofield, John. *Medieval London Houses*. New Haven: Yale University Press, 1995.

Thrupp, Sylvia L. *The Merchant Class of Medieval London, 1300-1500*. Ann Arbor: University of Michigan Press, 1968.

Waley, Daniel. *The Italian City-Republics*. London & New York: Longman, 1988.

—. *Siena and the Sienese in the Thirteenth Century.* Cambridge & New York: Cambridge University Press, 1991.

TRADE AND ECONOMY

Bolton, J.L. *The Medieval English Economy, 1150-1500*. London: Dent, 1980.

Braudel, Fernand. *Capitalism and Material Life, 1400-1800.* Miriam Kochan, trans. New York: Harper & Row, 1967.

—. *Civilization and Capitalism, 15th-18th Century.* Siân Reynolds, trans. New York: Harper & Row, VOL. 1: *The Structures of Everyday Life,* 1981; VOL. 2: *The Wheels of Commerce,* 1982.

Campbell, Bruce M. *Before the Black Death: Studies of the Crisis in the Early Fourteenth Century.* Manchester: Manchester University Press, 1991.

Carus-Wilson, E.M. *Medieval Merchant Venturers.* London: Methuen, 1967.

Cipolla, Carlo M. *Before the Industrial Revolution: European Society and Economy, 1000-1700*. New York: W.W. Norton, 1976.

Dodgshon, R.A. *A Historical Geography of England and Wales*. London: Academic, 1990.

Gras, N.S.B. *The Economic and Social History of an English Village.* Cambridge MA: Harvard University Press, 1930.

Holt, Richard. *The Mills of Medieval England.* Oxford: Basil Blackwell, 1988.

Lopez, Robert. *The Commercial Revolution of the Middle Ages, 930-1350.* Englewood Cliffs, NJ: Prentice-Hall, 1971.

McDonald, John. *Domesday Economy: A New Approach to Anglo-Norman History.* Oxford: Oxford University Press, 1986.

Miskimin, Harry A. *The Economy of Early Renaissance Europe, 1300-1460*. Cambridge & New York: Cambridge University Press, 1978.

Origo, Iris. *The Merchant of Prato: Francesco di Marco Datini, 1335-1410.* Boston: David R. Godine, 1986.

Orwin, C.S. and C.S. *The Open Fields.* Oxford: Oxford University Press, 1956.

Pirenne, Henri. *Economic and Social History of Medieval Europe.* New York: Harcourt Brace & World, 1966.

BIBLIOGRAPHY

Postan. M.M. *The Medieval Society and Economy.* Baltimore: Pelican Books, 1972.

White, Lynn, Jr. *Medieval Technology and Social Change.* Oxford & New York: Oxford University Press, 1964.

DIET, HEALTH, AND DISEASE

Arano, Luisa Cogliati. *The Medieval Health Handbook: Tacuinum Sanitatis.* New York: George Braziller, 1976.

Bennett, Judith M. *Ale, Beer and Brewsters in England: Women's Work in a Changing World, 1300-1600.* Oxford & New York: Oxford University Press, 1996.

Binski, Paul. *Medieval Death.* Ithaca, NY: Cornell University Press, 1996.

Cosman, Madeleine Pelner. *Fabulous Feasts: Medieval Cookery and Ceremony.* New York: George Brazillier, 1976.

Gottfried, Robert S. *The Black Death: Natural and Human Disaster in Medieval Europe.* New York: Free Press, 1983.

Hatcher, John. *Plague, Population and the English Economy 1348-1530.* London: Macmillan, 1977.

Hieatt, Constance B., Brenda M. Hosington, and Sharon Butler, eds. *Pleyn Delit. Medieval Cookery for Modern Cooks.* Toronto: University of Toronto Press, 1996.

Horrox, Rosemary, ed. *The Black Death.* Manchester: Manchester University Press, 1994.

Hughes, Muriel J. *Women Healers in Medieval Life and Literature.* New York: King's Crown, 1943.

Jacquart, Danielle, and Claude Thomasset. *Sexuality and Medicine in the Middle Ages.* Princeton: Princeton University Press, 1988.

Le Roy Ladurie, Emmanuel. *Times of Feast, Times of Famine: A History of Climate since the Year 1000.* Barbara Bary, trans. Garden City, NY: Doubleday, 1971.

McVaugh, Michael R. *Medicine before the Plague: Practitioners and Their Patients in the Crown of Aragon, 1285-1345.* Cambridge: Cambridge University Press, 1993.

Platt, Colin. *King Death: The Black Death and Its Aftermath in Late-Medieval England.* Toronto: University of Toronto Press, 1996.

Pouchelle, Marie-Christine. *The Body and Surgery in the Middle Ages.*

Rosemary Morris, trans. New Brunswick, NJ: Rutgers University Press, 1990.

Talbot, Charles H. *Medicine in Medieval England*. London: Oldbourne, 1967.

Williman, Daniel, ed. *The Black Death: The Impact of the Fourteenth-Century Plague*. Binghamton, NY: SUNY Press, 1977.

Ziegler, Philip. *The Black Death*. Harmondsworth: Pelican Books, 1970.

SOCIAL UPHEAVEL

Hanawalt, Barbara A. *Crime and Conflict in English Communities 1300-1348*. Cambridge, MA: Harvard University Press, 1979.

Harrison, J.F.C. *The Common People*. London: Fontana 1984.

Hilton, R.H., and T.H. Ashton. *The English Rising of 1381*. Cambridge: Cambridge University Press, 1987.

Justice, Steven. *Writing and Rebellion: England 1381*. Berkeley & Los Angeles: University of California Press, 1996.

Kaeuper, Richard W. *War, Justice and Public Order: England and France in the Late Middle Ages*. Oxford: Oxford University Press, 1988.

Miller, William Ian. *Bloodtaking and Peacemaking: Feud, Law and Society in Saga Iceland*. Chicago: University of Chicago Press, 1990.

Mollat, Michel, and Philippe Wolff. *The Popular Revolutions of the Late Middle Ages*. A.L. Lytton-Sells, trans. London: George Allen & Unwin, 1973.

INDEX

INDEX

INDEX

INDEX

267

INDEX

This Book Was Completed on August 1, 1997
At Italica Press, New York, New York. It
Was Set in Adobe Charlemagne and
Monotype Dante and Printed
on 60-lb Natural Paper by
Stanton Publication
Services, St. Paul,
Minnesota,
USA
★ ★
★